TIME *for a* TURNING POINT

SETTING A COURSE TOWARD
FREE MARKETS AND LIMITED GOVERNMENT
FOR FUTURE GENERATIONS

CHARLIE KIRK
with BRENT E. HAMACHEK

A POST HILL PRESS BOOK

Time for a Turning Point:
Setting a Course Towards Free Markets and Limited Government
for Future Generations
© 2016 by Charlie Kirk with Brent Hamachek
All Rights Reserved

ISBN: 978-1-68261-247-7
ISBN (eBook): 978-1-68261-248-4

Cover Design by Paul Romanowski
Jacket Photographs by Jill Jensen

Post Hill Press
275 Madison Avenue, 14th Floor
New York, NY 10016
posthillpress.com

Printed in the United States of America

1 2 3 4 5 6 7 8 9 10

*To my parents, for believing in me
when the world said this couldn't be done.*
From Charlie

*To Andrea, Sarah, Katy, and all children they may have.
It is for you we write, and it is for you Charlie fights.*
From Brent

TABLE OF CONTENTS

WHY I WRITE, WHY I FIGHT

"The only thing necessary for the triumph of evil is for good men to do nothing."

—EDMUND BURKE

Writing a book as a 22-year-old is a very humbling experience.

I'm so focused each and every day on the work and mission of Turning Point USA, the campus-based activist organization I founded, that I really don't ever stop to consider my age. I don't "feel" particularly young or old. That said, when I started to consider writing a book, it did make me wonder about the audacity (admission here that Barack Obama has made me cringe slightly at the use of that word) of the task and to wonder just how often in history other young people have attempted to impact the world with the written word.

So I turned to Google, that wonderful company born of a still relatively free market that has managed to turn a nonsensical company name into one of the most frequently used verbs in our language, and I *googled* "famous authors under age 23." Google showed me that there were roughly 289 million search results and I, being like so many other millennials and always in a hurry, selected the first suggestion on the first page: *23 Writers who were famous by the age of 23.*

There were a few things that surprised me. First, I had no idea that Mary Shelley was only 20 years old when she finished the manuscript for *Frankenstein*. (How could such a young mind have such a tortured view of medical science without exposure to Obamacare?) Second, imagine that at the tender age of only 20 Helen Keller had already experienced and overcome so much adversity in her life that she could write an autobiography. The third thing that struck me is that aside from Shelley and Keller, there were not many names on the list I recognized.

So this is not something that is done frequently by people my age.

Since so many supporters of my activities like to metaphorically equate the work we are doing with a "war" to restore American First Principles, I thought I would again turn to Google and google "famous young military leaders." I'm not for a minute positing that my efforts compare to those of a soldier in battle, but I thought the perspective would be interesting.

Alexander the Great, tutored by Aristotle and the seated King of Macedonia in 336 BC at the age of 20, was setting out on his first military campaign by the age of 21. When she was only 17, St. Joan of Arc led the French in driving back the English from Orleans in 1429. In 44 BC, 18-year-old Gaius Octavius, later to be Caesar Augustus, led an army of 3,000 into Rome and drove out Caesar's assassins.

Three great young leaders, two of whom met with fates that could easily cause me to reconsider my efforts if I felt the "war to restore America" were other than a metaphor.

Finally, I decided to search "famous young political leaders," since my efforts seem to make me most comfortably fit into that category. Surprisingly there were not a lot of meaningful results. I did learn that Egypt's famous boy-king Tutankhamun likely died as the result of sustaining severe traumatic injuries at the age of 19.

So there are numerous well-known names, many tragic endings, and some incredible accomplishments that have become the stuff of legends and sainthoods. But I'm not any of those people.

I'm just a 22-year-old who loves individual freedom.

I am writing this book as a young man who quite deliberately has chosen to commit my still early life to fighting to restore, perhaps finish building, an America that was envisioned by our Founding Fathers. It is disheartening to think that even the term "Founding Fathers" has fallen into a state of disrespect in recent times. The derogatory acronym DWEMS (dead white European males), which became popular in my parents' youth, is now replaced by more direct and caustic terms like racist, supremacist, and imperialist when discussing Jefferson, Madison, and Washington.

Those Founding Fathers, as an aside, do provide remarkable insight into the power of youth when it is joined together. Many of those Founders were quite young when the Declaration was signed in 1776. Hamilton (21), Burr (20), Monroe (18), Stuart (20), Madison (25), Ross (24), Lafayette (18) were all in the age range of today's college undergrad or postgrad student. Even an old man like Jefferson (33 in 1776) would qualify today as a millennial.

An entire generation of American youth is being taught to distance themselves from these people and America's beginnings. They are being taught that what was written in the Constitution isn't really what the Founding Fathers meant, or certainly isn't what they would have meant if they knew all the things we know today. The arrogance and condescension with which the idealists of 1776 are viewed in the early 21st century makes me angry, makes me saddened, makes me want to fight back. The quotation from Edmund Burke that began this chapter is one that hung on the wall of an 8th grade classroom of mine and one that I have made part of my core values ever since.

With the hostility to the people and principles of America's Founding comes hostility to capitalism and free markets. If somebody comes to the conclusion that individual liberty is synonymous with oppression, then the next logical conclusion for them to draw is that economic liberty is tantamount to indenturing the masses. The people who have had a strong philosophical influence on me (Hayek, Mises, Bastiat, Friedman) have led me to believe otherwise. There may not be a simpler sentence that better reflects an incontrovertible truth than the one used by Milton Friedman and others that there is no political freedom without economic freedom.

This deep and abiding belief in free markets and individual liberty is what drove me to start Turning Point USA immediately upon my graduation from high school, and what is now driving me to write this book. I don't for a minute believe that my commitment to these systems and values is any greater than was the commitment of great defenders of liberty who came before me. I do, however, recognize and feel an obligation to continue their fight using my energy, my passion, and my insight. I also intend on using the weapons of my time. Imagine what the oft-quoted quipmaster Benjamin Franklin could have done with Twitter!

One of the challenges I faced in approaching this project was how to separate myself and my own opinions and ideas from the activities and the mission statement of Turning Point. After all, this book hits the market as an offering of Charlie Kirk, not as a Turning Point USA issues pamphlet. After struggling with the concept, I finally realized that I cannot separate myself from Turning Point, because Turning Point and I share the identical goals. What Turning Point has become is the stronger, bigger, and faster version of everything that I have wanted to be.

In order to be able to deliver a message wrapped in individual liberty to the American marketplace of ideas, I needed a vehicle and I needed help. Turning Point is exactly that. While Turning Point uses Facebook as one of its tools, there is a sense in which Turning Point is its own Facebook. It has brought millions of young people together in a way that allowed them to find each other, to share their hopes, fears, and aspirations, and to then join with one another to act.

Because there were people like me out there before the organization was formed, you could say I didn't start Turning Point; I found it and made it available to others.

Of course, that may be a little too abstract. The simple truth is I did start Turning Point in June of 2012 and since then I have been joined by students and supported by donors from all around the country.

We have been tirelessly fighting against the well-oiled machinery of "Team Left" and we have been taking them on aggressively at every turn. We fight them with their own tactics and we fight them with new ones they haven't before seen. Mostly what we are trying to do is to move away from the apologies and counterpunches commonly associated with Team Right and hit preemptively and hit hard. I hope this book strikes one of those heavy blows by encouraging readers to join the battle on our side.

One of the more effective weapons, if not the most effective, that the other side has deployed is its use and control of language and speech. In the history of warfare, one of the most revolutionary inventions was that of the crossbow. While it's associated with medieval Europe, it was actually invented in ancient China, perhaps as far back as 2000 B.C. The Chinese were so certain of its profound power that they went to great lengths to keep it from enemies, and some evidence exists to suggest that they even considered "unilaterally disarming" from it. They knew it had incredible destructive capabilities.

Language control and political correctness have become the modern-day crossbow for Team Left and they are wielding their weaponry without conscience.

I want to better define the phenomenon we call "political correctness." The term has become so widely used that it is now almost impossible to go through an entire day, unless you are home sick with the TV off and your smartphone in airplane mode, without hearing it being used. Everybody knows that it means that there are only certain things you are allowed to say or do without them being considered "inappropriate." But what does that really mean and who is considering them inappropriate?

When you cut through it, political correctness is nothing more than self-censorship. It is forcing people to *voluntarily* stop behaving or speaking in certain ways. The driver for this becomes two base emotions: guilt and fear. Political correctness causes people to self-censor because they feel guilty about what they are about to say or do and they are afraid that they will "lose" something if they say or do it. The emotions of guilt and fear are such powerful drivers of behavior that people will stop themselves without even asking the question, "Who am I actually offending?"

Almost without exception the answer to the question is that you aren't offending any significant number of the people ostensibly being protected by the censored speech. What you are really doing is pushing back against some small, collectivist group that is seeking some sort of privilege or protection and does not want an honest, open discussion of the matter.

It doesn't matter what the topic is, the people who are determined to substitute collective decisions in the stead of individual freedom use the political correctness crossbow to set the acceptable terms of discourse. They do this so that people like me sound as though we are uncaring, insensitive, and downright evil to the untrained and otherwise overwhelmed public ear. If we discuss reasonable controls on immigration, we are xenophobic; if we are financially successful we are "one-percenters;" if we suggest that people should pay for their own discretionary choices in birth control, we are waging a "war on women" (Jonah Goldberg has done excellent work on this in his book *The Tyranny of Clichés: How Liberals Cheat in the War of Ideas*). It has become very uncomfortable and in some cases dangerous to academic, business, or public careers to use straightforward language to discuss straightforward issues.

Evidence of this reached the level of full satire in December of 2015 when filmmaker Ami Horowitz went on the campus of Yale University and asked students if they would sign a petition to repeal the First Amendment. The video, which is available on YouTube (another product of the free market), shows students enthusiastically wanting to sign and demonstrates just how Orwellian modern-day America has become.

I encountered efforts to suppress and control speech as far back as my high school classrooms, and Turning Point has encountered it on nearly every campus. Political correctness is a weapon that causes committed people who know better to voluntarily surrender. It is worse than being hypnotized, where it is claimed you cannot direct a person to do something injurious to himself or herself. All across America, on campuses and in offices, political correctness is getting freedom-loving citizens to take off their clothes, act like a chicken, and jump out of a 12-story window. I have no intention of surrendering our language to Team Left and I have every intention of doing what is necessary to recapture what has been lost. Wouldn't it be nice to hear the word "liberal" and know that it once again means somebody who values individual freedom and not somebody who wants to take away your 20 oz. soda?

This book will in part be an attempt to reclaim language and push the reset button, more effectively than Hilary Clinton, on the nature of the debate. There will be examples throughout the book of efforts that have been made to silence Turning Point USA on campuses, in social media, on television, and in living rooms. The stories you will find in these pages may or may not surprise you but I certainly hope that they motivate you. Opponents of ours hope that by limiting what we say and controlling how we are able to say it they will minimize our presence and our impact.

But they are mistaken. Neither I nor Turning Point is going anywhere and we are not going to change our message.

One of the key things I did not want to do when I started this project is to make it just another book about how messed up America is and how the hour of (*reader, please insert your favorite end of day's prophecy source*) is upon us. Everyone knows that things are bad and everyone is writing the book that tells us just how bad they are. I will spend some time on the current challenges we face and still a bit less on how we got here. Both are necessary in order to frame the situation and set our premises. Primarily, however, I want to create something that shows a vision of an America that I can see us being able to reach in my lifetime. Now, refer back to the beginning of this chapter. I'm only in my early 20s and I am assuming, perhaps naïvely, that I will live an actuarially normal life. I have more than 50 years remaining. This is going to be a long game. The challenges that America faces were not created just over the last several years under the Obama administration (although it certainly could seem that way).

In addition to sharing the vision of what I see for America, I want to show people the path that will get us there. Now, reasonable people can differ over the path that could or should be taken and I am the first to agree that there may be more than one workable path. That said, having watched the impact that Turning Point has had on college campuses in the past three-plus years with young people, the awareness we are creating, the conversions we are generating, the voters we are registering, I do believe that what I will offer you in these pages is viable.

One of the basic questions my collaborating partner asked me about this book before starting was, did I want it to be a work that was primarily a) philosophical b) factual or c) tactical? In other words, was this a book about what I think, what's the current situation, or what do we do about it? I found that to be an interesting way to approach the project. In the end, while it contains all three, and while I hope you agree with my suggested tactics, I truly hope you come away sharing my vision for an America that is just a bit further on up the road. If I succeed in that, then maybe someone out there smarter than I am can come along and help get us there faster and surer.

The reference made earlier to this being a long game is true. This means that for some people who aren't millennials there is a call to action you will hear that is one of the most difficult to answer. It is that call which asks of your time, treasure, and talent in order to pursue something which is going to be so challenging to obtain that you might not see it in your lifetime. Now, despite his historical prominence, and despite being played by a young and dashing Charlton Heston, very few people voluntarily sign up to be Moses, knowing in advance they likely won't see the Promised Land. What I'm counting on, indeed what I know, is that there are still many Americans who believe enough in the ideas of commitment and sacrifice that they will engage in order to make this country a better place for their children and many generations of children to come.

One of the most, if not the most, incredible stories of American courage (and there are many) that has made an impression on me is that of Operation Overlord and the June 6, 1944, invasion of Normandy by the Allies. First-day casualty estimates come in around 10,000 soldiers, but what I can't ever quite imagine is before those doors opened on the landing craft, what was going through the minds of the soldiers up front. They had to know, all of them, they were likely about to die. Their incredible bravery and sacrifice, made so that others could live, is hard for someone like me to fully appreciate. I've lived a life largely in peace, certainly without threat to my own physical existence. When someone compliments me on my courage in starting Turning Point, I thank them graciously but think to myself: Courage?

That said, there are some parallels. Our liberty is once again under attack, only this time from an insidious infestation of people who want us to lay down our liberty at the feet of some ill-defined, always corrosive, "greater good." Whether it's from the chaos coming from Obamacare, the bullets in a neglected and welfare-dependent urban neighborhood, or life on the streets brought upon by no jobs to be found, people's lives are in jeopardy. We all need to be able to step off that proverbial boat and fight and be thankful that we don't have to step off a literal boat in order to restore our freedom.

Yet.

So let me set some specific expectations for what we are going to do inside the cover of this book, be it virtual, skinned, or cloth-bound.

First, I want to make you familiar with Turning Point USA, the 501I(3) grassroots, campus-based organization I started back in June of 2012. While this isn't a book about Turning Point per se, it is a book entirely about Turning Point, as there isn't anything I envision for getting America from where it is to where it needs to be that doesn't require the people and the apparatus it provides.

Then we will take a look together at an America I can see approximately 25 years from now. To experience it we will look through the eyes of Julio, a fictionalized character offered in stark libertarian contrast to Julia, she of WhiteHouse.gov, who taught us how to go through the day taking advantage of every possible government entitlement program in order to survive but never thrive.

Next, we will take a look at where we are starting from today. We will examine the size of government (federal, state, and local), the crisis in education, the collapsing of our health care system, and the culture of dependency that is being created and becoming pervasive. As previously mentioned, this book will not be a long litany of problems. Unfortunately, a short litany is mandatory so we can all be on the same page (or pages).

After that we turn to what is necessary to advance our fight to restore free markets and individual liberty. I will take you inside the heart and mind of today's millennial and the up and coming youth to show you what they care about and how to motivate them. They are the foot soldiers of this movement. Nothing will be accomplished unless it matters to them and they become willing to fight. The messages and the media to be used will be described and, where appropriate, I will share examples about how our tactics will either mirror or surpass the tactics of the collectivist side. You will see that we are planning to cede them nothing and will contest them on every front.

Along the way the argument is going to get made for both the effectiveness and the justness of free market capitalism. For far too long someone wearing a T-shirt that says "I'm a Proud Capitalist" has been treated as if they were engaging in a public display of profanity. By the time you are done with this book, if nothing else, you will be able to morally and functionally defend capitalism from a college classroom to an Upper West Side Manhattan apartment. For this reason, in and of itself, it is worthwhile to keep reading.

I selected the collaborative author for this book, Brent Hamachek, because over the past two years he and I have worked together on an extraordinary amount of written material which has been published both personally and for Turning Point. We will draw from some of that material for use in this book because to most readers, it will be fresh and compelling and you will understand why it has been very effective in mobilizing people, both young and old, to join in the cause of First Principles restoration. Working together so closely on so much content has allowed us to share a thought process that would have been hard to create from scratch with anyone else. This has happened despite a 30-plus-year difference in our ages.

Now a note on what this book will not be. For anyone who hopes that this will be the moment in time when Charlie Kirk finally addresses social issues or national defense issues, I apologize. This will not be the book. My goal is to stick to the issues and the beliefs that drove me to start Turning Point. I can assure you that I consider these other matters and I have strong personal opinions and beliefs, but I am not yet ready to divert focus from my primary purpose. As I mentioned at the outset, I am young. Stay tuned.

This is very, very serious stuff that is going to be tackled in the pages that follow. Team Left takes this seriously. They fight with every weapon in their arsenal. Our team often seems to be fighting with forks and spoons against, well, crossbows. They see politics as a vocation, not as a hobby. If we don't match their level of intensity and commitment, then we are doomed to fail. Please don't get caught in the trap of thinking that all of our problems are going to work themselves out because everything is "cyclical" and the "pendulum swings both ways." Everything isn't cyclical; it is cause and effect. Right now, Team Left is doing most of the causing and enjoying a bountiful series of effects. As for the pendulum paradigm, I'd suggest that in terms of American liberty it looks a lot more like a guillotine.

As for those who think "we" need to focus on "winning elections" because otherwise we can't make a difference, let me assure you that Team Left keeps winning *and losing* elections without ever taking their eye off the target, which is making a permanent, structural difference. To prove this, think about how many issues are debated today where the "center" position is one that only a decade or two ago would have been considered to be the "far left" position. While many Team Right members get excited about a big midterm sweep, or a majority of Republican governors in the 50 states, the other side has studied physics. They know the incredible force that is inertia. Like they say in football, when we get in the end zone we need to act like we've been there before. We can't get so caught up in ephemeral celebration that we lose focus on how long a game this really is.

I want everyone who is reading this book to put it down at the end and feel invigorated, ready to answer a call to action. I don't want them to put it down and turn to a life of binge drinking and bulk lottery ticket buying because they feel despair and hopelessness. That, by the way, doesn't mean that the situation isn't serious or that there isn't an incredible amount of heavy lifting to do. It simply means that if you would be free people, if it's worth fighting for, and you think I'm on to something, then please join me. Help me. I can't help thinking of the famous words shouted by General La Rochejaquelein fighting against the first French Revolution: "Friends, if I advance, follow me! If I retreat, kill me! If I die, avenge me!"

So, get ready to challenge yourself. What follows is the path to doing something that our side hasn't tried before in the modern era, maybe in any era. We are going to show you what can happen when the ***principles*** of individual liberty and free markets are ***messaged*** properly to the right audiences, and then ***delivered*** through comprehensive machinery and infrastructure that takes those principles and splices them into every American's intellectual and spiritual DNA.

For anyone who has been waiting for a sunny day in America, maybe this book will show you a break in the clouds. Keep reading. This is going to be fun!

PART ONE

SETTING OUR PREMISES

CHAPTER 1

STOPPING BY A STARBUCKS ON A SNOWY AFTERNOON

"I'm taking the path less traveled by and it's making all the difference."

—CHARLIE KIRK, paraphrasing Robert Frost

There is not a variation of grey in the entire Crayola spectrum that quite does justice to the grey of the empty sky in Chicago during winter. On this particular late afternoon in December of 2012, the shade was particularly heavy and ominous. With the light snow falling and the slush darkening my shoes as I walked through the parking lot of a Rosemont Starbucks, the sky may have seemed more grey than usual because of my mood that day.

I was counting on a miracle.

My Turning Point associate, and Silent Generation mentor, Bill Montgomery, and I were meeting at Starbucks before heading to a political event in the city. My mood matched the weather as things were not looking good for the fresh-birthed organization that was Turning Point USA. It seemed like we kept taking one step up and then two steps back. We just weren't able to generate forward momentum.

I had no idea as I kicked snow slop off my shoes and walked into the coffee shop that this was about to be a turning point for Turning Point.

On that particular date, Turning Point USA was essentially broke. We had $3,000 in the bank and $2,600 in bills that were due. We were in the same position as was Jimmy Stewart's character, George Bailey, in the classic holiday film *It's a Wonderful Life*. The day that the run on the banks started, they were trying to make it to close with at least one dollar left in the vault. If they couldn't, they wouldn't be able to open the next day.

We were down to our last dollar.

At the moment of that Starbucks meeting, the atmosphere in the country surrounding what we call conservative political ideals was very dark. Mitt Romney had just been thoroughly beaten in an election that none of us thought was losable. I understood how America's voters had been tricked into voting for Barack Obama the first time, but with four years of objective evidence regarding his anti-American and anti-free market agenda, myself and others were certain that the American people would repudiate his actions at the polls. Besides, while Romney was far from the ideologist's dream candidate, he was a proven and successful leader and manager, so he should have presented a very acceptable, if not desirable, alternative to the incumbent.

Instead, everything had gone wrong. Romney had run a very bad campaign and managed to snatch defeat from the jaws of victory. Whether it was his inexplicable second and third debate performances, or his backing away from campaigning after Hurricane Sandy, or his inability to be unapologetic about his business successes, or some combination of those and other reasons, it really didn't matter. He failed, and now conservative Americans were discouraged and America would continue to suffer.

One of the reasons that Romney failed was his inability to attract young voters. After the election, Tufts University analyzed the voting behavior on that November 2012 election day. The study showed that Obama won voters in the age category of 18–29 by a 67–30 margin over Romney nationally. More importantly, in the swing states of Florida, Virginia, Pennsylvania, and Ohio, Obama won at least 61 percent of voters in each. If Romney had just been able to win 50 percent of the votes he would have carried all four.

This failure demonstrated the need to educate young people about free markets and to reach out to them in compelling and relevant ways. As an example, in Ohio back in late September of 2012, a young sophomore student at Cedarville University by the name of Josh Thifault was contacted by a gentleman he had met at an off-campus event. The gentleman thought the campus could be a good place for a political action group to set up a call center with student volunteers to generate support for Romney. He wondered if Josh could put him in touch with a student who could help with the project.

Having no background in this himself, Josh was interested. He asked how many volunteers the group was seeking. The caller suggested they were hoping to maybe get 12. Josh said he could personally do much better than that and asked for the opportunity. The caller was skeptical and said he'd get back to him. In less than an hour he called and suggested while they thought Josh was ambitious, he could give it a try. Josh was told if it didn't work they would have to pull the plug and get someone else.

Using pure energy and passion, Josh generated a volunteer staff of 280 students within a week! The PAC was shocked. Never did they dream that such mobilization could occur on a campus. They were, like the rest of the traditional establishment, completely clueless about how to reach out to young people and how important they could be.

Today, Josh is a full-time activist employed by Turning Point.

Another factor in Romney's failure was the clampdown by the IRS on conservative groups, in particular, anything having to do with the Tea Party. The story was still a few months away from breaking nationally, but those of us on the ground as activists were already very familiar with the chilling effect that the IRS had had on fundraising and activism. The impact can't be overstated. How else do you explain the incredible victories achieved in the 2010 election as a rejection of Obama and then not rejecting Obama, himself, when he ran again in 2012?

ᘓ   ᘓ   ᘓ

Sometimes even I wonder how I ended up becoming a political activist. I was born in Arlington Heights, Illinois, in 1993 and I grew up in the near-north suburb of Prospect Heights. My father is an entrepreneur with his own architectural practice and I grew up in that kind of pro-business environment. Mom is a mental health counselor and I'd like to believe she has taught me compassion. They have been great parents.

Politically, I would describe our home as low intensity Republican. My parents admired Reagan, support a strong military, and believe in free markets and low taxes. Political discussions were not frequent in my home. They read *The Wall Street Journal* and they watch Fox News but they don't leave it on all day as background noise. They have been supportive of my political efforts and I'm sure a bit puzzled, wondering where all this came from in their son. I have a sister whom I love but who does not share the same kind of interests as do I. I'm a family anomaly.

I was a bit of a contrarian right from the beginning. While attending Wheeling High School I did do some "normal" things for a boy my age. I played on the football and basketball teams, and I also played the saxophone. But I had an almost inherent interest in politics and current events. My first vivid memory of issue-oriented discussion was debating a teacher in sixth grade about climate change. I think that is almost the atypical definition of atypical.

My freshman year of high school was the year of the original "Hope and Change" Obama movement. With Wheeling, Illinois, being a very Democratic community and my being in a public school, there was significant pressure to comply with the pro-Obama school message. My contrarian side had me almost reflexively resisting the school's efforts to indoctrinate me, and I also took notice and offense to the fact that they were trying to indoctrinate students in general in an educational setting.

That campaign did get me to take an interest in economics in general, and free markets in particular, as my preferred economic system. I remember feeling very disappointed when John McCain lost in the general election, but the interest I had developed in the process was going to remain with me. McCain might have been finished as a presidential contender, but I was just getting started as an activist.

The next event to take place that had a major impact on shaping my positions and values was what happened in our neighboring state of Wisconsin with Governor Scott Walker and the efforts to recall him. Walker had made an enemy of the public sector unions when he called for the end to collective bargaining rights as part of necessary state austerity measures. Teachers from my school participated in organized group trips up to Wisconsin to participate in rallies against Walker and in support of public sector unions. Not to be outdone, I wrote a news column piece for my high school paper, which was published to the disdain of some of my teachers.

As this was going on, I was sharpening my arguments for free markets. Capitalism was becoming my bread and butter issue and I was reading the works of Hayek, Freidman, von Mises, and others. I wasn't certain what I was going to do with my life just yet, but I was certain it was going to involve promoting these ideas. In April of 2012, while still a senior in high school, I was asked to speak at a Tea Party rally in Lisle, Illinois. It was at that rally, after my speech, that I was approached by a gentleman named Bill Montgomery.

Bill Montgomery has been a serial entrepreneur for most of his life. He had success in the newspaper business, as an antique shop owner, and as the owner of the top-rated Cajun restaurant in the Midwest. Bill had the good fortune to be approached to buy his business operation just before the financial collapse in 2008. Having done well, he had turned his interest to politics and supporting conservative causes.

Bill told me I couldn't go to college. Now, this sort of advice is unheard of for an older gentleman to give to a high school senior. But there is nothing ordinary about Bill. He told me that the speech I had just given was a speech that every young American needs not just to hear but to learn. He encouraged me to consider starting a campus organization to spread the word and he committed to help me start it. It sounded like the craziest idea anyone had ever had, so I said what anyone would obviously say: OK. Let's do it.

On June 5, 2012, the same day that Scott Walker defeated his opponents who sought to have him recalled, I legally formed Turning Point USA. I was fully two days graduated from high school and used my own graduation gift money as part of the seeding. I was all in.

ç   ç   ç

As we sat in Starbucks that day, Bill knew I was discouraged. With the election loss so fresh, nobody on the donor side of things wanted to hear about messaging to young people and teaching them about free markets and individual liberty. I was coming up on what would have been the end of the first semester of my freshman year of college. I was thinking, if only I had done what almost every other high school graduate does and enrolled in a four-year university and moved on campus. Instead of sitting in a coffee shop near O'Hare Airport worrying about saving a fledgling organization, I would have been landing at O'Hare Airport and heading home to visit family and friends. Maybe it wasn't too late. Maybe I should just shut this down and head off to school. I could fight another day.

I signed on to the Starbucks Wi-Fi (a combination of two free market elements to be discussed later in this book) and using my Apple laptop (another great product of free enterprise which I will also discuss later) I showed Bill the Obama website. It was so good. Everything they did was brilliant in how they used modern technology, social media, and messaging to connect with young voters. They owned the collegiate world. Maybe if I just went back to school I could figure this out. I told Bill that many donors and other supporters I met kept telling me to just go back to school. Maybe they were right.

Bill told me no.

ç   ç   ç

A couple of days after starting Turning Point in June of 2012 I attended CPAC-Chicago. It was there that I first saw Foster Friess, a prominent conservative voice and influential donor who became an early and integral supporter of Turning Point. I used the local convention as a way to introduce myself to the people who were planning the annual national CPAC convention which takes place each winter near Washington, D.C. I was hustling them to allow me to have a role at the convention on stage. That effort eventually paid off.

Neil Cavuto caught wind of what we were doing and had me as a guest on his Fox television show in July. Immediately after that appearance, we raised $3,000 and I learned a lesson about the utility of television appearances to establish credibility. That was a lesson I have tried to put to good use over time.

In August of that year, Bill and I made the trip to the Republican convention in Tampa, Florida. This story is worth telling in some detail because of how important it was and because of the drama we experienced. We knew that the Republican convention was the epicenter of conservative political activity and that in attendance would be a Who's Who List of politicians, donors, influencers, and media personalities. At first we were going to make the 18-hour straight-through drive from Chicago to Tampa, but Bill saw fit to buy us a couple of airplane tickets. Without any scheduled meetings, without even badges, we set out.

Because of a travel plan mix-up, we ended up staying in Sarasota instead of Tampa, a good hour and 15-minute drive each way. We would drive into Tampa in the morning and camp out at either the downtown Hilton or the Marriot and look for opportunities to connect with people. Further complicating the matter was Hurricane

Isaac, which made its presence felt at the beginning of the convention. It was an inauspicious start for us.

Being new at the convention game, we didn't realize that getting into the convention wasn't as simple as buying a ticket. You need a pass, and they are more valuable than cigarettes in a maximum security prison. We were spending our time working nearby and offsite to try to get someone to let us have a pass. No success. It was starting to look as though the entire trip was going to be wasted, and we didn't have the time or money to waste on anything.

Prior to the convention, there were two things I had done that wound up becoming very important. The first was that I made a connection with Evan Draim, the youngest delegate at the convention. Because of our age and enthusiasm, Evan and I were kindred spirits. The other thing I had done was to try to turn myself into a living version of FBI facial recognition software by studying the faces of the well-connected Republicans and conservatives.

I was attempting repeatedly to reach Evan Draim via text to see if he could get us a pass. No response. I reached out to Fox News, Neil Cavuto's show in particular, to see if I could get interviewed. They responded that they would love to but that I needed a pass to get in first. I was in the middle of a Joseph Heller novel.

I plugged in my phone to charge in the lobby of the Marriot with only 2% battery left. When the charge reached 9% I received a text from Evan. He had a one-hour pass for me if I could get to the center and meet him right away. I grabbed my phone with almost no battery and sprinted over the center. I met Evan and got my one-hour pass. I was in the door. Now what?

I called the producers of Cavuto's show and told them I was in the building. Could I get an interview? They said maybe tomorrow (and of course I'd need a pass). I explained my situation and asked if there was anything they could do. They told me Neil was entering the facility shortly and they told me at which gate I could meet him. Perfect. One problem, however: my one-hour badge was about to expire.

I found an elderly gentleman in the lobby looking as though he was getting ready to leave. I approached him and asked if I might be able to use his pass. I explained that I had a very important meeting but I needed an extension of my pass and was looking for a solution. He gave me his and I ran to find Neil. Success! I found him; he greeted me warmly, and asked his staff member to get me a pass for the next day. The next day I was a guest on his show live from the convention floor. The ripple effect from that national interview on that stage would become very valuable from a donor and public awareness perspective.

Things weren't quite done yet. After the Cavuto show, it was time for Bill and me to leave. We were out of time and out of money. We had generated a national television appearance and that was a primary goal. It could have been more productive, but it wasn't a waste. Bill then reminded me that "it isn't over until it's over." He had no idea how right he was.

As we were leaving the building and coming down a stairwell into a nearly vacant corridor, there was a nicely dressed man wearing a cowboy hat and giving an interview to a reporter. My FBI mental software kicked in and I told Bill the man was Foster Friess.

I went up and introduced myself. I told him that I wanted to create the MoveOn.org of the right. MoveOn was founded in 1998 in response to the Clinton-Lewinsky scandal, and by 2012 was an incredibly powerful force for anti-American propaganda in all 50 states and had a strong campus presence. I asked for his help. He gave me his card and told me to reach out. As Bill and I walked away we were amazed at the luck of running into him. I asked Bill if he thought he would really donate to our cause. Bill told me only if I reminded him. I did remind him a few days later and he sent me a check with a note that said, "Go start the MoveOn of the right!"

As the fall semester started on college campuses, we had no real presence of any sort. We were using social media to generate awareness and interest in the concept. A couple of the schools where we got good first responses were actually surprising: the University of Wisconsin in Madison and Marquette University in Milwaukee. Both of these schools have reputations for very liberal campuses. We concluded that we were likely going to receive cries for help from students who felt like a silenced minority. They were looking for a voice.

In October I was asked to speak at CPAC Colorado as part of a panel with Guy Benson. While my presence on the panel made Guy look old (he is eight whole years older than I), he forgave my youth and from that moment forward has been a key supporter of Turning Point efforts and events. I also continued my lobbying efforts with the national CPAC people about the upcoming conference. They assured me I'd have a role to play.

We worked hard through the election season and felt like we were making connections. With the help of Foster Friess, Neil Cavuto, and others we had raised $30,000 in a few months, and had done so during an election season which I would come to learn was a hard time to raise money for non-campaign-type causes. That said, we were still small potatoes and we were on the ropes.

ϲ   ϲ   ϲ

As the snow kept falling and the skies got greyer, Bill Montgomery understood my weariness and concern, but he believed so strongly in the importance of our mission that he encouraged me to continue. His thought was that we could work in six-month stages and keep reevaluating at each six-month juncture. He reminded me of the Team Left activist group, MoveOn.org. I admired their tactics and detested their messages.

Bill asked me how I thought they might have felt after the 2004 election when George Bush won a second term. With all their infrastructure and efforts, they couldn't defeat a controversial president who had lost the popular vote during his first election. Bill reminded me that they didn't give up. They doubled down and were now a public opinion-shaping powerhouse. Bill knew he was pushing buttons with me because many times I had said that Turning Point was going to be the MoveOn.org of the right.

Bill suggested that we get a list of everyone who had donated to the Romney campaign and that we start right in our own backyard of Illinois. He also urged me to try to get as many media appearances as possible (we had learned already they helped to raise money). He said to get our logo in plain sight wherever we can and to work on disseminating the Turning Point message in a concise way to build a brand.

In the end, he sold me. When I walked out of Starbucks I wasn't optimistic, but I wasn't pessimistic either. I was reassured and resolved. If I remember right, the color of the sky had even changed from "Chicago grey" to a pleasant hue of blue.

ℭ   ℭ   ℭ

From the moment I left that coffee shop, Turning Point began to experience a forward trajectory with an increasing rate of acceleration. In this early post-election stage, there were key people who had an incredible impact on Turning Point. I'll mention several of them because their involvement and the connections they made created a logarithmic multiplier for us.

Right after that coffee shop turning point, I made a connection with Mike Miller, a Barrington, Illinois, jeweler and conservative cause supporter. Mike was down after the election results and was admittedly struggling with what he wanted to do next, if anything, in terms of political support and involvement. When I met with him and shared what we were doing, he seemed enthused, but as a jeweler, it was also the busy Christmas season. He said he'd get back to me after the holidays.

With one of Bill's directives to me being that getting on national TV as a 19-year-old was a big deal, in early January of 2013 I headed to New York to see if I could find my way back onto Fox. On January 10, I was a guest on both Stuart Varney's show and Neil Cavuto's show. That accomplishment caught the attention of Mike Miller back in Barrington. He wrote us a check and adopted our cause.

About this time, I was asked to be the Master of Ceremonies for CPAC 2013 in Washington. It was an incredible honor. It was hard to imagine that less than a year earlier I was a high school senior. Only a couple of months earlier I was ready to throw in the towel.

Mike Miller invited me to attend a fundraising event featuring Newt Gingrich. I had learned from the self-help books I'd read the importance of meeting people, so I immediately accepted. At that event I met Joe Walsh, now a former U.S. congressman and a radio talk show host. Joe became a very vocal and influential mouthpiece for Turning Point. I also met Chicago business owner Gary Rabine, founder of the national paving company The Rabine Group. Gary would go on to become very important to Turning Point and to me.

When I eventually appeared at CPAC, Gary sent his son Austin to meet me and see me speak. Austin went home and told his dad about me and about Turing Point. Gary reached out to me and became what I call my first "earned" contact. Gary invited me to be a speaker at a conference in West Palm Beach. I eagerly accepted and while I was there I drew the attention of an amazing lady by the name of Allie Hanley. Allie would reappear in my life in a few months and make an incredible difference.

In March of 2013 I also had an opportunity to meet a man who had aspirations to be the governor of Illinois. Bruce Rauner loved what Turning Point was doing and became a supporter financially and vocally. It was an incredibly important relationship because of his influence right in the middle of our home turf, which was the greater Chicago area.

In August of 2013 we hosted our first event for donors and students, at the Chicago Prime Steakhouse. We were able to showcase our programs and our plans. The event validated us in the minds of the people who were there and marked another turning point. Our campus presence was growing and our messages were taking hold.

October of 2013 saw the return of Allie Hanley to my life. She called and invited me to a David Horowitz event. I attended, and a new world of influential conservatives migrated into the Turning Point family. Allie Hanley opened the entire southern corridor for us. Allen Witt and Greg Gianforte would do the same for us in the West.

Turning Point wasn't just taking over campuses; we were taking over the passions and interests of very influential people.

Along the way in all of this, we made a key hire. Crystal Clanton was a young and passionate devotee of free markets and liberty. She wanted to come and work with us to help build Turning Point. It was the best hire we ever could have made. Crystal's attention to detail and ability to organize turned us into a business operation instead of just a movement. She has skills and talents that I don't have. The organization is deeply indebted to her.

In July of 2014 we needed to hire staff. We started with 10, funding in part made possible using donations from an appearance I made earlier in the year at the Horatio Alger Event (invited by Foster Friess). Our model was going to be to flood the market with materials and messaging that could be disseminated by Turning Point, and by other groups already in existence that could benefit from our ability to create appealing and sticky ideas. We approached this as if we were trying to build a business, not start a think tank or social club. Conversions would be our measure of profits.

In August of 2014, after an arduous legal battle, Turning Point USA was finally granted its 501(C)(3) status. The floodgates opened. This was what so many donors had been waiting for; especially institutional donors and foundations. The status was granted, by coincidence, on the night of our second anniversary party. The atmosphere was enthusiastic to begin with, but when I announced the IRS approval, the room erupted in applause. Everyone in attendance knew what this meant. It was simultaneously humbling and exhilarating for me.

In the fall semester of 2014 we launched a program with a controversial title on every campus in the country where we had a presence. We called it "Big Government Sucks." For 10 weeks we had a different theme that used posters, literature, and personal engagements to hammer home the message that government was too big and was jeopardizing our freedom. While some of our donors were nervous at first, they came to realize that we knew how to connect with people of our own demographic. It worked and generated national attention.

In 2015 as we continued to grow we hosted three student conferences that were new and unique. First, we had a Young Women's Leadership Conference where 125 conservative high school and college females from around the country attended. Then we held a Young Latino's Leadership Summit with 50 attendees. Finally, we conducted our High School Conference with 110 students from around the country. Nobody had ever done anything like this. As this book is written, attendance for all three conferences in 2016 is expected to at least double for each event.

At the date of this writing, Turning Point USA has a field staff of 83 part-time and 60 full-time paid members. Our 2016 budget is at $5.5 million. At the first CPAC we attended we brought four people. In 2016 we had 300. We have charters for Turning Point on more than 280 campuses and some form of presence on more than 1,000. On Facebook we are reaching 30 million people per week. We have a Twitter army of 10 million. Every number I'm sharing will be obsolete by the time you read this. Our growth is incredible and a result of incredible people, very hard work, and luck.

¢   ¢   ¢

What has happened in the time that's passed since I walked out of that Starbucks on a snowy afternoon is something that could not really have been imagined. I know I didn't imagine it. I just kept going. The contributions of the people along the way and the daisy chain of connections were so fortuitous they defy explanation.

We have had a lot of luck. Luck is a funny thing. To be a recipient you have to show up and be standing there ready to receive it. Every single member of Turning Point has been showing up and growing up relentlessly since we started. It might be luck but it isn't an accident. We have put ourselves in position to benefit from events. It's working.

We live and breathe by celebrating capitalism, individual liberty, and limited government. We keep it simple. It connects with students of every imaginable demographic group. No matter how you slice them, they respond to these three elements. Of course, these are the three things that have been under assault in America for quite some time. We know that what Turning Point is doing is a long game. We need to arm a generation with facts, arguments, and passion.

Our approach is different than other groups that have come before us. We are street fighters using modern technology as our weapon. We are taking a road less traveled, and it's making a difference.

Now I want to show you what we are working toward. I want to show you an America where today's Turning Point members have come of age and created change. What follows in the next chapter is what we can do if you let us and if you help us.

CHAPTER 2

Back to America's Future

*"Optimism is a strategy for making a better future.
Because unless you believe that the future can be better,
you are unlikely to step up and take responsibility for making it so."*

—NOAM CHOMSKY

In May of 2012, the Barack Obama Re-Election Campaign posted on their website a slideshow entitled "The Life of Julia." The idea was to take an ordinary woman, Julia, and show how through the course of her life she would not only be able to benefit from big government programs, but how her quality of life would be greatly impeded if those programs didn't exist.

Starting at age 3, when Julia entered into the Head Start program, and culminating at age 67, when she retires and starts to benefit from Medicare and Social Security, Julia was created by Team Obama specifically to contrast her hypothetical subsidized life with what it would be if the cold and calculating Mitt Romney were to become president.

Beyond Julia's alpha and omega with government assistance mentioned above, there are a variety of other stops at the trough throughout her life journey. For example, a cartoon depiction of a faceless Julia (I suspect they made her faceless so as not to offend people whose faces looked different from hers) standing at a bus stop, ostensibly waiting to be picked up for work, is accompanied by the following caption:

> **Under President Obama**: *Because of steps like the Lilly Ledbetter Fair Pay Act, Julia is one of millions of women across the country who knows she'll always be able to stand up for her right to equal pay. She starts her career as a web designer.*

In each of the slides about Julia's life there is some sort of unwritten but automatically and involuntarily inferred message about what fate would have awaited her without the presence of big government assistance. In this case, we conclude that Julia would not be able to stand up for herself, prove herself, or assert herself in the workplace without a government booster seat. Just being determined and capable wouldn't be enough because she is a woman. What was once condescension has now become sound policy.

Continuing with Julia's "assisted living" arrangement in the Oppressive States of America, we address her need to try to prevent pregnancy. She stands in what appears to be a doctor's waiting area but with a full shelf of medicines mounted on the wall as if they had been stocked by Procter & Gamble. The caption for that slide reads:

> **Under President Obama**: *For the past four years, Julia has worked full-time as a web designer. Thanks to Obamacare, her health insurance is required to cover birth control and preventive care, letting Julia focus on her work rather than worry about her health.*

For anybody reading this for the first time you can immediately understand why the site generated countless web-based parodies. Just imagine the 20-something young professional sitting at her desk, chewing on a pencil, and unable to concentrate on her work out of fear of suddenly becoming pregnant. The viewer is drawn to the inescapable conclusion that without government assistance a woman would just not be able to do anything to control or protect her own body and health.

As a final illustration of Julia's protected path to success, let's consider what happens when she decides to start her own business and begin the journey to become a member of the much maligned "One-Percenters":

> **Under President Obama:** *Julia starts her own web business. She qualifies for a Small Business Administration loan, giving her the money she needs to invest in her business. President Obama's tax cuts for small businesses like Julia's help her to get started. She's able to hire employees, creating new jobs in her town and helping to grow the local economy.*

Even going to borrow money to start a business now needs to get kick-started through a government program. There is particular irony in this because if you look back in history to when what is now called "capitalism" (it had no such name at the time) was first truly unleashed during the initial Industrial Revolution in early 18th century England, one of the key components was the financial intermediary service provided by what have now evolved into commercial banks. These intermediaries collected money from people who had a surplus and "invested" it for them into business activities to generate a return. Et voila! Enter financial leverage. Now in 21st century America, Obama supporters were telling Julia that without government assistance the cornerstone in the foundation of free markets could no longer support her or others.

In each of these slides where Julia is told how "Big Sister" takes care of her, there is a section below that explains what happens if she turns to the dark side of the Force and votes for Romney. In the case of her business loan, she is warned:

> **Under Mitt Romney:** *The Romney/Ryan budget could cut programs like the Small Business Administration by 20%.*

This is simple and to the point: If you vote for Mitt he is going to make it less likely that the government will help you get a loan.

Of course, they know that Julia is gullible enough to then figure out that without the government she could never get a loan on her own merits in a free market. Ironically, in today's America, where the banking industry has become an embedded partner of government, it *is* difficult to get a small business loan without the government's help. That, however, is not a failure of free markets. It reflects the *absence* of a free market in banking.

So, Julia becomes the animated representation of Obama's 2008 campaign slogan "Yes We Can!" The emphasis is on the "we." There is nothing about the life of Julia that leads us to believe that she is able to accomplish anything on her own. She is dependent; she is incapable; she is a victim ready to happen. The collectivist Obama "we" is a subliminal call for many to join together to take from and oppress many others. It is their duty. They must. If they don't, poor Julia will be left to fend for herself, and she is simply not capable.

For many people who think like I do that America has lost its way, this story of Julia might seem like it is much more than campaign spin; it might seem like it is inevitable reality. But I am optimistic. If I weren't optimistic I certainly wouldn't have committed my life and efforts at the age of 18 to trying to change the trajectory of America.

The 1998 film *Sliding Doors*, with Gwyneth Paltrow, famously shows what the life of a young woman would become depending upon whether she did, or didn't, catch a train immediately after having just lost her job. The "Life of Julia" shows one possible version of America. Allow me to slide the door closed on her and that bleak, dependent future and instead open the door to a very different America.

An Alternative American Story Line

I'm not buying Julia's story; not for a minute. It is not at all paradoxical to see that the only reason that Julia is in need of government assistance to get through her life is because government itself has so interfered with the workings of free markets and has so corrupted the initiative and self-confidence of its citizens that barriers have been erected to success and self-actualization. These barriers are both structural and spiritual. For decades our political leaders have created an America that fosters feelings of entitlement, dependency, and victimization in too many Americans.

If we could eradicate those three feelings and replace them by making Americans feel like they are self-determining, independent, and always on the offensive in confronting whatever circumstances are presented to them, then we have a chance to live in an America that is more in line with what the Founding Fathers envisioned. How we get to that America will require some hard work, and that process will be described in this book. But before we get to the "how" I want to share with you my vision of the America that should be. This is an America that I see materializing in my lifetime. I'm going to be called naïve by some and a fanciful idealist by others. To both those groups I respond with a giant millennial Whatever! If somebody thinks this vision is unattainable, then I will spend the remaining pages trying to persuade you that it isn't. If after that you still think it's too difficult, then let's part agreeing to reconnect in 30 years and see what's happened in between.

Since Comrade Obama chose the life of the faceless cartoon Julia to illustrate the fruits of collectivism, I present to you Julio. If Julio were a cartoon character, he would have a face. The face would be one that reflected at once strength, determination, and loving kindness. It would be the face of a man who just at a glance conveyed a very simple image.

An image that says, "Yes I can."

I give you, "The Life of Julio."

Julio at Age 5: Julio Starts His Education

Julio is holding his father's hand as he walks up the sidewalk approaching his new school. It is his first day of kindergarten. Julio heard someone mention that kids are often scared on their first day but he feels no fear, only anticipation and excitement. In the short walk to school from his home on the near northwest side of Chicago all he could think of were his father's words telling him that "today was the day he gets to start becoming whatever it is that he wants to be."

As they get closer to the front door of the school, Julio notices all of the different colors and features of all of his new classmates. Everyone looks so different, but they also look the same: excited. Julio thinks it is good he is going to meet so many different people, each as excited about school as he is.

The school itself is only a few years old and started because of the voucher program recently put into place for primary and secondary education. With the elimination of the U.S. Department of Education a decade ago, control of schools and funding returned to the individual state level. The voucher program, coupled with the decertification of teacher unions, led to the creation of numerous schools staffed by smart and experienced people in neighborhoods which previously only permitted access to poorly managed government schools (unless a family was already wealthy enough to send their child to a private school). As a result, everybody now had access to the school of their choice. Julio thinks his family has made a really good choice.

Julio is proud of his parents. His mom and dad came to America 10 years ago from Mexico. They were able to take advantage of a new and simplified immigration program that allows people to enter the country for a probationary two-year period in order to find work. His parents signed papers that said if they agreed to not commit any crimes or attempt to apply for any taxpayer-funded benefits or services during those two years then they would be eligible to apply for full citizenship after that time. Both of Julio's parents are now full-fledged U.S. citizens and both are gainfully employed.

Mom told Julio that for years there had been anger and fear in the United States over people like his parents coming to live there. She said it was because some Americans felt that people were coming here to take advantage of government-supported welfare programs and that working Americans shouldn't have to pay for noncitizens to live here. Once the system was changed, Mom said that the problem corrected itself almost overnight. Only people who want to work come here and Americans welcome them because they know that they have come to the United States for the same reason their ancestors had come: to live better lives as a byproduct of their own efforts

As a result of the new immigration system, an entire industry sprouted up overnight to serve people living in that two-year window. There are medical clinics, language centers, employment search centers, and job skill training facilities. All of these arose completely unplanned and without any sort of intentional coordination between them. Even so, when Julio heard his dad talk about them, it was almost as if each of them had deliberately worked together to help him. It was like an invisible hand was guiding them.

When he arrived in the United States, Julio's dad took a job as a laborer on a farm outside of Chicago and was now a supervisor. There were lots of these small and profitable farms around. Once the USDA and other agencies were stripped of their power to regulate who could grow what, and who could charge how much, small farms were once again able to flourish. The end of price supports had caused some pain and disruption in the economy for a while, but nobody went hungry and now, with the government out of the agriculture business, many individual farmers could get back into the agricultural business. Some people had warned that if the government didn't regulate what and how food was produced that farmers would be able to poison consumers.

Julio didn't know about anyone who had died from their food being poisoned.

As his dad pulled open the big red wooden doors he looked down at Julio and said, "Now remember, son, there is nothing more exciting in life than learning. Learning is how you discover all the things that your life has to offer and which of those things you want to explore. Go inside and start learning. Every single day you spend inside this school is going to be amazing."

Julio walked down the hallway thinking, "I want to be like my dad. I want to be like me."

Julio at Age 18: Julio Goes to College

Julio is ready to begin preparing for the rest of his professional life.

Having graduated from high school with honors, Julio is now ready to pursue the path he is certain is right for him, that of a computer software design engineer. He is going to miss high school. Outside of the fellowship with diverse classmates, he learned so much about American history, math, science, literature, and grammar that he actually had a hard time deciding what interested him more. His thorough and well-rounded secondary education exposed him to much, but ultimately he decided to choose the demanding world of high-tech.

The school that Julio will be attending will provide a three-year program that combines intensive study in his chosen field with higher level academic education. Julio plans to supplement his coursework in software engineering with studies in accounting, business law, and marketing. He has a plan that someday he would like to start his own business in the technology field and he wants to make sure he is prepared by taking relevant courses with true utility.

Julio also plans to take electives in philosophy and logic. He wants to learn how to make decisions and reason through situations by applying consistent and thorough analysis to each matter at hand. During high school, Julio noticed so many times when he was involved in some sort of stressful or complex situation that teachers or other adults were saying and doing things that just didn't seem to make sense. Julio could think of numerous times where he was watching the activities of adults and thinking that they were getting so emotional they weren't making good decisions. It struck him as being dangerous and it made him wonder how often people, businesses, even countries found themselves in trouble because they didn't stop long enough to put aside emotion and instead employ reason?

Anyway, he thought some logic and philosophy might help.

A higher education was a lot less expensive than it used to be. In the not too distant past the federal government had control of the entire university financing system in the form of the various student loan programs. Working in lock-step with the universities themselves, the government made student loans easy to obtain. This allowed the universities to increase their tuition as much as they wanted, triggering an increase in the level of student loans the government would provide. There was a quid pro quo between the schools and the government as the schools could continue to get richer while the government was guaranteed to receive graduating class after graduating class of young people who were financially indebted and beholden to the state. Unfortunately for the students, they found themselves more often than not graduating $30,000–$50,000 in debt with a four-year degree that could not even help get them a job.

It took some time and the university system experienced some serious delirium tremens from the detox, but once the government exited the higher education funding market, tuition charges declined, programs became leaner with more focused offerings, and more specialized schools emerged. It was this type of school that was going to provide Julio with the skills and the specific knowledge required to make him immediately successful and eventually top-notch in the career he was choosing.

Julio is grateful that the system had changed before he ever had to enter college. His father actually knows someone who just finished paying off his student loans last year. Student loans still existed but now they are different. For the most part they are provided by one of the many new community banks which have emerged over the last 20 years since the repeal of Dodd-Frank and numerous other banking rules and regulations. Each bank has its own rules for making the loans and each family has to make an educational choice based upon what their circumstance could support and sustain. Julio knows that there are some assistance programs out there for families who are truly in financial need, but fortunately his mother's and father's hard work make it unnecessary for him to seek that sort of assistance.

Julio had a small loan to start school and he also had funds that his family had saved through special educational accounts. Between the two he had almost all of his tuition, but the balance of it came from a new and, for Julio, exciting source. Julio is going to be an intern.

Businesses are able to take advantage of a program that creates tax deductions for any educational contribution or any tuition assistance. There are no limits on the tax deductions so companies are increasingly investing in schools that graduate trained and competent workers. Many of these companies also offered internships along the way so that an employee can start with them at the beginning of school and possibly continue on after graduation. Julio has found just such a company that is going to provide him on-the-job experience while he gets his education and will also round out his tuition. In the past, these kinds of arrangements could only be offered by large Fortune 500 companies. Now the playing field has been leveled and any company willing and able to make the investment can do so. The result is a better trained workforce graduating from a more diverse group of schools.

Julio is about to begin an exciting educational experience. In just three short years he will master a skill, learn the business basics he will need to launch out on his own someday, and see the inner-workings of a real business that he could stay with after he graduated. He felt like running as fast as he could until he couldn't run any further. The energy he felt for this next phase of his life was exhilarating. He knows that the only impediment he will face will be Julio; nothing or nobody else. Only he could get in the way of his success. Julio isn't worried about that. He has never let himself down before.

Julio at Age 28: Working on a Dream

College had been a good ride for Julio. While completing coursework that ultimately led him to graduate with high honors, he found time to become involved in numerous campus activities, including serving as president of the campus chapter of Turning Point USA. Turning Point was a campus watchdog group that kept an eye out for professors or student groups that wanted to return to the days of big government control. Whenever Turning Point spotted a threat to freedom they would speak out to convince others on campus not to be tempted. Julio learned the history of Turning Point and knew they had been instrumental years earlier in the role of an activist group to turn the tide against big government.

It is seven years after his college graduation and he is still at the same company that had helped to put him through school. He feels a special bond with the people who run the company. It wasn't obligation. They had invested in him and he had worked and repaid that investment. This feeling was more akin to respect. He knows that the owners of the business had made a risky decision to invest in him and others and then they followed through knowing full well the risks of Julio and others not performing. They were committed. He admires that. Perhaps he would be able to do the same thing for people in the near future.

Julio is getting that entrepreneurial itch.

While Julio was making his way to a supervisory role in his company, he was also saving his money to be able to start his own technology company in the near future. Not content to just save money from his paycheck, Julio had taken a second job in order to save more money faster. He worked as a "car concierge" for the transportation pioneer Uber. Uber had started its private driver company years ago and stood against the joined forces of municipal governments and taxi cab companies to provide low cost and reliable transportation to passengers. Because of Uber's fight, the barriers to entry were eventually torn down and now private car services flourished, with consumers benefiting by having more choices and competitive fares. While Uber had long since moved to computer-driven cars, some people still liked the extra value of having a "driver" in the vehicle. For a slight premium Uber provided that service, and Julio was one of those people.

Julio's savings were growing. Since the elimination of the broke and bureaucratically bloated Social Security Administration, people like Julio were allowed to put away unlimited amounts of money for their own future and retirement. Julio laughed every time he thought about "retirement." Retire from what? Productivity? Creating value? Having fun? He couldn't imagine a life without activity. It was the things he did each day, at and away from work, which gave him the joy in life he always wanted to experience. Julio figured he'd let other people retire and then tell him what it's like.

Julio also put money away each week into his medical savings account. That account makes him feel like he is prepared to handle the kind of medical emergencies that can arise that don't require the use of your actual medical insurance. He is managing his risk and controlling his insurance costs. He has a sense of balance.

The various savings programs that had been introduced into the economy had helped lead to the rise of commercial savings institutions that were more flexible and community-based. These institutions also like to make loans into the community in which they operate. Julio has been talking to one such bank about what would be required to get a loan to help him start a business. He isn't quite ready yet, but he has a plan. He doesn't want to start his business too soon and borrow too much money because he knows that would make it harder to succeed. As much as Julio can taste the instant gratification of being his own boss, he also is going to be patient and do it when he can afford to do it. He figures that being a brave businessman doesn't equate to being a foolish businessman.

Julio's boss had called him into his office yesterday and told Julio that he was doing a great job and that he was glad he had invested in him years earlier. He also told Julio that he knew he was destined to start his own business someday. He could see it in Julio's eyes. He just wanted to let Julio know that it was ok with him and he would support him however he could. He asked Julio just to give him an early head's up when he thought the time was close. Julio promised he would.

Julio hopes that when he becomes an employer he will have the courage and character to speak so honestly and openly with his employees. He wants his employees to think as well of him, to respect him, the way he respects his boss. Without that kind of respect, what was the point in assuming the obligation of employing others?

Julio at Age 35: Ribbon-Cutting Day at Julio Tech

The day Julio had been planning and preparing for since he entered college has finally arrived. He is about to open the doors for the first time at his own computer technology company.

Julio stands outside the rented commercial office space with his wife, their two children, and his first 10 employees. They are going to cut a ribbon he has hung across the door. Julio is a student of history and he had found it interesting that ribbon-cutting ceremonies likely originated as part of marriage ceremonies, where the bride would cut the ribbon as the groom came into the church to symbolize the obstacles they had to overcome in order to finally be joined together. Julio liked the image that conjured for him. He knows how difficult it was for him to get this far and he feels like he is using that experience to form a bond and commitment with and to his employees.

In order to start his business, Julio had been saving money for years. He would not have been able to save as much money if his past employer hadn't paid him such a fair and healthy wage. In fact, Julio knew that all of the people at his past employer's company were paid well. Julio wondered if his boss had paid the workers so well because he was benevolent or because competition in the labor market forced him to offer very competitive wages. He decided that the motives of his boss didn't really matter. What matters is that because his boss was acting in his own self-interest, Julio was able to save enough to realize his dream.

Julio didn't have all of the money he needed to start a business. In order to open the doors and hire his people he needed a loan from a commercial bank. He went to a bank that had opened just down the street from his last employer several years ago, a bank that was started by business leaders in the community, and he asked for a loan. The process turned out not to be as complicated as Julio feared it might be. The bank asked him questions about his plan for the business, had him provide some financial information, and told him he had to personally stand behind the business by guarantying the loan. Julio thought all of these things were reasonable, including that guaranty. After all, if he didn't believe in what he was doing why should anyone else?

Before opening his business doors, Julio had to find vendors for the parts he needed to assemble his technology products. He had been able to source everything he needed from companies that were based in the United States. He recalled being told how at one time it was virtually impossible to source any kind of product from U.S. companies because the prices were so much higher than they were overseas. Fortunately, because of the dramatic reductions in government regulations imposed upon business operations and the significant lowering of all tax rates, especially taxes on businesses, American companies now all had lower cost structures and were able to compete.

He had learned in high school history the story of the copper mines in the northern Midwest which ultimately could no longer afford to operate because they weren't cost-competitive with other countries. Tourists would be taken on a guided trip of an abandoned copper mine and then led to a souvenir shop, where they could purchase copper trinkets that were actually made somewhere in Africa. Julio was heartened to know that he would be selling a product that was created with American labor and ingenuity, and then bought primarily by American consumers.

Julio loves his children and family and has found himself naturally drawn to other people who have similar life circumstances. Perhaps not coincidentally, eight of his new employees each have young children. Julio has hired someone to come on site each day and run an informal nursery for his employees' toddlers. The cost of adding such a program is a deductible business expense, and because there is no government red tape regarding licensing a day care facility, Julio was able to use his knowledge of people and his educated sense to pick the right person for the job. He knows this is going to lead to a happier and less distracted work force. Even he looks forward to being able to peek in on his own kids during the work day!

Something interesting happened a couple of days earlier while Julio and his employees were doing some preopening work around the office. A man came and knocked on the door and asked if he could come in and talk to the employees. He told them that he was from a "union" and wanted to know if they would like to organize themselves and join. One of the employees asked him what would happen if they joined the union. The representative explained that each week they would send the union money from their paycheck and in return the union would try to get more money out of Julio for them and it would lobby the government to try and get special protections for them.

After saying "no thank you" and closing the door behind the befuddled representative, one of the employees turned and looked at the others and asked them why anybody would ever voluntarily join such a group. After a collective shoulder shrug, all of the employees went back to work, preparing for the opening of a brand new business.

Julio was thankful for their support. He was thankful for the support of his former employer. He was thankful for the support of those who helped to educate and prepare him along the way. He was thankful for the support of his family.

In general, Julio was very thankful.

Julio at Age 47: Julio Gets Sick

As he walked out of the doctor's office holding his son's hand, Julio was thinking he has had better days. He has recently also had worse.

Several months ago Julio was diagnosed with an autoimmune disorder that was serious, rare, but treatable. While it wasn't dampening his spirits, it was definitely draining his energy.

Fortunately, Julio was prepared for the onset of this illness, both medically and financially. He had been saving money for years without penalty or forced withdrawal in a medical spending account for both him and his family. Years of good health had allowed that account balance to grow quite large and Julio was able to contribute as needed to his treatment.

Julio and his family also have regular access to health care providers of all types and levels based upon their needs. The deregulation of the health care industry has permitted the establishment of all types of clinics and various treatment centers with relatively low overhead and easy access. Getting medical care has become similar to going to a restaurant. You can call ahead for a reservation or just walk in and get served as soon as there is availability. You can choose a "gourmet" setting, or grab something quick. The best part is that there is an abundance of quality providers filling whatever need you have in a timely, professional manner.

When it came to paying for services, Julio likes the way the system works. As a business owner he appreciates being able to know the price of something that includes all of the available options and then deciding what is really needed based on the cost and the circumstances. Prior to the doctor performing any treatment or issuing any prescription, Julio is told the price of the service. Julio then asks questions regarding different options or alternatives. He can open an app on his smartphone while he sits in the doctor's office and compare prices, even getting "insta-second opinions" from doctors online suggesting alternatives he might want to explore.

Once Julio decided what he wanted to do, he agreed to the procedure and the price with his health care provider. They then "closed the sale." Julio pays for the service (or is billed), and he submits the bill to his insurance provider. There are never any surprises in the process because even with the insurance carrier, once Julio knows what he is doing with the physician, he again turns to his smartphone and opens his insurance app. A few swipes later it lets him know immediately what they will pay and what he will pay for the procedure.

Julio knows that in the old system the patient never knew what anything was going to cost until the bill came in the mail from the insurance company. Sometimes the patient was pleasantly surprised that they owed little or nothing. Sometimes they were forced into financial ruin. Because all of the costs and all of the reimbursements were set as part of an agreement among government, the health care provider, and the insurance company, the actual consumer or patient was left out of every aspect of the process except the part that involved paying. Julio was glad he wasn't part of that system. In the process they have today he feels like he is in command of his own health care choices and costs.

Once direct third-party paying had been eliminated, and once the government was prohibited from mandating what could and could not be charged by providers and paid for by insurers, then all of the costs in the industry dropped dramatically. With costs no longer subsidized by the government, the medical industry became like every other industry. It could only charge what patients were able and willing to pay. The quality and quantity of medical information and doctor availability through web-based platforms made the medical market work much more efficiently than it ever could have under government direction.

Julio's insurance coverage and premiums were top-notch. Shopping for the right insurance was somewhat complicated, but in a good way. There were so many choices because insurance companies could compete with each other nationwide that Julio's biggest challenge was making sure he didn't miss finding the best deal. He liked to call it a "first-world problem."

According to his father, the biggest change that patients felt was the decrease in the cost of medication and the speed with which new drugs were coming onto the market. With the Food and Drug Administration's role reduced to investigating reports of unsafe medications, big pharmaceutical companies lost their oligopoly grip on the development and issuance of medications. Drug innovation flourished. In addition, more patients were being saved because the tortuous process of getting a new drug approved through the clinical trial process was no longer controlled by bureaucrats. Very sick people could gain access to very new treatments sooner and without restriction.

Julio had been able to be the recipient of just such an experimental drug. His doctor told him that just a few years ago Julio may not have been able to have the chance to try the new medication that was making him better. He may have even been given a "placebo" as part of a control group just to make certain the test satisfied the government. Unfortunately, the placebo group was often synonymous with the "death sentence" group because they weren't really being treated at all.

So as Julio got into his car that day he looked at his son and was grateful that he hadn't come down with his affliction 20 years ago. He was going to be fine and his family wasn't going to lose all that they had earned just to get him better. His son told him that he wanted to be a doctor someday so that he could save lives and become rich.

Julio told him those were both very noble goals.

Julio at Age 60: Julio Cashes Out

Twenty-five years after he cut the ribbon, Julio is ready to move into the next phase of his life. Some of his friends told him they can't imagine him retiring. He insists to them that he isn't retiring, he is just transitioning. Julio never has felt like he was stopping anything; he has always felt like he was starting something else.

He and his wife have four grown children. One is a doctor, one an instructor at a technical school, and the other two, a son and a daughter, work in the family business. It is to those two children that Julio is selling his controlling ownership interest. When he told them he had decided to sell them the business, he also told them that he was going to sell it to them for the actual value and not at a discount just because they were his children. They would have to pay full price. Upon hearing that from their father, the children both replied in unison by saying, "Of course. Why wouldn't we pay you what the business is worth?"

Julio knew then that he and his wife had done a good job as parents.

Julio now had 180 employees in his company. Many of them have been there for years and five were part of the original 10 who opened the doors with him a quarter-century earlier. All of those employees had been contributing to health and retirement savings accounts over the years and have acquired a sense of financial security. Low tax rates have allowed Julio to pay them more and allowed them to save more of what they have been paid.

It made Julio smile when he stopped to realize that these employees had been able to use their wages from this business he started to buy homes, to raise families, to live a complete and fulfilling life. He had always known from early in life that he wanted to help others, and he had done much with private charity along the way. What fascinated him was how he had provided so much help to so many people just by opening his doors each morning and asking them to come to work.

Most of the employees own their homes. Home prices are much more reasonable than they had been decades earlier when the federal government was busy pumping money into the mortgage market so politicians could gain favor with voters. After the system collapsed for the second time and tens of thousands of families suffered immeasurable loss, the government finally exited the mortgage market. Now, most mortgage loans are made by smaller banks that know neighborhoods and know the values in those neighborhoods. There was much more stability. People no longer buy homes primarily to bet on an increase in value to help them in their retirement. They now buy homes in order to have a nice place to live, and they save for their retirement with the right sort of financial investments.

Julio's children are getting a loan from the same community bank that had made the loan to Julio to start the business. The bank has grown a lot since then but still serves the community well. Two other banks that had started in the same area of town were keeping them responsive to the local market needs. Every borrower and depositor in the community has benefited from the competition among them.

Julio's employees take turns standing on a podium in what was now a massive rotunda entrance to the business facility. Each of them makes remarks as to how the business that Julio started with his own money and his own credit has benefited their lives. They express sincere gratitude.

When they finish, Julio stands up before them all and thanks them for their hard work and support, recognizing that without them he would not have the chance to move on to the next chapter of his life and do the things he was about to do. He tells them it is a wonderful thing when people could join together and be successful without anyone feeling as though anyone else had taken advantage of them. All of them have earned this success through their own efforts, hard work, and sacrifices. He reminds them of the sign just outside the main entrance to their building: *Self-Reliance Leads to Self-Satisfaction.*

Julio at Age 75: The Bohemian Life of Julio

As Julio promised, he never really retired. He just keeps going. His life now was like splashes of color on a Jackson Pollack canvas. He is doing so many different things and experiencing the joy of life in so many different ways, his only hint of regret is that he couldn't escape mortality. Even in that case Julio is convinced it isn't the end of life, just the start of the next one.

Julio spends time each day in a mix of activities that include painting, sailing, and even taking voice lessons. There had been so many things he had wanted to do all those years he was working inside his business that now he is devoted to working inside himself. He seems to discover a new passion or interest almost every day.

As Julio looks out his bay window sipping a glass of lemonade, he watches as his grandchildren set up a lemonade stand near the end of the driveway. To think that there was a time when a police officer might have driven by and written his grandkids a ticket for operating a lemonade stand without a license. Julio finds that hard to imagine. Now he can just sit and watch with pride as they enter into their own free market experience.

He takes satisfaction in knowing that his kids and grandkids will have a nice financial safety net after he and his wife pass on. Tax laws favorable to the creation and accumulation of wealth have allowed Julio to save more than he and his wife will ever need. It is also comforting to know that it will pass on tax-free to his heirs. He cannot believe they used to tax money that a father would leave to his son when that money had already been taxed at the time it was earned. There was something about that tax that really rubs him the wrong way. Imagine not allowing a parent to just give a child whatever it was they owned without penalty. Hubris, he thinks. Pure hubris.

After the grandkids "stock out" of lemonade, Julio and Grandma get them all in the car and they head downtown into the city. Julio likes the city. It is safe and clean, as are most of the cities in America. He knows how fortunate they are compared to other countries, where the inner cities are a place where people congregate because they are beholden to government assistance and subjugated by the ruling class. Without hope, they turn to crime and dependency. The United States has its problems with crime and poverty to be sure, but nothing like what exists in other parts of the world, where free markets haven't been enthusiastically embraced.

Julio and his wife take the kids into a theater, where they see a rollicking swashbuckler that utilizes 3D technology, now so advanced, the action actually appears to take place inside the audience. After the movie, they head off to the Museum of American History, where the latest exhibit is titled "Turn into 21st Century America." The exhibit features such things as cars you had to drive, phones you had to dial, doors you had to push or pull to open, and televisions that required a screen in order to project. Julio is amazed at what capitalism had accomplished in his and his father's lifetime.

After all that, they stop for ice cream. Ice cream is the one thing that Julio felt has not improved at all since he was his grandkids' age. It still tastes the same: perfect. It is good to think that maybe perfection isn't just an unreachable abstract goal.

It's time to head home. Julio needs to get to his part-time job as an Uber concierge. He doesn't need the money but he still loves the people. He feels as though he will be guiding folks through Chicago for as long as he can get in and out of those hovering, self-driven cars.

Julio vs. Julia: Who do you want to see? Who do you want to be?

If you compare the alternate versions of the idyllic life as presented by Barack Obama (Julia) and by me (Julio), the differences go far beyond someone relying primarily on government and someone relying primarily on herself or himself. The differences are more fundamental and have a broader impact than you might realize after just a superficial glance.

Everything that Julia does requires her to take from others; to take from society. She has to "get" at every level. She is a draining force. Julia's message to the world around her is, "Help me. I can't figure this out or get this done on my own." She confronts each life problem by asking, "What source can I turn to that will take care of this for me?" Julia exists on the backs of her fellow citizens.

Julio is exactly the opposite. His relentless focus on doing things for himself generates opportunities for everyone around him. Julio wanted to start a business, be his own boss, and provide for his family. As a consequence, 180 other people were able to find work and provide for their families. Julio is always looking at what is "next" and then turning to his instinctive thought, which is, "What do I have to do to get there?" The thought of how he could ask someone else to do it for him, whatever "it" was, would never occur to him.

Julio is always reaching out a hand to pull someone out of the undertow. Julia is always holding someone else down under the water so that she can get a breath.

There is another key difference between them. While the cartoon character of Julia may be featureless, there is a sadness that you can still see written on her empty face. Julia has a life that is absent real joy. Julia lives a life that is about getting through, a life that is about being done. Julia is like so many other people today who seem to spend their lives watching the seconds tick by on a doomsday clock. Julia plays life safe, just hoping to not get thrown off the island by the other "survivors."

Julio has a life that is all about joy, and in the process of living that life he is always bringing joy to others. Julio couldn't begin to think about retiring because Julio wouldn't know from what he would be retiring. As opposed to ever thinking about being "done," Julio is always thinking about "doing."

I believe that a life that is lived in freedom is a life that is always being lived. A life being lived in some state of dependency is a life that is always just being managed and endured. Right now in America there is a siren's song that calls people to become dependent. It wants them to place their future, their lives, into the hands of government.

Hillary Clinton says it takes a village to help build an individual. No it doesn't! It takes a lot of self-built individuals living and working with one another to make that village thrive. Hillary has it backwards.

If you like the vision of an America I see in my lifetime, if you like the life of Julio and pity the life of Julia, then keep reading as I share what I believe it will take to get us there. First, however, we need to spend a chapter looking at the current state of America and identify some of the problems we face. These problems have been created because of bloated government at every level and the culture of dependency and victimization it has created.

One thing is absolutely certain: the choice of the kind of America we get is still in our hands. Each of you reading this book needs to ask yourself whether you want Julia's life and world or Julio's life and world. It is my strong belief that most Americans want the life of Julio even if they don't see it clearly in themselves. It is the obligation of people who do see it to help others recognize it and act on it. Only through that sort of mass awareness can we open a different set of doors and walk into a different America.

CHAPTER 3

BIG GOVERNMENT SUCKS!

"We have met the enemy and he is us."

—WALT KELLY, satirical cartoonist (as expressed by his character Pogo,
who was lampooning America for harming itself unnecessarily)

I stated in the opening to this book that I would not make it be about all of the things that are wrong in America today. Enough of those books have been, and will be, written. My intention is to give a view of a different America (Julio's America) and then talk about how to get there. I'm trying to stay positive.

That said, it is important to at least panoramically create a view of the current setting to illustrate just how much we have to overcome and how much work will be required. America hasn't gotten to where it is at this moment over just the last couple of election cycles. It has taken years of government growth and invasiveness to place us in the situation we are in today. It is going to take some time to reverse.

The "Big Government Sucks" theme is one that Turning Point USA has used successfully on college campuses; so successfully, it was even co-opted by candidates early in the 2016 presidential campaign. Later in the book I will share the story around the message but for now let it suffice as a chapter heading because I believe it succinctly sums up the most compelling argument against a leviathan state.

When it is at its "best," big government replaces individual responsibility, choice, and initiative with reliance, limitations, and lethargy. In the United States today we are certainly seeing signs of each of these negative attributes. What can be deceptive is when we get caught witnessing the exploits of successful innovators or entrepreneurs, we can allow ourselves to think that things are great. After all, how else could they have become successful?

The problem with that reasoning is that it ignores all of the things that are not being accomplished by all of the people who have been consumed by the tidal wave of big government. Averaging out estimates, there are approximately 320 million people in this country. Imagine what could be if all 320 million woke up every morning feeling like Julio and not like Julia. America would become limitless.

At its worst, big government makes everyone a slave. History is filled with far more examples of that than it is with examples of freedom. Most of history has found people shackled and drawn at the hands of tyrants. We can't let the United States get to that point.

I'm going to take a look at the size of government from several angles. Each one of these has had entire books written about it and I would encourage anyone reading to engage in further research in any and all areas of interest. For my purposes, I just want to create a comprehensive sense of the enormity of the problem. The yet-to-be-born Julio is going to need some help in readying the earth before he arrives.

Government Spending

In mid-December of 2015, Turning Point USA was hosting a conference of students from around the country during their winter break. The event was held in a modest hotel in West Palm Beach. Before the conference opened, we held a daylong meeting for our advisory board members to discuss what we had accomplished in 2015 and what we had planned for 2016. There was an almost palpable level of energy and enthusiasm present.

And then news came in regarding the vote, first in the U.S. House and then in the Senate, regarding the $1.15 trillion spending package that had been passed in order to avoid a government shutdown. Throughout the remainder of the conference, our conversations were preoccupied with the disbelief over what Congress had just done.

It was just over a year earlier that Americans had elected a majority of Republicans in both the House and Senate, ostensibly to prevent the exact kind of spending from taking place that those same Republicans had now approved. The Republicans controlled 54 seats in the Senate and 247 seats in the House. They had seemed to have won a mandate to rein in government. Yet they clearly had other intentions and gave the openly big government-supporting Barack Obama nearly everything he had wanted. The Republicans had positioned themselves a year earlier as being the supporters of limited government, low taxes, and reduced spending. Look what they had done.

The numbers have lost all sense. Total spending for the 2016 fiscal year is estimated at $3.59 trillion. Tax revenue for that period is estimated at $3.17 trillion, leaving a deficit of $420 billion. At that level of spending, the federal government is laying out $11,219 for every person in the United States. Consider that according to the Census Department, in 2014, the last year for which numbers are available at the time of this book, U.S. per capita income was $28,889. The same survey showed that median household income (the income level which half of the household in the United States fall below and half rise above) was $53,657. This level of spending is disproportionate to the amount of money people make through their own efforts.

The U.S. Treasury Department breaks down spending into three categories: discretionary, mandatory, and interest on debt. The discretionary spending is the part of the budget that gets fought over seemingly every year and which was the source of our consternation in December 2015. Discretionary spending includes such items as national defense, most of the various government agencies (such as the Environmental Protection Agency, the Department of Education, and so on), and international affairs. It accounts for less than half of the overall spending of the federal government.

Mandatory spending is less talked about because of the use of the word "mandatory." If politicians talked too much about it, they might cause Americans to start asking the questions: "Why exactly does it have to be mandatory? Since we made the rules, can't we change the rules?" This type of spending is governed by "authorization laws" that by statute require Congress to set aside money every year to cover the obligations to fund the programs. Examples of mandatory spending include Social Security, Medicare, and Medicaid. Spending under these types of programs is roughly two and a half times the size of spending under discretionary categories.

The final spending category is interest on the federal debt. We will get to that in a moment. The key thing to remember is that when you hear the news coverage each year addressing the battle to approve a budget and prevent a government shutdown, they are talking only about approximately one-third of total federal spending. The rest of it is on autopilot and it's traveling at a high rate of speed, completely off course.

The spending is delivered with incredible inefficiency through a myriad of government agencies, many of them with overlapping or outright duplicative responsibilities. The Office of Management & Budget lists 19 U.S. government agencies plus an "other" category to break down spending allocations. Tops on the list is the Department of Health and Human Services at $982 billion in FY 2016. The Social Security Administration comes in at $905 billion (but don't worry about that, it's uncontrollable and mandatory). The Defense Department is allocated $527 billion and often finds itself at the center of controversy over the size of its budget and cuts that could be made to their "guns" before we start taking people's "butter" off the table.

What is forgotten in those arguments made against the Defense Department is that defending the country is the only mandatory function given to the federal government in the Constitution. Most of the powers granted to it are permissive in nature. Only defense is mandatory.

In March of 1975, then Senator William Proxmire of Wisconsin sent out a news release naming the first monthly recipient of his "Golden Fleece" award. The award was designed to satirically recognize some incredibly wasteful and frivolous uses of taxpayer money. The award ultimately turned into a book deal for the late senator, and since he started the award, numerous examples have been published identifying outright silly government programs. At Turning Point, we created a publication titled *50 Wacky Ways the Government Spends Your Money*. It has proven to be our most popular book with college students. With a nod to Senator Proxmire, here is a small sampling:

▸ The National Endowment for the Arts gave a grant of $15,000 to the Colorado Symphony Orchestra, which it used to produce "Classically Cannabis: The High Notes Series." The provocative concert was put on to attract the younger crowd to classical music.

▸ The National Science Foundation gave $202,000 to New York University and Yale researchers to study if gender bias existed on the website Wikipedia. One example of sexism found in the study showed that some women writers were listed as "American female novelists" instead of just "American novelists."

▸ The Securities and Exchange Commission spent $3.9 million rearranging desks at their Washington, D.C., headquarters.

▸ Approximately $194,090 of taxpayer money was used to conduct a study wherein text messages are sent to "heavy drinkers" warning them not to drink and then monitoring whether they do, in fact, get drunk anyway. Some subjects get a text at 3 a.m. reminding them of the consequences of heavy drinking.

▸ Since 2006 the National Institutes of Health has issued $2.4 million in grants to companies attempting to reinvent the condom. One such company is Origami, which is currently developing a condom with accordion-like pleats that will make a condom easier to don for the user.

Senator Proxmire would be proud.

Federal spending is also eating up what we produce in this country. Since the recession started in 2007 and the financial markets collapsed in 2008, federal spending has settled in consistently at or above 20 percent of our Gross Domestic Product (the monetary value of all the goods and services produced within our borders over a particular period of time). If you add in state and local spending, it has been consistently around 35% of GDP. Government transfer payments (e.g., Social Security) are excluded from GDP but other spending is included. Once you sift through all the mathematics, the simple conclusion to be drawn is that government has spent its way into a significant portion of our economic activity.

The spending has led to a bloated bureaucracy. The Bureau of Labor Statistics indicates that government at all levels now employs almost 22 million people. That is more people than work in productive manufacturing jobs by a margin of about 1.8 to 1. Study after study shows that in virtually every case, government agencies run at much higher overhead levels than do comparative operations in the private sector. More people working less efficiently and with a wage and pension scale (especially at the state level) that is not constrained by market forces has led to runaway costs and too many dollars spent—our dollars.

What is important to remember is that every time the government spends a dollar it is substituting the choice of bureaucrats for the choice of Julio and others like him who want to use that money for their unique activity. The argument is made that there is no difference between a dollar spent by government versus a dollar spent by a private citizen. That isn't true. Because the bureaucrats spending the dollar have no vested interest in the earned value of that dollar, their use is random and errant.

The government taking money out of the economy and throwing it back in has the effect of a pigeon hitting a helicopter's rotor. The pigeon is still accounted for in terms of total mass, but its functionality has been greatly reduced.

All of this has led to an enormous level of national debt that is so large it is hard to actually appreciate. Like the ever expanding, never-ending universe, it defies most people's ability to comprehend. At the time of this writing the federal debt is $19.3 trillion. Some people like to translate that number into some sort of context to make it "graspable," as if you stacked that many dollar bills together they'd extend to...well...somewhere far away. I'm not sure there is a need. Anybody with a pulse knows that $19 trillion is a lot of money. With a GDP just over $17 trillion in 2015, that means the U.S. debt is larger than what the entire economy produces in one year! That does not include debt of government agencies or obligations under Social Security.

There are specific concerns about this level of debt beyond the obvious one of just its pure size. The first is that over one-third of this debt is held by foreign countries. China is the largest holder at just over 7 percent. This means that we have become reliant upon the investment of other nations to fund our excessive appetite for big government. If they stop buying, we won't be able to sell enough. Then we will default. The ripple effects would be cataclysmic in world financial markets.

The next problem is what will happen when interest rates increase. For years now, interest rates have been held artificially low because of the Obama-friendly monetary policy of the Federal Reserve. This means the borrowing cost for big government has been artificially low. When you consider that every year the government is spending more than it is taking in (deficit), which adds to the debt, you understand that the government is borrowing money to pay the interest on the money it has already borrowed! If interest rates rise by five percentage points, it will add almost a trillion dollars a year to the debt. Paying interest on interest has a compounding effect. It is a disaster waiting to happen.

The federal debt per person is around $60,000 at this moment. Imagine the burden this is placing on our nation. The numbers might be too large to grasp but we had better start trying.

I could address Obamacare at the end of this section on government spending, but I won't.

Taxation

Our Founding Fathers wanted to make certain that the people of the United States would not face taxation without representation. It likely never occurred to them that we would tax ourselves into oblivion, voluntarily, *through* our representation. That is exactly what we have done. If there were to be the equivalent today of the Boston Tea Party, we would have to make it a progressive party and make stops along the way to throw income, real estate, cigarettes, cell phones, hotels, and gasoline overboard.

We are now taxed everywhere. States have so worn out their welcome with citizens over high taxes they have resorted to tapping into vices in order to raise revenue. Through lotteries and casinos, the revenue slot machine just keeps showing 777 for state and local governments around the country.

It is always the federal income tax that receives most of the attention when the matter is discussed. Subjectively, it is probably state income taxes and then property taxes that come in second and third. This is likely the case because these three taxes are the largest for most people and the easiest to see. With my focus in this book being on large-scale challenges (that can be reduced to smaller-scale analogies for each state and locality), I'm going to focus on taxes at the federal level in general, and on income taxes, personal and corporate, in particular.

It is so easy for us to fall into the trap of thinking what is always has been (that will come up again later in the book). I am amazed at the number of young people I encounter who think that the United States has always had a national income tax, so what's the big deal? The truth is that the United States survived without one until 1862, when Abraham Lincoln signed the Revenue Act, which created a 3 percent tax on incomes above $800. This was, of course, necessitated in order to help fund the Civil War effort against the South. Considering that I would not likely be writing this book, or any book, if the North hadn't won, I have made my personal peace with Lincoln's decision. The income tax was eliminated in 1872 but was brought back in 1894. In 1895 the Supreme Court ruled it unconstitutional.

In 1913 the constitutional problem was solved with the passage of the 16th Amendment, which established the income tax on both individuals and corporations. It effectively also created the Internal Revenue Service, although that name wasn't assigned until the 1950s, when the agency was changed from a political patronage appointment system to a professional civil servant institution; simply a stunning improvement.

The withholding tax came about in 1943 in an effort to even the flow of revenue collections during the Second World War. It is more than ironic that one of the primary architects of the withholding tax was future Nobel Prize winner and small government advocate Milton Friedman. Friedman helped create the idea during the war while working for the government. More irony, the IRS actually opposed the idea, saying it was too complex and would never work. In his later years Friedman would say he didn't regret the move because at the time it was necessary. He did wish there had been some other way and that the withholding tax could somehow be repealed.

The highest marginal tax rate for personal income in U.S. history was 95%, found during 1944-45. A history of ups and downs has brought us to today's rate of 39.6% at the top individual bracket (above $415,000). This places the United States about in the middle worldwide in terms of rates.

While that number looks favorable, consider it differently. Just because everyone around you is doing something self-destructive doesn't mean that you should be happy doing something less self-destructive than they're doing. In the United States, we have created a measure known as "Tax Freedom Day." Tax Freedom Day is the day that the nation as a whole has earned enough to pay its tax bill for the year. According to the Tax Foundation:

- ▶ In 2016, Tax Freedom Day falls on April 24, or 114 days into the year (excluding Leap Day).

- ▶ Americans will pay $3.3 trillion in federal taxes and $1.6 trillion in state and local taxes, for a total bill of almost $5.0 trillion, or 31 percent of the nation's income.

- ▶ Tax Freedom Day is one day earlier than last year, due to slightly lower federal tax collections as a proportion of the economy.

- ▶ Americans will collectively spend more on taxes in 2016 than they will on food, clothing, and housing combined.

- ▶ If you include annual federal borrowing, which represents future taxes owed, Tax Freedom Day would occur 16 days later, on May 10.

So nearly the entire first third of America's year is spent just paying for big government. This makes it more difficult for Julio to have the disposable income he needs to save money and start a business. It also makes it harder for him to do less adventurous things, like eat.

Politicians like to make political hay from the statement that the upper 1 percent "doesn't pay their fair share." According to the nonpartisan Tax Policy Center, the top 1 percent of Americans paid 45.7 percent of the individual income taxes in 2014—up from 43 percent in 2013 and 40 percent in 2012 (the oldest period available). The bottom 80 percent of Americans paid 15 percent of all federal income taxes in 2014 and the bottom 60 percent are expected to pay less than 2 percent of federal income taxes.

Facts displacing rhetoric is always so refreshing.

If I haven't won you over on the incredible burden of personal income taxes, take a look at the corporate tax picture. Among Western nations, the United States has the highest marginal tax rate at 39.1%. Only Chad and the United Arab Emirates have higher rates anywhere in the world. The average corporate tax rate worldwide is 22.6%. This has created the phenomenon known as "tax inversion" wherein a large company based in the U.S. moves its corporate "headquarters" to another country to lower its tax rate. According to Bloomberg, since 2012, 20 large U.S. companies have gone through this process, with more on the way.

The specious argument that corporations are businesses so taxing them is fairer than taxing individuals doesn't take into account that only actual human beings are the ones who pay any taxes. If IBM writes a giant check out of profits and sends it to the government it means that either prices were higher, they bought less, they paid less, or their shareholders received less. All of those are human-felt financial losses. No matter how you want to turn the tax hologram, the picture is the same. People are paying too much in taxes and losing too much freedom.

The IRS itself now holds an incredible amount of power. Its scrutiny of "Tea Party-type" groups and their donors leading up to the 2012 election had a chilling effect on conservative voters that can't be overstated. If you look at the 2010 midterm election results, where Tea Party enthusiasm raised money and rallied voters, and then look at Barack Obama's election coattails in 2012, you have to ask yourself, "What changed?" A big part of that was the clampdown orchestrated by IRS band leader Lois Lerner and the Taxocrats.

When you combine personal taxes with corporate taxes, and then factor in the complexity of the tax code, the U.S. ranks 32 out of 34 within the Organization for Economic Cooperation and Development (OECD) nations in terms of burden. Too much money taken and too much power wielded

My firm belief is that we need to get the point where the tax code is reduced to such a simple level and such a reasonable amount that avoidance is unnecessary and evasion is simply not profitable enough to take the risk. My targeted number is a flat 10 percent across the board with no deductions. It will take a while to get there. The entire U.S. economy has been built upon the manipulation of the tax code—to exploit loopholes and minimize liability. Imagine a world where business and personal financial decisions are based solely upon their merit and their likelihood of success instead of passive losses and tax credits.

Elsewhere I will suggest using the tax code in order to help us transition from our current state of crisis into a less inhibited market-based economy. Those kinds of steps will be intermediate. Long term, I want Americans to pay their taxes after they've done something, not worry about their taxes before they've done anything.

I could address Obamacare at the end of this section on government taxation, but I won't.

Redistribution of Wealth-Transfers and Entitlements

One of the main drivers for Julio's success is that he doesn't have the option of just staying home and being taken care of through the efforts of others. Julio is living in a world where initiative and effort are not hoped for, they are expected. Right now in America, the federal and state governments have created such a culture of dependency and entitlement that potential Julios cannot easily develop. They can too easily end up settling for subsistence and leisure time instead of pushing themselves to the extreme levels to which their skills and talents could otherwise carry them.

The history of the growth of entitlement and wealth redistribution programs in this country is too lengthy and complex to delve into for my purposes here. There have been very consequential presidents and events over time that have greatly increased citizens' dependency on government. FDR, Lyndon Johnson, and George W. Bush each played significant roles. Under President Obama, however, we have witnessed the near perfection of the welfare state.

People have increased their level of dependency in virtually every area. In 2015, 47 million Americans were receiving aid under the Supplemental Nutritional Assistance Program (SNAP or Food Stamps). That means one in seven Americans was receiving that form of relief. With regard to disability payments, after the first five years of the Obama presidency there were more than 10 million people receiving disability payments, which was up from 8.9 million when he took office. Mental disorders and musculoskeletal and connective tissue disorders made up the majority of the claims. I'm not suggesting we cannot afford to help the truly disabled, but does anybody besides me think that maybe, just maybe, there are people out there who are milking the systems?

Other examples abound in terms of dependency under Obama. This isn't by accident. We will see it below in health care and later when discussing student loans. Creating dependency on government ensures the continued growth of government. There are a lot of people with both a dream and a stake in making sure that happens. Barack Obama is just one of them.

These transfer payments have an incredible impact on state governments, as well. Often the states are required to fund programs mandated at the federal level. This has led to higher taxes, larger deficits, and flights of businesses and citizens from states with high tax and dependency rates to states in better "states" of repair. You can argue that it serves them right to lose populace and jobs, but the truth is that we are all Americans. Not everyone can move from state to state and the idea that those who get left behind in big government wastelands somehow are getting what they deserve is counterproductive for every American.

It isn't like we didn't see this coming. One of the most vocal canaries in the dependency coal mine was the late Senator Daniel Patrick Moynihan, who warned about what the growth of reliance upon transfer payments could do to a people. Back in the mid-1960s, the early stages of the Great Society programs, Moynihan, then a social scientist, discussed a graphical analysis that would come to be known as "Moynihan's Scissors." The graph showed two intersecting lines traveling in opposite directions. One showed the level of welfare payments rising; the other showed the rate of African-American male employment declining. Moynihan would spend the balance of his life as a nearly lone voice in the Democratic Party warning of the perils of a culture of dependency.

Nobody on Team Left was listening.

I could address Obamacare at the end of this section about the redistribution of wealth, but I won't.

Regulation

How did we ever get to the point in this country where people seem to have come to the conclusion that every good idea ought to become a law?

Let me take politics and government down to the local level for a moment. Every reader knows somebody in their community who has run for city council, or the zoning commission, or the school board, who feels really passionate about something. They decide that they have a really great idea to address something that sincerely bothers them. They run and get elected to the appropriate governing body that controls their pet peeve. Once they are on that board they make their argument to their peers, people nod their heads and say "that sounds reasonable," and then they pass an ordinance.

Then they do it again, and again, and again. Ultimately, there are so many rules in the community that it becomes impossible to know them all, and almost impossible to go through a single day without becoming some sort of "civil criminal." On the local level this creates emotional confrontations between citizens that sometimes escalate to the point of the police having to become involved. Nobody likes to be told what to do in general, and in particular they don't like being told what to do when their actions only involve the inconveniencing, not harming, of others.

On the national level the impact of regulations becomes even more significant. The single most compelling reason is that federal regulations are universal. If one local community becomes especially difficult in which to conduct everyday life or business, there is the option to move to the city next door. When the federal government imposes a rule, it requires a Johnny Depp-style move to France in order to escape. American businesses have been doing just that. For individuals, it is much more difficult.

The father of all this madness of government intrusion into the marketplace was the first of the Roosevelt presidents. Theodore "Teddy" Roosevelt took office in 1901 and immediately went to work dismantling the separation that had for the most part existed between government and commerce up to that time. Roosevelt is frequently hailed for being a "trustbuster" by filing 44 separate lawsuits against large companies in an attempt to break them up.

While his activities against the railroads are the ones most commonly referenced, Roosevelt also made it a point to go after the meatpacking industry. The socialist rag *Appeal to Reason* paid writer Upton Sinclair to go to Chicago to create a fictional and inflammatory account of meat processing practices, which was ultimately, and infamously, published as a book, *The Jungle*. Teddy decided he needed to lean things up. Roosevelt's regulations, supported by the big players in the meatpacking industry, had the effect of restricting entry into the space, raising prices, and lessening competition. The exact same scenario would be re-created in the steel industry.

Teddy Roosevelt is hailed in revisionist history as a champion of the common man who fought against big business in order to protect the weak. It simply isn't true. Roosevelt changed the trajectory of America with his presidency and began the bridge-building between big business and big government that makes life more challenging and costly for every entrepreneur and citizen today.

Compliance with government regulations is costly. Since the Roosevelt regulation revolution, the federal government has increasingly added more and more regulation, now covering nearly every single aspect of economic activity. In every instance, big business interests will publicly decry the new regulatory encroachment, but privately they work behind the scenes with lawmakers in order to produce final rules that they can afford to manage. The rules are so complicated and costly they prevent new entrants from coming into their space.

Nowhere is this better exemplified than with the Dodd-Frank legislation that became law in 2010. Its official name is the Dodd-Frank Wall Street Reform and Consumer Protection Act. The title itself is offensive because the two legislators after who it is named, Christopher Dodd and Barney Frank, were serving in oversight capacities with regard to financial institutions in the run-up to, and during, the financial market collapse. Whether through complicity or incompetence or a combination of both, they hold some degree of responsibility for many Americans losing a substantial portion, if not all, of their net worth. Wall Street gets blamed, but the politicians were right there letting it all happen.

Dodd-Frank is the most sweeping addition to financial market regulation since the Great Depression. The big bank groups helped the federal government draft the original law and now, six years later, the regulations that place the teeth into the law are still being written by various federal agencies. These regulations make it difficult for small, independent banks to continue to operate, and they make it almost impossible for new banks to start up. The commercial banking industry is consolidating at an alarming rate. Less competition means fewer and poorer choices for consumers and a rigidness of rules that can't take into account the unique circumstances of each individual or business borrower. This means that the loan that Julio is going to need to start his business a few decades from now is very hard to get at the moment and it's getting harder.

This is satirical at a *Saturday Night Live* level. Big government and big business conspire to milk and destroy the financial markets, individuals and privately owned businesses are left in total ruin when the system collapses, and then big government and big business get together to write new rules to "protect us" from them! This is a theme that has been recurring in the United States for more than 100 years. It has led to an incredible fortress of rules and regulations inhibiting freedom and markets.

According to an article in *The Hill* in December of 2015, the year saw the largest number of pages ever published in the *Federal Register* (the daily journal of federal regulations). According to the report, 81,611 pages of regulations were entered, which beat the record year of 2010 when Obamacare was signed into law. At the end of 2014, the last year data was available as this is being written, the *Code of Federal Regulations* (CFR), which is the codification of all rules and regulations promulgated by federal agencies, stood at 175,268 pages at the end of 2014 compared to 22,877 pages in 1960.

Every single rule comes with a cost. Each rule has someone who favors it, or is favored by it, at the expense of someone else who is harmed or hindered.

Each regulation started out as something somebody thought was a good idea. It then went through a process of being turned into the power of law, so no matter who was impacted or how, everyone had to comply. Most of these regulations are written well out of the public view in a process that is so secretive it is understood only by insiders. Participation is limited to a few who seek to use the new rules as a way to gain some form of advantage for themselves.

If you take nothing else from this chapter bemoaning big government, please understand this: People justify and defend regulation by saying that those "other people" in business are greedy and need to be controlled, and "those consumers" are unintelligent and need to be protected. But if people are inherently greedy and ignorant, what evidence do we have that the people writing rules that take on the power of law are virtuous and intelligent?

I could address Obamacare at the end of this section on excessive government regulation, but I won't.

Health Care

Now, I will address Obamacare.

Just a handful of years ago, the subject of health care would not likely have made it into a chapter of any book that was titled Big Government Sucks. Today, with the advent of Obamacare, it not only gets mentioned, it gets its own special section. The federal takeover of one-sixth of the nation's economy was such an extreme and pervasive extension of government reach into our lives that there is almost nothing in American history to which it can be compared.

Obamacare's legislative name is the Patient Protection and Affordable Care Act of 2010 (ACA). It was signed into law in March of 2010 along with its amendment, the Health Care and Education Reconciliation Act of 2010. At 2,700 pages in length, and now having over 28,000 pages of regulations in the *Federal Register* so far, it is one of the largest, most comprehensive and sweeping pieces of legislation ever passed in U.S. history. Almost more importantly, it is the only piece of legislation EVER passed of this significance without a SINGLE vote from the minority (Republican) party in support.

Obamacare creates a national mandate for citizens to obtain health insurance, either through the purchase of a policy themselves or with government assistance if they cannot afford a policy on their own and qualify for aid. In addition to mandating insurance coverage, the legislation broadly expands the role of the federal government with regard to regulating the health care and insurance industries (which were already heavily regulated before the law's passage).

Insurance is offered under "exchanges," managed by either the states or the federal government, where citizens can apply for the preset level of coverage they wish to have and find out if they qualify for some form of welfare assistance to pay for all or part of their premium. Some states have participated enthusiastically in the program and some not at all. Regardless, any citizen can seek coverage through the Federal Exchange.

The law originally (Obama continues to unilaterally modify it through executive fiat to suit his purposes) required all employers with more than 50 full-time employees to provide health care coverage for those workers. It also imposes certain minimum standards for what all insurance policies must cover, regardless of whom the insured is or what their needs are. It eliminates the exclusion of preexisting conditions as grounds for an insurance company denying coverage to an applicant and it allows young people to remain on their parents' insurance policy until the age of 26.

Some of these features sound good, some seem harmless, and some just a bit mysterious. But no matter how they might appear, each and every one of them represents an interference with free markets, voluntary choices, and patient-doctor relationships. Obamacare has firmly taken control of over 16% of the U.S. economy and as a result, all of the inherent waste, preferential treatment, and interruptions of both service and innovation that go hand in hand with big government are now beginning to impact how you and your family members are able to prevent yourselves from getting ill, and how you can get help to get better once you are ill.

Obamacare was sold to the nation as a law that was necessary to stop the widespread abuse of insurance companies denying people coverage and, more broadly, to provide a method that would cover the 46 million Americans Team Left claimed to be uninsured. Supporters pointed to a lack of preventative tests being covered under many insurance plans, how people with preexisting conditions could be denied coverage and left to die, and the arbitrary decisions of big-insurance executives forcing people to be kicked out of hospital beds too soon and sent home at great risk to themselves and others.

They also cited those 46 million who had no coverage at all and were left to wander into emergency rooms in order to get treated for a simple common cold. All of these arguments, at face value, sounded compelling and made it seem as though the government had to do something to help citizens in need. Unfortunately, they were actually a ruse to disarm and deceive Americans into surrendering access to their doctors, their hospitals, and their treatments in order to serve the "greater good."

What was the truth? The supporters of Obamacare universally cited the "fact" that almost 46 million Americans were uninsured. They used that statistic to argue that if one-sixth of the population of the richest country on earth couldn't get insurance then the system was broken, and people who didn't want to fix it simply lacked compassion. However, as is always the case when people seek to obtain power and control over others through the use of a "factual" argument, when closely examined, those facts start to look more like a magician's sleight of hand.

The 45.7 million uninsured "citizens" number comes from the Census Bureau report in 2007 indicating that was the number of people in the United States without health care coverage. Clear enough. However, when you start to look at what the report actually says it isn't quite the case.

The report stated 9.7 million of the uninsured people in the country were not U.S. citizens. That brings the number down to 36 million. Of those people, it was estimated that 17.6 million had incomes in excess of $50,000 per year and could have afforded insurance had they chosen to buy it. Add to that a study by Blue Cross Blue Shield that 14 million of the uninsured already would have qualified for Medicaid and SCHIP (State Children's Health Insurance Program) and, allowing for some liberal rounding of data and applicable margins of error, you can conclude that the number of uninsured Americans who just couldn't manage coverage at the moment was less than 10 million.

Supporters of Obamacare deliberately overstated the number of uninsured to get compassionate Americans not armed with the facts to sign on to the idea of universal coverage and sign away their freedom in the process.

The other compelling argument made by Obamacare supporters was that because insurance companies refused to cover people who had known preexisting health conditions, those people were left to slowly die if they lost the coverage they currently had or if they did not have any at all. The problem with the argument is that it is literally impossible to insure something that is preexisting.

Insurance is built on the concept of having a large pool of shared diversified "risk" levels wherein each member contributes relatively small amounts of money in order to pay for those who become victims of that risk. When someone has a preexisting condition their situation is certain. You do not insure against certainty. When insurance companies are forced to cover the treatment of someone for something they already have, that is not insurance. It is a transfer payment or welfare. Obamacare was designed to force insurance companies into the welfare business.

In order to gain control over a people nonviolently you need to get them to surrender their freedom voluntarily. One of the better ways to do that is to convince them that by surrendering their freedom they are helping out others. The best way to do it is to convince them that they are helping themselves. Obamacare supporters pushed both of those buttons to get people to surrender.

There were two fundamental goals with Obamacare. One was to gain control of one-sixth of the American economy, which is what the health care industry currently represents. The other was a derivative of the first and far more important. Once you take responsibility for people's health care you can use that to take control over nearly every other aspect of their daily lives. The argument goes something like this: Since society has taken on the responsibility of making sure that you have health care coverage, then the leaders of society have the obligation to make certain that you make choices that are consistent with preserving your health.

Much has been made of the actions taken by the Obama Administration to push back implementation dates for elements of Obamacare. There is a reason for that. Originally, the law was not scheduled for any real implementation, except for the preexisting condition protection, prior to the 2012 presidential election. Obama knew the negative impact would hurt his reelection chances. Further delays were ordered to try to help Democrats running for election in 2014. Full implementation has been pushed back beyond 2016 because Obama does not want to deal with the carnage while he is in office.

He and his people know, and knew, exactly what has been done to our health care system. This monstrous vehicle, which includes every element from this chapter (spending, taxing, redistribution, and regulation), is going to so negatively impact the quality of American life that we will suffer for generations if it isn't repealed.

And as big government grows and envelops the health care industry, and there are fewer doctors, with less discretion to exercise the care of more patients, people are going to die.

There are some simple ways that the health care system could have been improved, and still could be improved if our ruling class of politicians can summon the courage to do something that is not often enough done in America: repeal a law. If the ACA can be eliminated, here are some free market-based reforms that would make an incredible difference in the delivery and cost of health care:

▶ Allow insurance companies to compete across state lines: Currently, health insurance companies are not allowed to operate interstate. This means that each Blue Cross Blue Shield organization in each of the 50 states must be its own separate legal entity. Allow insurance companies to operate in any state they wish and let the competition drive the cost of insurance lower. This prohibition is currently the result of different individual state laws. Interestingly enough, later I'll discuss how the assertion of the Commerce Clause to remove these barriers would actually be a legitimate use of the constitutional provision and consistent with the original intent.

▶ For people with preexisting conditions, provide taxpayer subsidy for care: Nobody wants to see someone left to die because they have a chronic or acute condition requiring care but because they recently lost their job and their insurance they can't afford to pay. It would be relatively simple and cost-effective to subsidize people in such a circumstance the same way we subsidize dependent children or unemployed workers. Insuring for something that already exists isn't insurance by definition. We need to stop calling it insurance and call it assistance. With honest language perhaps we can get an honest solution.

▶ Make health insurance portable: For decades the majority of people got their insurance from an employer's health care plan. If they left that job they could continue their coverage for a period of time but ultimately it ended. If people were allowed to carry their individual policy with them, we could help eliminate the "structural" level of uninsured people in the country primarily caused by people losing their employer's policy coverage.

▶ Eliminate direct payments from insurance companies to hospitals: One of the reasons that health care costs have skyrocketed is because the patient doesn't ever get to see the real charges ahead of time. Nobody asks "what's this going to cost?" People get their care, the hospital submits the charge to insurance company, and the patient gets a statement in the mail saying what was charged, what was paid, and what they owe. Too late! By that time the damage has already been done. If hospitals were required to go through the charges at time of service with patients and show them what treatments would cost before and after their insurance was applied there would be a whole new level of cost-consciousness introduced to the process. In addition, if patients were required to submit charges to insurance companies for reimbursement then further awareness would be generated.

▶ Subsidize insurance premiums for low-income individuals/families: If we want to make certain that everyone has access to some sort of health insurance, we don't need to have big government take over the system. All we have to do is 1) create a means test for assistance 2) establish an amount that equals an annual policy premium for acceptable coverage and 3) make that amount available to tax filers in the form of a tax credit. This in and of itself would provide for the opportunity overnight for everyone to have health insurance and would do it at a fraction of the cost of Obamacare.

ↄ ↄ ↄ

There are a number of other ways I could have chosen to point out the threat created by big government. I could have discussed its invasion into our privacy. I could have discussed its policing powers. I could have discussed its censorship capability. Finally, I could have talked about its detrimental impact at the state and local level when those government entities become too large to be sustained by their tax base and end up essentially bankrupting themselves (states and cities can't print money to cover their debts).

Those topics and others will have to wait for a future volume. I think I've shown enough to paint the picture of an America that resembles an egret trying to take to the air after touching down in a BP oil spill. The weight our nation is carrying is simply too great to allow for uninhibited free flight. We need to start cleaning up the enormous spill of collectivism that has created the hazardous conditions.

Enough about our problems. Now come with me as I discuss what we need to do to help Julio.

PART TWO

THE PIECES
WE NEED TO JOIN

CHAPTER 4

THE TIMELESSNESS
OF FIRST PRINCIPLES

"The equality of people before the law, the purpose of government as servant
of the people and protector of an individual's inalienable rights, are universal
and timeless principles. The Declaration of Independence states them;
the Constitution is intended to give them life. Commitment to
these principles allows a people to govern themselves and be free."

—DAVE SHESTOKAS, author of *Constitutional Sound Bites*

Across human history there have been an almost unknowable
number of governmental systems that have been implemented in
order to organize the behavior of the citizens. Until the United States
was formed, however, never in human history had a group of framers
and designers of a societal structure intentionally tried to put limits
on the size and power of the state.

The prevailing viewpoint until the Founding Fathers was that
unlimited centralized governmental power was the only way to keep
peace and order amongst the citizenry. The founding fathers took a
calculated, well-researched risk to try something radically different.

They decided to put in place a framework that intentionally creates checks and balances to limit the power of the state and maximize individual liberty.

Dissenting voices of the time argued that if you gave people too much freedom anarchy will ensue. Never before did a government have a set of rules and boundaries that protected personal and economic freedom.

It is important to note that the founders did not know this experiment would work. They were making an educated, well researched guess that it would. The founders studied every failed civilization in the history of the world. At the center of each was a power-hungry centralized state that deprived its people of freedom and liberty. Our framers learned from this and charted something far different. They made people be in charge of their government. Not government in charge of the people. They put limits on rulers' power and they went out of their way to limit the extent that power-hungry representatives could abuse such power.

From Babylon, to Ancient Egypt, to the Chinese empire, to Ancient Greece, to the British Empire, there was never a group of people who tried to limit their own power and the influence of the state. Their constitutional experiment resulted in the creation of the most exceptional society in the history of the world. The principles created by our founders spread like wildfire across the Western world and became aspirational to nations of all populations, ethnicities, and religions. They remain so to this day.

The American constitutional framework gave rise to more than a country. It trailblazed a culture in the west that embraced merit, the limited rule of law, individual liberty, and capitalism. The framers did more than start the greatest country in the history of the world; they liberated billions of people from oppression under the ruling class of the state. They gave the world a glimpse as to what a free society looks like and what a free people can do.

In a very real sense, the work that I do each day, the reason for the formation of Turning Point, is directly because of the First Principles embedded in our Declaration of Independence, the Constitution, and the Bill of Rights. Each idea I and Turning Point promote, without exception, came from our Founding Fathers and those documents. Without their work, I think it is fair to say I wouldn't have been smart enough to originally think of the things they thought of more than 200 years ago. Our fight is designed to preserve their work. It has been dying little by little, piece by piece, for more than 100 years.

It is common in my travels across the country to college campuses to hear students speak in a dismissive way about the founders and First Principles. As mentioned earlier, the dead, white, European male (DWEM) concept still exists as it did during my associate writer's college time more than 30 years ago, only it is worse. Now there is a sentiment that what the founders created was, in fact, not the greatest nation in history, but the most oppressive in history. The American success that has been produced by their work has created American guilt for all of that success.

I don't feel the least bit guilty about being an American or enjoying the fruits of the founders' labor. The people who criticize America today from within don't realize that they are criticizing it against a set of standards that the Founding Fathers created in the first place. Each and every criticism I hear is that America is falling short of its ideals. But those ideals wouldn't exist if the Founding Fathers hadn't attempted to codify them.

Father Andrew Greely, the late Catholic priest who also became an award-winning novelist, once intoned that those who wanted to be part of a perfect church should seek it out. If they found it, they should immediately join it, but they should know that the moment they joined it that it would cease to be perfect. That sentiment should be kept in mind when viewing the founding, and the subsequent growth and development, of the United States. Our country was doomed to miss perfection the moment the Constitution was ratified and men began to uphold it. But that misses the point.

The relevant point is the standards that were set and what has been accomplished since our nation was designed in the late 18th century. We have gotten to the point where we have lost track of those standards and have been trying to replace them with more "contemporary" notions of what is right and just to serve as the organizing rules for society. We look at the founders and their work as if to say, "Well, this is what they *really* meant. Certainly it is what they *would have* meant if they were as enlightened as we are today."

The same students I encounter who are dismissive of First Principles and the founders are also quite willing (at least the more erudite ones) to quote Socrates, or Hegel, or Marx, as if those famous philosophers and theorists are still relevant and credible but our Founding Fathers are not. This points to the greatest fallacy with regard to America's founders, and even Constitutional supporters are guilty of promoting it: The Founding Fathers are always credited with pulling from the greatest minds and political thinkers who had come before them in order to do their work. But the Founding Fathers were, themselves, perhaps the greatest minds, philosophers, and political theorists in the history of mankind.

In the world of architecture, there is a need for the theoretical work of the physicist, the mathematician, and even the chemist. Their work tells the designer everything he needs to know about load capacity, structural shape to withstand weight and stress, and material composition to ensure stability and resist deterioration. Once all those contributions are made, along must come the building engineer to take all of that theoretical work and apply it in a way that actually gets a building built. No application of theory results in no action of meaning being taken. The formation of America is an exact duplication of the process of building design.

Our Founding Fathers took the work of Locke, Hume, Paine, Smith, and others and asked themselves, "How do we incorporate all of these theories about limited government, individual liberty, and free markets into an actual functioning nation?" The United States of America was their work product. Our founders weren't just aggregators of the philosophy of others. Men like Franklin, Madison, and Jefferson were brilliant political philosophers in their own right.

These men weren't disciples of Locke; they were intellectual peers. Their ideas translated into action have made the United Sates powerful, influential, and rich even beyond what they could have imagined. Ironically, their ideas made us rich enough to forget their names.

ʗ   ʗ   ʗ

One reason for the disregard and condescension shown today toward our First Principles and the founders is the myths that surround our founding documents. These myths have led the ill-informed to conclude that these were a bunch of old and privileged men, who were racist, who didn't respect women, and who pretended to give us a democracy that never worked as intended. All of these things are incorrect.

One of the more interesting aspects of discussing the Founding Fathers is actually deciding who falls into that category. Obviously there were many, many people involved in both the Declaration of Independence and the Constitution, but who were really the core founders? It is a debate where in reasonable people can differ, and have, over the last 200 years. It isn't really relevant for my purposes but for illustration, let's use the seven identified by historian Richard Morris in 1973: John Adams, Ben Franklin, Alexander Hamilton, John Jay, Thomas Jefferson, George Washington, and James Madison.

The average age of those constitutional fathers in 1776 when the Declaration of Independence was declared was 39. Ben Franklin, by then in his eighth decade, greatly skewed those numbers. Remove Franklin and the number drops to 32 for the remaining six. They were joined by many others of similar age. As I mentioned earlier, these were essentially the millennials of their time. Gouverneur Morris of Pennsylvania was only 35 years old when he authored a major section of the Constitution a few years later.

The founders were not remarkably rich, either. Of the 55 delegates to the Constitutional Convention, only a few were extremely wealthy, George Washington and Robert Morris topping the list. Almost all were financially stable, which would be expected from people who had attained a level of recognition to be asked to contribute to such an undertaking as nation-forging. Forty-one of the 55 had previously served in the Continental Congress, all but eight were born in the 13 Colonies, and almost all were well-educated. In fact, education was the unifying element amongst them all. These were very bright people.

To the notion that the founders were all racist so their ideas should be automatically discounted as being inherently unfair, I offer words from none other than the great abolitionist Frederick Douglas, who said, "Abolish slavery tomorrow and not a sentence or syllable of the Constitution need be altered....[The government created by the Constitution] was never, in its essence, anything but an antislavery government."

When America was founded there were about a half million slaves in the country, the vast majority found in five southern states. While many of the founders owned slaves (Washington, Jefferson, Madison), many did not (Franklin, Jay, Hamilton, Adams). Regardless, because it was a set custom for some and abhorrent to others, compromises needed to be reached in order for a nation to be formed. There are three areas of the original document that are relevant to slavery: enumeration, the slave trade, and fugitive slaves. By the way, it is important to note that the words "slave" or "slavery" never appear in the original Constitution.

With regard to "slaves" only being counted as three-fifths for the purpose of representation, it is a myth to say, as is commonly said on college campuses, that this meant that the founders were saying slaves weren't fully human. The simple fact is that southerners wanted them counted as full citizens (even though southern slave owners afforded them no rights) so that they would have greater representation in the new government. Northerners did not think they should be counted because it would give southern states too much power and influence. The three-fifths figure was a compromise. Even though the southern states considered slaves to be property, the Constitution recognized them, albeit imperfectly, as people. From the moment the Constitution was signed, the end of slavery became inevitable.

The other two issues related to the regulation of the slave trade and the fugitive slave clause. Regarding trade, the compromise was reached that the federal government would be given the power to control and to tax the trade but that the power would not take effect for 20 years after ratification. This created a "sunset" period for pure state control. The "Fugitive Slave Clause" was incredibly controversial and tediously negotiated at the time because they related to the returning to slave owners their escaped "property." The nuances of this go beyond my scope but the bottom line is that the Constitution stopped short of sanctioning the practice of slavery and left it clear (Dred Scott 60 years later notwithstanding) that if a fugitive slave escaped to federal land, or a state which did not have slavery, they would cease to be a slave.

For anybody reading this who believes the fact that the Constitution is irrelevant as a document of freedom because it did not resolve the issue of slavery all at one time, I would suggest that you need to adopt a more realistic view how change takes place within human society. Nothing, and I mean nothing, happens overnight. Every movement in the United States since the Constitution has taken years for its general acceptance. Later in this book I will talk about movements such as Women's Suffrage, American Labor, and Civil Rights. All of these took time. The Constitution was not just a discrete data point on a historical timeline of documents; it was a continual movement along a progressive timeline of human improvement. It was an inflection point.

Another myth is that the founders were "antiwoman." It is a theme on college campuses among young women that the Constitution isn't relevant because it was only written by men and for men. In the language of the time, the use of the masculine pronoun "man" was used to refer generally to "mankind." Other references in the Constitution are to "persons" or "citizens." All of the rights granted to men in the Constitution are granted to women.

Because of sometimes careless and sometimes deliberate deception, young women have been led to believe that the Constitution and the Founding Fathers deliberately denied women the right to vote. The fact is that the Constitution didn't create the right to vote for anybody. It left it to the states to decide the rules for the activity. Just like with slavery above, it was going to take time for conventions to change. They have.

Of course, the United States is not a democracy. Every time a reporter or a politician or a professor uses the term to describe our country, they are doing it a disservice. We are a republic. The founders were very familiar with what a pure democracy would mean in terms of the "tyranny of the majority" famously mentioned by John Adams. They did not want a society where 50 percent plus one could always impose its will upon the other 49 percent. They gave us a republic where the people would elect their representatives to vote in their place. They also structured the representation in the republic to reflect both the population of people (House of Representatives) and the importance of each individual state to the whole regardless of population (the Senate).

Another great myth is the idea that to "...promote the general welfare" meant that the government should be passing laws to transfer wealth, regulate health care, or limit the size of the sodas we can purchase. The "general welfare" is mentioned twice in the Constitution: once in the preamble and then in Article 1, Section 8. In the preamble, the sentence reads in full:

> WE THE PEOPLE of the United States, in Order to form a more perfect Union, establish Justice, insure domestic Tranquility, provide for the common defense, promote the general Welfare, and secure the Blessings of Liberty to ourselves and our Posterity, do ordain and establish this Constitution for the United States of America.

In the context of the three duties mentioned it is clear to anyone not intending to use the word "welfare" as a weapon that the preamble is just referring to the obligation of the government to keep people safe. It is not a mandate to do all of the things the government has since done because, if it were, the founders would not have spent so much time limiting the power of the government in the first place.

In Article 1, Section 8, the term is used at the beginning of the section, which enumerates government powers and obligations:

> The Congress shall have Power to lay and collect Taxes, Duties, Imposts and Excises, to pay the Debts and provide for the common Defense and general Welfare of the United States; but all Duties, Imposts and Excises shall be uniform throughout the United States;

Again, notice the absence of a comma. Common defense and general welfare are grouped as a single item in string. This is another clear association with our simple safety; not interfering with every aspect of our lives for our own sake or for the sake of another.

These myths are the ones I find to be the most destructive and inhibiting in terms of getting to Julio's future. Interestingly, they have two completely contradictory effects, usually within the same person. The first is to have them invalidate the Constitution as being relevant today because it is an ancient document of discrimination and privilege. The second is to cite it as the document that gives legitimate authority to take collectivist action.

I believe that there are some very core First Principles that need to be restored before we can pave a road to limited government, free enterprise, and individual liberty. I am going to walk through a few different areas where I feel there has been abuse and offer what I think is a necessary return to original intent in order to be free.

In Article 1, Section 8 of the Constitution, it grants the power "to regulate commerce with foreign nations, and among the several states, and with the Indian tribes." This short sentence, referred to commonly as the Commerce Clause, has been used as the justification for the federal government to interfere with the free market since very early days.

At the time of the Constitution's signing, there existed among the states a series of tolls and tariffs which punished one state's goods from entering another. It was the original intention of the founders to be able to prohibit such tactics so that there would be, in effect, a free trade zone among the states. Today, the original intent of the Commerce Clause has been so forgotten that in one area in particular where it could and should be applied—state rules prohibiting out-of-state insurance entrants into their health care markets—it has sat essentially dormant. This has served to protect big business, this time the health insurers, because in each state they wind up with an oligopoly situation (very few providers controlling the entire market) and they can make preferential deals with state governments to protect their turf.

Destructively, the Commerce Clause has a long history. As far back as 1824, the revered Supreme Court Justice John Marshall wiped his nose with the founder's original intent by declaring in *Gibbons v. Ogden* that the power under the Commerce Clause "like all others vested in Congress, is complete in itself, may be exercised to the utmost extent, and acknowledges no limitations, other than are prescribed in the Constitution." He went on to argue that commerce is "something more than traffic." Marshall essentially opened the gate to allow the federal government to take a shot whenever appropriate to use the Commerce Clause to see if they could expand government control over market activities.

Remember that when the government expands control into the free market it's not as if that is an area that is somehow outside of the rest of our lives. Our entire lives are impacted by the market at almost every moment of the day. Since Marshall in *Gibbons*, the government and the Court have exploited the Commerce Clause to allow intrusion into every single aspect of our lives. There is really nothing you buy anymore that has not been impacted by the application.

Presidents from Roosevelt, to Roosevelt, to Obama have used it as justification for aggressive assertion of federal power. In Obama's case, it actually turned the entire Commerce Clause into parody by using it as an argument for the imposition of Obamacare. Obama and the architects of his health care program were afraid to call the program a "tax" because they knew Americans would reflexively recoil upon hearing the term. Instead, they said the law was justified under the Commerce Clause. When the Constitutionality of the Act was challenged, the case made its way to the Supreme Court.

Obama's attorneys argued that the law was constitutional because of the federal government's well established right to regulate interstate commerce. Chief Justice Roberts, in writing for the majority in support of upholding the constitutionality of Obamacare, said that it wasn't permitted under the Commerce Clause but that it was permitted as a tax. So by fiat he defined it as a tax. This is big government so intent on regulating and controlling our lives that they can't even get their stories straight. A group of 10-year-olds could cover up the truth behind a broken window with more cohesion.

In order for Julio to have the opportunity to freely innovate, grow a thriving business, and employ well-paid workers, the federal government needs to be out of his way. Many of the regulations written about in the prior chapter are justified through the Commerce Clause. A return to original intent is needed so that individual states cannot impede commerce among themselves and the federal government plays the role of referee to make sure they don't. The key to making this happen is an informed citizenry understanding the concept and electing politicians who will reverse the trend. That is part of the Turning Point message.

¢ ¢ ¢

During the Obama Administration, it has been alarming to watch the boldness with which the president exercises his executive authority through the issuance of executive orders. In January of 2014 the president quite arrogantly declared, "I've got a pen and I've got a phone—and I can use that pen to sign executive orders that move the ball forward." This was clear confirmation that the president had no intention whatsoever of working with Congress to see if laws could be passed through debate and compromise. He was simply circumventing them, and has, to serve his own purpose.

At the time of this writing, Obama has issued 235 executive orders. This compares to 291 issued by George W. Bush before him. My associate writer for this book likes to tell the story of a conversation he had with a friend during the last Bush administration. His friend was enjoying the fact that Bush had gone around Congress to get something done. My colleague warned him that Bush was setting a dangerous precedent and he wasn't going to care for it when a successor came into office with whom he didn't agree and started exercising the power of an imperial presidency.

He was right. His friend doesn't like it and neither do a lot of Americans. The problem is that there doesn't seem to be a lot being done about it. Congress has appeared impotent in responding to much of Obama's activity. While Bush had more executive orders, Obama's have been more consequential. From Obamacare modifications, to unilateral changes in enforcement of immigration laws, to the handling and classification of drug criminals, President Obama has been making a mockery out of the lawmaking process.

The founders probably erred a bit when it came to restricting executive authority. The president was given executive power to act as:

- ▶ Commander in Chief of the armed forces
- ▶ Head of the executive branch
- ▶ Chief law enforcement officer of the United States
- ▶ Head of state

The founders anticipated George Washington as being the likely first president of the United States. Of course they were right, but they had a great deal of trust for Washington and rightly so. The problem was that their trust of him likely caused them to take their eye off the ball when it came to limiting power. From the perspective of those original Constitutional Convention delegates, much of the problem they had encountered with Great Britain stemmed from the British Parliament. It was then in the areas of the House of Representatives and the Senate that they focused most of their attention.

They did, however, give Congress the "power of the purse:"

"All Bills for raising Revenue shall originate in the House of Representatives; but the Senate may propose or concur with amendments as on other Bills."

—U.S. Constitution, Article I, section 7, clause 1

"No Money shall be drawn from the Treasury, but in Consequence of Appropriations made by Law; and a regular Statement and Account of the Receipts and Expenditures of all public Money shall be published from time to time."

—U.S. Constitution, Article I, section 9, clause 7

Repeatedly, Congress has abdicated its responsibility to use this power to shut down executive authority. Citing concern over voter backlash about a government shutdown, Congress continues to be unwilling to contest executive action by simply defunding the activity. We saw them essentially validate the president's unconstitutional action in his immigration orders by passing the funding measures that would permit them to take place. Whether you support the actions or not, you can't support it when our system of checks and balances turn into checkbooks with unlimited balances for the Chief Executive Officer. Enron had tighter oversight.

Keep in mind that story from before regarding the friend who supported President Bush's executive orders, only to be subsequently angered by Obama's. This centralization of power into the hands of one person needs to be stopped. There is an arbitrariness and whimsicalness to the actions of a king when they are at their best. At their worst, they can be devastating to large groups of citizens and can greatly curtail freedom. If we allow big government to get bigger, simply by letting one person use a phone and a pen, then big government can get as big as any one person wants it to be.

Another term that in and of itself has corrupted original intent is that of "states' rights." The states don't have "rights" under the Constitution; they have powers. The 10th Amendment reads:

> The powers not delegated to the United States by the Constitution, nor prohibited by it to the States, are reserved to the States respectively, or to the people.

There is in a very real sense a way to view the 10th Amendment in conjunction with the Ninth Amendment, which reads:

> The enumeration in the Constitution, of certain rights, shall not be construed to deny or disparage others retained by the people.

When you view the two in combination it is clear that the founders wanted to attempt to concentrate power into the smallest unit, the smallest of which would be the individual (Ninth Amendment), and then below the federal level it would be the states (10th Amendment). The interlocking theme of the two is to make it clear that if the Constitution didn't expressly grant the power to the federal government to do something, then they didn't have the power to do it.

Going back to the Constitution's writing, one of the great debates was whether a Bill of Rights was necessary or desirable. There were founders who believed that a Bill of Rights was not only superfluous, but it was dangerous. It was viewed as unnecessary because they felt the Constitution was so clear that there were only certain things the government could do, that listing specific exclusions was not required. They felt it was dangerous because if you started to list things the government couldn't do specifically, nefarious future leaders might infer that it meant you could interfere with anything else.

The other argument was that there were certain practices that were so fundamental to the success of a free nation, an experiment at that time, that they needed to be specifically cited and excluded from governmental interference. Sadly, both sides seemed to have been right with regard to their pessimistic view of future leaders. State power is an obvious example of this.

As I noted earlier, the Constitution only addressed the federal government and the rules which applied to its structure and the constraints on its power. In 1868, after the Civil War and the abolition of slavery, the 14th Amendment extended all of the protection due to citizens from the federal government to the same types of protections from the state governments. This meant the Bill of Rights in particular so that no state could behave in a manner contrary to federal standards by limiting individual liberty in key areas.

Once we were at that point, I would argue that America had been, in some real sense, constitutionally perfected. By that I mean that the incredible work of codifying freedom that had been committed to words by our founders now applied, clearly applied, to every state government, as well. If we had stopped there we would have been in really good shape, with limited and fair government preserved at each level. Unfortunately, we didn't stop there and the federal government has continued its march into states' issues, and states have increasingly found ways to work around Constitutional restrictions; at a minimum, in terms of spirit.

The federal government was intended to leave activities such as policing and education to the states to provide and control. Today, the federal government has expanded its reach into those areas and others. In addition to education and policing, they mandate various social welfare and redistribution programs with which states must comply and find ways to fund.

In 1985, the Supreme Court ruled in *Garcia v. San Antonio Metropolitan Transit Authority* that the federal government had power under the Commerce Clause to extend the Fair Labor Standards Act to state and local governments, requiring them to have employers pay minimum wages and overtime to workers. This decision overturned a decision by the Supreme Court a decade earlier in *National League of Cities v. Usery* that said such an extension would violate the 10th Amendment!

That simple above-cited court incursion into the Constitution, state powers, and original intent is a powerful example of just how far we have fallen. The steady seepage of centralized power into our lives is relentless. Just 10 years after having been rebuked by the Court in an attempt to interfere in state labor issues, back the feds came, from a slightly different angle, and with a new slate of judges to whom to argue. They were then able to take the ground they failed to take in the previous offensive. My use of military terminology is deliberate. The federal government has been steadily invading our individual liberties for a very long time. In the *Garcia* case, they used the weaponized Commerce Clause to once again take ground inside the smaller entity.

Controlling power is best wielded from the highest perch. Liberty is best preserved at the closest, local level. To the extent that we continue to move away from local control to federal control we will continue to loose liberty. Big government doesn't just suck, it makes dependent slaves out of all of us. Our Founding Fathers knew these dangers, took great steps to prevent this from happening, and yet we have found a way to chip away at everything they built for us.

When people talk about First Principles, the debates can get very esoteric. People argue over original intent and they argue over every word. While they are right to carefully examine each word (Madison said, "Every word in the Constitution decides a question between power and liberty"), they spend time fighting over those words absent broader context. Madison also wrote in Federalist 51:

> "Men are not angels; their passions and self-interest often get the better of their reason and sense of justice, so we need government in order to protect our rights against those who would take them away.... Government must be limited because people in government have passions and interests too."

The entirety of the preserved debate and writings surrounding the Declaration, the Constitution, and the Bill of Rights is filled with variants of this language. None of our founders can be found to have been foreshadowing Marx and trying to set the stage for collectivism. None of our Founding Fathers were trying to make ready the new nation inspired by Locke and others like him to "progress" to something Rousseau might admire.

The entire context of every meaningful word of the Constitution is liberty and restrained government. When it is interpreted it needs to be interpreted in that context. That is what should be meant by original intent. It is simply impossible to argue while sober that any of our Founding Fathers would have supported the idea of Obamacare, or that they would have supported the federal government taking complete control of the entire funding mechanism for higher education. Nobody can make that argument unless they do so disingenuously for their own self-serving purpose.

Woodrow Wilson was the first sitting president to criticize the Constitution while in office by arguing that the separation of powers, embedded by our founders in the Constitution, prevented truly democratic government. As already mentioned, our founders didn't want a truly democratic government because of the inherent risk of mob rule and the tyranny of the majority. That is why they gave us a republic. Wilson was saying, in essence, that he was simply more enlightened, more highly evolved, than were the founders. I disagree. Wilson was nothing more than a frail want-to-be despot. He wasn't more enlightened than our founders, he was as dark as was any would-be tyrant the world had seen a thousand times before him.

In January 1944, Franklin Roosevelt, during his State of the Union Address, announced his new proposed "Economic Bill of Rights." FDR was frustrated by the founders and their work because he felt it tied the hands of government to do things for people. Of course, when a politician wants to "do things" for people what he really wants to do is to extend his control over them by increasing government influence in their lives. Some of FDR's "economic rights" included:

- ▶ The right to a useful and remunerative job in the industries or shops or farms or mines of our nation;
- ▶ The right of every family to a decent home;
- ▶ The right to a good education;
- ▶ The right to adequate medical care and the opportunity to achieve and enjoy good health.

For some readers, you might be surprised to know that FDR's "economic bill of rights" has never become law. When you look at those items, you can see that the federal government has made ingress into every single area. The federal government has inserted itself into the world of employment both directly by hiring workers and indirectly by mandating employment arrangements for companies doing business with the government and setting wage standards.

They have interfered in the housing market through the Federal National Mortgage Association (Fannie Mae) and the Federal Home Loan Mortgage Corporation (Freddie Mac), the activities of both then leading to the mortgage market collapse in 2008. Through the bloated Department of Education, they have stepped into education and significantly wrested away control from local school boards. Obamacare is the ultimate unconstitutional incursion into the private sector, and has taken away control of our own health care from us and our physicians.

What is the solution to restoring us to a nation that honors and observes the original intent of our Founding Fathers and restores First Principles? So much damage has been done that it is clear that reversal will take a very long time. With every expansion of government power there follows the expansion of personal privilege for those who command that power. This creates a spoils system for people who are in the system, both as legislators and as hangers-on, that is self-perpetuating. Those who are in power want to stay there and those who are outside of it see the trappings and want to get there.

In his seminal work *The Ruling Class*, first published as an article in American Spectator and then later as a book, Angelo Codevilla describes the culture that has developed inside American government. I highly recommend the book, which unveils the cabal between both parties (Republicans as the comfortable minority) and special interests. I feel so strongly in the merit of Codevilla's work that I think what we need to do to restore First Principles is to destroy the ruling class. There is only one way to do that: term limits.

I know that term limits isn't an original argument but it would be an original solution. I mentioned at the beginning of this chapter that the founders were not all career politicians. That doesn't mean they hadn't served but it does mean they did not seek to stake their entire careers of drinking from the public trough. It seems that every entrant into the political arena starts by telling people that they just want to go to Washington for enough time to make a difference and then return to their outside vocation. The problem is that once they get there and become members of the ruling class, they never leave.

One argument against term limits is that is an admission by a people that they can no longer govern themselves and that we should not be making that admission; that it somehow makes us seem weak and incapable. I understand that argument but here is the contemporary problem: It isn't about voters making better choices, it is about the people who run for office either intentionally before they run or organically after they get elected becoming part of the ruling class. Even the purest of intentions can get corrupted once they are surrounded by what elected office provides for them.

There is a lot of work to be done. Our elected officials have to start rolling back regulation, get a handle on the fiat power of the courts, control spending by making tough choices on cutting favorite entitlement programs, and taking numerous other actions. These tough choices are always going to run up against the pressure to get reelected and knowing that losing office means losing privilege. If we don't send them there knowing the privilege is fleeting by design, we can't expect them to all be so strong and resolved so as to resist its temptation.

People also say that governing and government has gotten too complex to constantly be filling leadership roles with rookies. Exactly! If we shorten the lifespan of politicians we will necessarily force them to reduce the size and complexity of government. We will also immunize them to the corrupt influence of lobbyists and big business, both poisoning our system so severely that big government ought to mobilize the EPA to come clean it up.

I want to go further than just the politicians. Staffers should also be limited in their service. The career bureaucrat also has to go. Public service has become job entitlement. There needs to be reasonable limits on employment duration so that every public service job turns over with new people. Then public service can become exactly that.

Congress should have shorter sessions; 10 weeks at a maximum. Everything they do needs to be televised. Congress should also take its show on the road, holding sessions in different cities for each convening. That way they would become closer to the people. If national security dictated secrecy, then there could be secrecy. This would be the exception, though, and not the rule. The Star Chamber in Washington could be left for significant events or emergency situations. Legislate for the people, near the people.

If we can't get back to First Principles, then all is lost. There needs to be recognition of just how great this work of our founders was and remains. Everybody who wants to attempt to replace it, modify it, or update it needs to ask themselves: Just what could I possibly create that in totality would provide a nation of people with a greater opportunity to be free?

The Constitution was not written for the times; it was written to stand the test of time. We hold in our hands the opportunity and the responsibility to make sure that it does.

CHAPTER 5

THE EFFECTIVENESS OF FREE MARKETS

"There's no limit to what free men and free women in a free market with free enterprise can accomplish when people are free to follow their dream."

—JACK KEMP

Big government has been around for a very long time. Long before capitalism was unleashed. I want to focus on which has accomplished more in a shorter period of time.

To do that I'll start as would any economist or writer trying to show the effectiveness of free markets. I want to quote scripture. Consider the following passage from the King James version of the Christian Bible:

> And it came to pass in those days, that there went out a decree from Caesar Augustus, that all the world should be taxed. (And this taxing was first made when Cyrenius was governor of Syria.) And all went to be taxed, every one into his own city." *Luke 2:1-3*

The Romans created written text in several ways, including using wax tablets, thin leaves of wood, or papyrus (most commonly used for legal documents). When Augustus issued his declaration of a tax to be levied, it would likely have been written on papyrus leaves and transported to all corners of the Roman world using the "cursus publicus," the Roman postal service. According to Britannica, the postal carrier network could cover as much as 170 miles per day. That pace of message transmittal was not exceeded in Europe until the 18th century.

In a world without modern capitalism, it took nearly 1,450 years from the time that Augustus' tax decree was handwritten, one copy at a time, on papyrus leaves, until the invention of the printing press by German-born Johannes Gutenberg. At the time he invented the printing press, he was a member of the Roman Empire—*The Holy Roman Empire.* The world had changed so greatly in its political and religious configuration that the empire written about by Luke which predated Christianity had long since fallen and been superseded by the Christian Church.

The first book typeset by Gutenberg and printed on his press was *The Gutenberg Bible* (aka "The 42-Line Bible"). The project took him approximately three years to complete.

The transportation of the finished book would have been by means no faster, typically slower, than those employed by Augustus. The original book sold for 30 florins each, which was a considerable sum of money at the time—more than a year's wage for most people.

Today there are estimates ranging from 22 to 48 copies of the original Gutenberg bible that are known to exist. No auction has been held in years but if one were to be sold, say at Christie's Auction House in New York, it is speculated that it could fetch as much as $100 million. The buyer of that book, living perhaps in Rome, could have it delivered to them in two days, or overnight with special provisions, by FedEx, a product of the American free enterprise, capitalistic system, founded in 1971 by Fred Smith.

For those either religious or curious who are unable to afford purchasing an original Gutenberg bible, there is some consolation. They can simply go to an "App Store" from their smartphone and download a complete copy of the King James version of the bible for free in a matter of seconds.

The key element to creating Julio's future is the unleashing of free markets. Everything that happens in his world is either a direct result, or a byproduct, of free enterprise. Writing back in 1949 in his magnum opus from the Austrian School of Economics, *Human Action*, Ludwig von Mises described the central role economic freedom plays in creating an environment for other freedoms to exist:

> Freedom, as people enjoyed it in the democratic countries of Western civilization in the years of the old liberalism's triumph, was not a product of constitutions, bills of rights, laws, and statutes. Those documents aimed only at safeguarding liberty and freedom, firmly established by the operation of the *market economy*, against encroachments on the part of officeholders.

Since most Americans alive today have lived in mostly stable, peaceful times, it is easy to mistakenly think that the way we live today is the way that we have always lived. It is even easier to conclude that the political and economic systems we see in the world today are as old as mankind itself. The truth is that forms of government and economic systems that promote individual freedom, choice, and responsibility are relatively new to the human experience. Capitalism in particular has a relatively short history, both in terms of existence and application. That said, what it has allowed people to accomplish is indisputable. Virtually all of the means and media used by opponents of capitalism to condemn it today would not exist for them to use without capitalism.

Instead of citing statistics about GDP in countries around the world or discussing relative poverty levels in order to promote free markets, I am going to describe some of the more current examples of the successes of capitalism. By sharing stories about products and services created by entrepreneurs and now enjoyed by tens of millions of Americans, I hope you come away convinced of the power of private enterprise and why we need to embrace it, not deny it. As you're reading through some of these examples, consider how increasingly taxed and regulated our free markets have been over the past several decades and then just imagine what else could have been accomplished.

If after this chapter you still want to protest a free market system and suggest some other form of big-government directed economic order, then you should take out your feather, dip it in ink, scratch out your thoughts on a papyrus leaf, and let your voice be heard.

Perhaps the most impressive feature of capitalism, the system that has allowed for a disproportionate number of mankind's greatest inventions and innovations, is that it was not "invented" by anyone or any government. Capitalism evolved out of people's desire to become better off and using their own creativity and initiative to make it happen.

Adam Smith is often credited with having "invented" capitalism and documenting that invention in his famous work *An Inquiry into the Nature and Causes of the Wealth of Nations*. What Smith actually did in that work was to identify and describe what he was seeing begin to operate inside 18th century Great Britain during the first Industrial Revolution. Up until that time European economies were governed by "mercantilism," which had governments directing the activities of a nation's economy for the purpose of accumulating a surplus of "riches." A variation was "merchant capitalism," which was more agrarian-based and had economic activity financed through small private funding sources, primarily for commodity production.

But the Industrial Revolution changed that. As the need for the financing of production grew, and as the complexities of sourcing and pricing component parts of complex manufactured items increased, innovative and self-interested people began to find ways to finance and facilitate the growth. Smith keenly observed this process and described how an "invisible hand" was at work, efficiently and effectively coordinating all of the activities in the marketplace to ultimately deliver finished goods to the consumer at the best possible price. Smith, a philosopher by trade (his *The Theory of Moral Sentiments* remains, to this day, a classic in the discipline), was identifying a naturally occurring process and pointing out the different attributes.

His work can best be thought of as that of a Scottish Enlightenment diagnostician. He was watching certain market behavioral symptoms manifest themselves and then pinpointing their causation.

Smith never even used the term capitalism. In fact, the *Oxford English Dictionary* locates its first usage in English in 1854 by William Makepeace Thackeray in his novel *The Newcomes*, some 13 years before Karl Marx wrote *Das Kapital*. What the American Founding Fathers did in reading Smith's work and incorporating his analysis of the power of free markets and private property ownership into our nation's First Principles was *not* trying out Smith's "invention." It was simply recognizing the power of what he identified and allowing it to be unleashed.

Capitalism created itself, just like an energy source, and free men have learned how to harness it in order to improve the human condition in ways that would never have been imaginable in the age of Caesar Augustus.

If we go back to the time of Caesar Augustus and the collision of B.C and A.D., or Before the Common Era (B.C.E.) and Common Era (C.E.) for those who prefer, it is interesting to examine the progress of invention and innovation. In this chapter I will focus on events in the Common Era.

There are numerous sources available that discuss the history of inventions/innovations and show timelines for those that are most important. Of course, reasonable people can differ over what defines "importance" but setting aside those kinds of coffee shop debates, consider just a couple of different web-based listings of important inventions & innovations and see if it is a normal or skewed distribution.

The website *DatesandEvents.org* publishes an inventions timeline that shows 98 significant inventions since the start of the Common Era up to the year 2001. Of those, 31 were made prior to the start of the Industrial Revolution (generally cited as commencing in 1760) and 67 have come since. That means that 68% of their list of significant inventions happened in the 12% of history which incorporates the applied principles of capitalism. The much-maligned but often used

Wikipedia cites 113 inventions over essentially the same time period with 61, or 54%, occurring since the Industrial Revolution. More interesting in their listing is that starting in the 1820s they begin listing the inventions by *decade* rather than by *century*. Of course, with the United States only coming into actual existence in 1789, the 1820s begin to reflect its ramping up to greatness.

Because so much of my work is directed at making young people aware of the power of free markets, I want to take a look at some of the innovations that have taken place over recent years that are popular with students who are in college today. Some of these companies didn't exist when current 2016 college students were born, and definitely didn't exist in their current form. As each company is discussed, I'm going to go back in time and show just how long it took civilization to progress in each company's or technology's area prior to the emergence of capitalism and its subsequent identification by the intellectual diagnostician Adam Smith.

The Internet

Despite the common perception that Al Gore invented the internet, the real story is even more interesting. According to InternetSociety.org, the first written conceptualization of computer networking came in 1962 through a series of memos by J.C.R. Licklider of MIT wherein he discussed his "Galactic Network" concept. Licklider became the first head of computer research at the Defense Advanced Research Project Agency (DARPA) and introduced the concept to his team.

The development, which began at that point, experienced a series of milestones all leading up to the true commercial launch of the Internet in 1990 when Advanced Research Projects Agency Network (ARAPNET), the first network to have used the Internet protocol, was dismantled. In 1995 the National Science Foundation Network (NSFNET) was decommissioned and the Internet fell completely into the hands of the free market and clasped with the invisible hand of capitalism.

Twenty-plus years later, the Internet, with the information it transmits and the commerce it allows to be conducted, has revolutionized the world. While everyone knows that its impact has been extraordinary, there is literally no way to effectively measure it. It has impacted almost every aspect of mankind's existence.

Imagine that since the beginning of the Common Era, it took 1,833 years before the first observation of a semiconductor property by Michael Faraday in *Experimental Researches in Electricity*. From that point, it took only 123 years for John Bardeen, William Shockley, and Walter Brattain to be awarded the Nobel Prize in Physics for their invention of the transistor, sometimes called the most important invention of the 20th century. The Internet was developed and released into commercial hands only 39 years after that. Capitalism is more than an economic system; it's a logarithmic learning curve.

It is often pointed to by big government supporters that the Internet was a government program originally, and without the government the generation of information and wealth created by the Internet could never have taken place. This point of view is shortsighted at best and flat-out mistaken at worst. The Internet was the product of great minds being allowed to think freely. Only in a capitalistic system can university members have access to the developments in the outside world economy that allow their imaginations to dare create "what's next."

The creation of the Internet never could have happened, in government or elsewhere, if capitalism hadn't provided for the surrounding technology. Once the government had it they had no idea what to do with it or how to monetize it. No person, agency, or collective group could possibly design what 300 million free people could design. All guided by an invisible hand of which Adam Smith caught a glimpse more than 200 years ago.

Google

Capitalism is such a powerful force that it doesn't just increase the offering of products and services, or simply facilitate the creation of great wealth and a higher standard of living for all: I can turn a proper noun into a verb. It has probably been within the last several hours that either you have or have heard someone say "Let us *google* that."

According to Compare Business Products, on average, Google is subjected to 91 million searches per day, which accounts for close to 50% of all Internet search activity. Google stores each and every search a user makes into its databases. After a year's worth of searches, this figure amounts to more than 33 trillion database entries.

Google was founded in 1998 by Stanford University graduate students Larry Page and Sergei Brin. While at Stanford in 1996, Page and Brin began developing their first search engine, BackRub. In 1998, they established their first data center in Page's dorm room.

At the advice of Yahoo founder David Filo, Page and Brin decided to start a company. They first raised $100,000, and eventually $1 million, and started their company in a friend's garage in 1998. Today, Google has a massive corporate complex in Mountain View, California, and has more than 70 offices in 40-plus countries. It is now in the process of launching a "smart car" that drives itself and its own wireless network. There is nothing in the area of technology it will not attempt to enter and conquer.

None of this could ever have been accomplished if a room filled with central planning government bureaucrats had set out to invent Google. They never could have envisioned it. The founders them-selves could not have envisioned what they have since created. Can you imagine a government program progressing from search engines on the Internet to powering smartphones to driving automobiles? Only an invisible hand and the creative passions of entrepreneurs could have possibly guided a journey like the one Google has taken in less than 20 years.

But at its very core, Google is still recognized as a search engine. If you think about it, an online search engine is really a library where the Dewey Decimal System is replaced by some strokes on a keypad or the tapping of a mouse (or now your voice saying, "OK, Google...").

Prior to libraries becoming widely available to the general public, they were found primarily on university campuses or in monasteries. Often, universities and monasteries would collaborate to provide library offerings to students, academics, and the privileged.

It was in England where public libraries were truly born near the end of the 16th century. One of the first was Francis Trigge Chained Library in Grantham, Lincolnshire, in 1598. It would be until the Public Libraries Act in 1850 before the U.K. Parliament mandated that cities populated with 10,000 or more were asked to pay taxes in support of public libraries. By 1877 the number of cities with free libraries exceeded 75 and by 1900 the number had grown to 300.

So, 1,598 years for the first significant public library with mass-printed books, and only another 400 years for Google. Today, the U.S. Library of Congress states that it has on hand more than 37 million books and other printed materials, the vast majority of which were produced using the invisible hand of capitalism; the one Adam Smith saw. Compare that to Google's 91 million search requests per day.

Google has also been disruptive for cartographers. Google Maps and the navigation system it has created that gives you precise, real-time directions, adjusted and recalculated instantly as necessary, and sends them to your smartphone, has made it possible to get to places without actually having any idea of where they are. Map or compass reading is no longer necessary. It took Western man 1,300 years into the Common Era to discover the modern compass. It took Google only a few years of operation to turn the compass into a keepsake and the map into a placemat.

Amazon.com

Anybody who sits in front of a laptop, lays an electronic notepad on the arm of a couch, or holds a cell phone in the palm of their hand to holiday shop, needs to be grateful to Jeff Bezos and the idea he had in 1994 to take the relatively new Internet and turn it into the world's shopping destination. Bezos was only 30 years old and already very successful as a senior vice president with Wall Street investment banking firm D.E. Shaw & Co. He learned of the incredible rate of growth of Internet use by doing research for his day job and decided to make an entrance.

Legend has it that he made a list of 20 possible items that could easily be sold online. He settled on books because there were so many titles that no single bookstore, no matter how big, could ever carry them all. An online store, however, could carry many multiples of what could be held inside a Barnes & Noble.

Bezos chose Seattle to be the home of his new company because of its high-tech labor pool and because it was proximate to Ingram Book Group, which had a large warehouse, filled with salable product. Bezos raised $1 million from family and friends as an initial investment, found a place to live, and started Amazon.com in his garage.

In July 1995, Amazon.com started doing business with the tag line of "Earth's Biggest Bookstore." They initially had more than 1 million titles. Since then Amazon has shown great innovation in how it structures its shopping experience for customers. They patented and trademarked the "one-click" payment method and name for returning customers. They have used state of the art algorithms to offer suggestions for shoppers who have bought items from them previously. They created a loyalty program, rare for online retailers, which allows you to buy a membership to avoid shipping charges, sales taxes in some locations, and avail yourself to various "Prime" member benefits.

Today, Amazon.com is the largest of all online retail stores and is the place that merchants want to have their items listed for sale, even if they have their own e-commerce site. They gave the market its first electronic book (e-book reader) through its introduction of the Kindle in 2007.

If you go on Amazon.com you can buy a first-edition of *Atlas Shrugged*, a 24-foot extension ladder, or a collection of all the digitally remastered Beatles music for the baby boomer in your life. If that isn't enough, you can order an Xbox system and have it delivered to your home tomorrow with no charge for shipping, or you can log into Amazon Prime Video and have recent seasons of *Game of Thrones* stream onto your iPad for immediate viewing.

During a *60 Minutes* interview in December of 2013 (at the time of the broadcast it was disclosed that Amazon had more than 225 million worldwide customers), Bezos created a stir when he revealed that Amazon was planning to have packages delivered to customer doorsteps using a small drone. Safety controversy aside, it was a breathtaking concept and one of the most dramatic answers to the instant gratification culture that we have now heard so much about. On the Amazon horizon are its own smartphones and a home delivery service. One thing is certain, it will continue to innovate.

In its simplest form, Amazon.com is the world's largest department store. According to Christine Larson, writing in the *Washington Monthly*, it took us 1,870 years before the first department stores opened in Victorian London. She writes:

> When the first stores opened in the 1870s and '80s, they were cavernous, no-frills storerooms that stocked a hodgepodge of items once available only from specialty merchants. The different merchandise lines were known as "departments." At these one-stop Victorian shopping destinations, the sales staff might not have known silk from twill, or how to trim a jacquard vest, but the prices were low, and one could pay in cash—an innovation at a time when most retailers required annual credit lines that were extended only to wealthy regular patrons.

From this beginning, the invisible hand of capitalism spread the stores "across the pond" to the United States. The free market is always searching for better ways to deliver products and services in the most efficient and cost-effective manner to consumers. Since their British beginnings, names like Woolworths, Hudson's, Marshall Fields, Kmart (almost) have come and gone while others—Walmart, Target, and Amazon.com—have emerged in their stead. It is fascinating to imagine what comes after Amazon.com.

Apple

In April of 2014 it was reported by numerous news outlets that Apple had more cash on hand than did the federal government. At that moment in time, according to information from Bank of America, Apple had approximately $165 billion in cash balances and the Treasury only had $48 billion. Not to fear about the federal government going broke; it can always just print more money, so it does have that advantage over Apple.

The innovation that has come from Apple has changed the world. So compelling are its products that now a whole new cottage industry of therapy has sprung up trying to help people cope with their addiction to Apple devices and the copycats that have followed. The recent list from just the past 20-plus years is breathtaking:

▶ 1998: iMac desktop computer.

▶ 2001: iTunes music library—the most complete and affordable library of music.

▶ 2001: iPod—made your entire music library able to be clipped to your belt.

▶ 2006: MacBook Pro laptop computer—now the gold standard for the creative world.

▶ 2007: iPhone—launch of the smartphone that has revolutionized communication.

▶ 2007: Apple TV—bringing all of the Apple user experience to a big screen.

▶ 2010: iPad—does anybody want to take notes or read books any other way?

▶ 2015: Apple Watch—in case everything else isn't enough, let's link them together on your wrist.

The beginnings of Apple go back to 1976, and illustrate what we've already uncovered as being the most important element of successful entrepreneurship: If you want to be successful, you need a garage.

Steve Jobs and Steve Wozniak started what would become Apple in Jobs' garage in Los Altos, California. Their goal was the creation of a user-friendly computer. They certainly fulfilled that dream.

Wozniak stayed with the company until 1983, when he left to form his own company. Jobs left in 1985 to form his own company, NeXT Software. He then bought Pixar from George Lucas, and everyone who has been a kid or had kids since that time is very familiar with the groundbreaking work of Pixar.

After Jobs and Wozniak left Apple, the company continued to perform successfully, largely from the momentum they had created. In 1990 it posted the highest profit it had up until that point. However, the company began to struggle and lose market share, due, in part, to a decision Wozniak's successor made not to work with Microsoft founder Bill Gates to license its software. Microsoft became Apple's biggest market challenger and took over the business user world because of its MS Office suite of products. Apple's market share continued to decline and in February of 1996, *BusinessWeek* published an article, "The Fall of an American Icon." In it they pointed to all of Apple's mistakes and wondered what, if anything, the company might be able to do to reverse course.

In 1997 Apple would find the answer in the form of its co-founder, Steve Jobs. Apple purchased his NeXT Software, then made Jobs the interim CEO (he called himself the iCEO). Jobs made a deal with Microsoft to create a compatible version of its Office software, and the rest is very, very successful history.

Of all the things that Apple has innovated, each in its own way important, it is hard to argue that the "smartphone" is not at the top of the list. The smartphone delivered a full computer into the owner's hands and allowed them to essentially do anything they wanted in terms of communication and research from wherever they were at the moment. It provided instant access to the world of knowledge and the world of contacts.

From a business perspective, the smartphone has accelerated the pace at which commerce takes place. An attorney can now read a legal brief saved as a pdf file while riding in the back of a taxi cab on the way to court. College students can look up a complex algorithm they forgot to study just prior to walking into their midterm exam. Every person standing on a busy street corner becomes a potential photographic or video journalist for a crime or other event taking place. People can text for no charge from around the globe to stay in touch with each other: Instantly!

There is a great debate taking place today as to what extent the smartphone is damaging real "human to human" communication. Critics say that everyone is spending all their time walking around with their heads down, staring at their smartphone, instead of looking up at the world around them. There might be some element of truth to that, but it won't last forever. Right now, because of Apple and the invisible hand of the free market, people are just staring down because they cannot believe what they are seeing.

The computer age which dawned in the early-to-mid 20th century is marked by numerous milestones in its early phases, and who gets credit for what came first is not as clear-cut as might be the case with other "inventions." There were many simultaneous and complementary steps being taken by different people and groups at a very high rate of speed.

The Computer History Museum in Mountain View, California, just outside San Jose, does list the first key event in the development of computers as taking place in 1939. You are not going to believe where it started: in a Palo Alto garage used by David Packard and Bill Hewlett. Their first product was the HP 200A Audio Oscillator, which became a popular piece of test equipment for engineers. Walt Disney Pictures ordered eight of the 200B model to use as sound effects generators for the 1940 movie *Fantasia*.

From there, a series of developments take place, including the creation of the "counting machine," or Bombe, as it was properly named, designed with the participation of Alan Turing of *The Imitation Game* movie fame. The museum does cite 1950 as a key moment in time for the commercialization of computers. That was when

Engineering Research Associates of Minneapolis built the ERA 1101, the first commercially produced computer. They sold them to the U.S. Navy and by today's standards they operated with the sophistication of an abacus.

To refer back to our timeline of economic progress, the naturally occurring force of capitalism began to be unleashed in 1760 CE. From that point forward it took less than 200 years for the development of the first commercially sold computer and, after that, only 56 years until the smartphone e changed the world.

As for the telephone itself, it was in 1876 that Alexander Graham Bell was awarded the patent on the first telephone. There has been considerable debate over the past century and a half as to whether Bell or his contemporary counterpart, Elisha Gray, actually "invented" the phone. Those debates aside, and with an acknowledgment that both men were brilliant, what is not contested is that it took humanity almost 1,900 years into the Common Era to invent the phone. Once that happened, however, it only took capitalism roughly 100 more years to get us to Apple's smartphone. As an aside, it took less than 100 years after the start of the Industrial Revolution for Samuel Morse to send the first telegraph message, the precursor to the telephone.

Uber

The taxi cab industry has long been one of the inexplicably government-protected industries in a nation that, from its very beginning, embraced free markets. What could possibly be more basic than allowing someone with a valid license and access to an automobile to give a ride to someone who needed one, and charge them a few dollars for so doing? Despite that, the truth is that taxi cabs have been heavily regulated and protected, especially in major urban centers, for decades and have restricted entry to the marketplace and kept rates unnecessarily high and service demonstrably poor.

Enter Travis Kalanick and his App-centered car service Uber. An article in *Gulf Life Magazine* tells the basic story of Uber's beginnings:

The story of Uber takes us back to 2008, when the co-founders, then still friends and not aware they'll be at the head of one of the most successful startups to date, were attending LeWeb conference in Paris. Travis Kalanick and Garrett Camp, like old pals, were complaining about the many crappy things we all have to deal with in life, including finding a cab...[The] next thing you know, these two "uber" kids were already brainstorming, thinking about ways to solve this global issue of finding cars at the right place. And the right time...[The] solution had to be mobile and fast. Garrett took the lead.... It didn't take long before Travis joined the ride to work with him on what would later be known as Uber. Fast forward to January 2010 and Uber was already rolling a couple of black cars in the city of New York to simply test the service out.... Soon after, San Francisco joined in to host Uber, and the rest, is history.

It is worthwhile to stop for a moment in the discussion of Uber and take note as to Adam Smith's invisible hand coming into play in this instance. Cars, phones, and computers all wound up being integrated together to provide the service. There is no way to believe that when Steve Jobs' Apple came out with the iPhone in 2007 that they were planning to have somebody else design an App, that tapped into the Internet through its computing integration capability, that would revolutionize the world of automobile "taxiing." The free market directed one into the other and came up with something that the largest room of brilliant government central planners could never have designed back in 2005, even if they had lunch brought in so they could keep working.

Today, Uber operates in more than 200 cities and in 58 countries around the globe. The company demonstrates a social consciousness found only in nongovernmental entities by committing to get 1 million women Uber drivers behind the wheel by 2020. They have even recently begun to deliver Uber Ice Cream. (*Melts in your mouth, not the backseat?*) The service is used by college students making their way around a university town and by Hollywood celebs out for an evening of merriment. The company's universal appeal reflects the quote from its co-founder cited at the beginning of this section. The only thing "red" or "blue" about Uber is the color of some of its cars.

Uber has faced predictable resistance from predictable sources, namely politicians who are closely aligned with the traditional taxi cab industry. One of their chief nemeses is current New York City Mayor Bill DeBlasio, who has never met a free market solution he didn't dislike. In the summer of 2015 he was forced to temporarily back down from an attempt to severely limit the number of Uber vehicles on city streets. Even the Democratic governor of New York, Andrew Cuomo, weighed in on the side of Uber.

New York has long been famous for the fact that the cost of a single taxi cab "medallion" (the city-issued symbol required to be displayed on the side of a cab to allow it to legally pick up passengers "hailing" from the street) was $1 million. This eliminated entry into the space for the poor and essentially made drivers regulated—market-slaves to the medallion owner. Since the advent of Uber, prices for medallions in New York City have dropped to roughly $700,000. It shows the power of the free market and the pricing mechanism directed by the invisible hand to make more goods and services affordable to all.

At the time of Caesar Augustus, at the beginning of the Common Era, the development of the roadway system was of great importance. Augustus sought to develop an infrastructure of roads for military and economic use. The roads themselves were built with simple stone paving blocks and had drainage ditches on each side for runoff. The roads were almost never used for recreational travel; such a thing didn't exist. They were used by diplomats, mail carriers, soldiers and traders. Many rode on horseback and the very wealthy might actually be carried lying down on a litter or sitting in a sedan chair carried by slaves.

As for the taxi industry, it goes back to the beginning of the 17th century. A horse-drawn hackney carriage operated in Paris and in London. It didn't take long for big government to regulate it. In 1635 the Hackney Carriage Act in London was proclaimed to regulate the number of carriages which could operate. In a world controlled by kings, lords, clerics, and all other forms of managed-economy sorts, it took more than 1,600 years to create a taxi industry. No worries, free markets were about 100 years away, and Uber right around the corner from that.

With regard to cars themselves, it took 1,885 years from the beginning of the Common Era for Karl Friedrich Benz to invent the gasoline-powered automobile. From the start of the Industrial Revolution, however, that car was only about 120 years away from pulling out of some inventor's garage.

Netflix

For anybody in college today between the ages of 18 and 22, at the time of your birth the blockbuster in the world of home entertainment was Blockbuster. At their zenith in 2004, they had 9,000 stores and 60,000 employees. In 2010 they filed for bankruptcy and by 2011 they were vapor. What happened?

Part of what happened was Netflix. According to *Forbes* magazine, in 2000, Reed Hastings, founder of a fledgling company called Netflix, flew to Dallas to propose a partnership to Blockbuster CEO John Antioco and his team. The idea was that Netflix would run Blockbuster's brand online and Antioco's firm would promote Netflix in its stores. Hastings got laughed out of the room.

Started by Hastings in 1997 to offer online movie rentals, what Netflix has done is change the way people spend their entertainment time and dollars. It has also changed the way television executives and movie producers create and disseminate film content. When you combine the entertainment deliverables of Netflix with the technology of Jobs and others, learning how to operate a remote control almost becomes mandatory vocational training for a happier adult life.

Netflix launched its subscription service in 1999, to provide unlimited rentals for a flat monthly subscription fee. They had their IPO in 2002 and had more than 4 million subscribers by 2005. Their video streaming platform with which we are now so familiar started in 2007. Since then they have moved into original programming, like the award-winning *House of Cards*.

At the end of 2014, Netflix had more than 57 million subscribers, and generated $1.48 billion in revenue in just the last quarter of that year alone. Its market value is many times greater than Blockbuster's ever was, even in it best years. Netflix continues to expand into overseas markets and has spawned imitators such as our friend from pages past, Jeff Bezos at Amazon.com, with their Amazon Prime program for streaming video. All of the competition will make certain that Netflix will not be able to strangle the market and raise its prices to an unaffordable level. If it tries to, the invisible hand will direct competition to step in and drain market share from them so that they either adjust their strategy or get a tombstone right next to Blockbuster's.

There are great names associated with the development of photography and film (Claude Niépce, Charles-Émile Reynaud, Eadweard Muybridge, Étienne-Jules Marey, George Eastman, and others), but the best known is Thomas Alva Edison, who first patented the "Kinetograph" in 1891. When you consider that the first still photograph was taken by Niépce in 1827, the progression time is incredibly rapid. Mankind went more than 1,800 years in the Common Era before reliably capturing an image (although the first photograph took more than eight hours to fully expose). From that point it took only a few decades for Edison and others to transfer still photos and images into "film."

None of these great scientists was directed or inspired by government. They operated freely, allowing their creative minds to theorize, hypothesize and test. Once the technology developed, the free market took it and never let go, bringing us to where we are today with the next season of *House of Cards* always looming.

Starbucks

Starbucks has had an incredible impact on the coffee industry by changing the way we consider the entire experience of the beverage and the coffee shop. It has created a proliferation of coffee shops that combine a wide range of beverage selections with specialty pastries and other food offerings, and place them in an atmosphere that becomes a virtual office setting for the ever increasing number of people who work remotely or independently. In short, Starbucks has created an entire coffee shop culture that has taken the old European model and thoroughly "Americanized" it.

The story of Starbucks has been told many times and can be found concisely on numerous websites. It actually began in Seattle in the Pike Place Market area of the city. The three founders, Jerry Baldwin, Zev Seigl, and Gordon Bowker, sold whole bean coffee and coffee-making equipment only; no ready-to-drink beverages. In 1981 the three hired a young Howard Schultz to be their director of retail operations. Schultz tried to convince them to sell beverages, but the group declined.

Disenchanted, Schultz left the group. He toured Italy, learned about the world of coffee, started his own coffee company, Il Giornale, and ultimately returned to Seattle and purchased Starbucks from its founders in 1987. In June of 1992, Starbucks went public at $17 per share. An analysis done by Joshua Kennon in 2012, 20 years after that public offering, showed that a $100,000 investment in Starbucks the day it went public would be worth $9.2 million two decades later. What Schultz and Starbucks have done since the mid 1990s is difficult to imagine when you understand that it is built, at its core, around a beverage that is thought to have originated natively in Ethiopia and which was being traded in Arabia as far back as the 9th or 10th century.

Think of what Starbucks has done to change our language and create the proliferation of competitive products: Frappuccinos, Lattes, Chai Teas, Red Eyes, Black Eyes, Tall-Grande-Venti-Trente; all these terms and ideas have infiltrated the way people have come to think about a coffee shop experience. Starbucks has had this impact because the chance to operate in a free market, or near-free markets, has enabled it to establish a footprint of more than 21,000 stores in 65 countries. They are literally almost everywhere and their influence is pervasive.

Walk into any Starbucks today and you will find people sitting at virtually every table with their MacBook Pro fired up and working on something while they people-watch and sip the beverage of their choice. This was a scene completely unknown in America 20 years ago. Now it is not only commonplace, but Starbucks has created additional competition, and a race to make a beverage and dining environment also into an office environment. Rival Panera Bread introduced in Chicago in 2014 built in computer screens, web access, and cell phone charging and synchronization *right into their countertops*. What will develop in this arena is difficult to imagine and *impossible* for any group of bureaucrats to plan. Only the invisible hand of the free market knows where it is heading, and it isn't talking.

There is no possible way to give credit to all of the great outputs that capitalism has generated in the past 20 years from the inputs of human ingenuity and individual freedom. For example, Facebook, founded in February 2004 on the Harvard University campus, was originally limited to Harvard University students. It then expanded to other Boston universities and from there to the world. Facebook now has more than 1.2 billion active monthly users.

There is Groupon, the online daily deal coupon provider launched in 2008, born, legend has it, from a bad experience co-founder Andrew Mason had in trying to cancel a cell phone contract in 2006. The company became so successful that in 2010, two years after it was founded, it turned down an offer from Google to be purchased for $6 billion. In 2014 Groupon had sales of $3.2 billion. It has completely changed the marketplace in terms of electronic special offer couponing and has created smaller knockoffs in various municipalities around the country.

In early 2005, Chad Hurley and Steve Chen were taking video at a party held at Chen's house. After shooting the video they decided that they needed some way to share it with others. They decided to start a company where people could post video online. YouTube was born. A year and half later they sold the still-new company to Google for $1.6 billion. Today, it is almost impossible to think of any particular video you might want to see that is not on YouTube. You can have a YouTube app on your iPhone, next to Groupon and Facebook if you arrange them that way, and you can view or post video anytime and from anywhere.

None of these free market miracles were planned by central government.

ᑕ   ᑕ   ᑕ

All of the achievements of the entrepreneurs I've mentioned above came about because they were able to unleash their ideas and their passion through a free enterprise system. It is easy to look at their success and ask why I think there's a problem. The answer is that the free market window through which innovation can pass is closing. Big government has been aggressively raising the barriers to entry by increasing levels of taxation and regulation. It is getting harder and harder in America for the entrepreneur to hurdle these artificial barriers to entry.

It is ironic that when an activist, or a student, or a politician takes to social media to criticize capitalism they are using the tools that only capitalism could have provided. As they go to Twitter to send out 140-character assaults on the free market, as they take selfies with demonstrators on the street and post them on Instagram, they are using the creations of a free market in order to attack a free market. There is great ignorance to be found in anyone who picks up a tool they intend to use for battle and then uses that same tool to strike down the toolmaker.

Critics of free markets, whether on television or in a campus lecture hall, would do well to consider how effectively they could deliver their message, or how comfortable they would be when they get home that night, if it weren't for the array of life-accentuating innovations provided by capitalism. Perhaps they would like to write their message on papyrus leaves and have it carried by a horseman around the countryside? The hardworking, dirty shirt of freedom has given them much for which to be thankful.

The difference between the people I've mentioned in this chapter and the people who lived, say, 600 years ago, is that these people lived in a time when they could turn their ideas into realities through the use of a free market. They also benefited because several generations before them had the same opportunity to develop their ideas. Those developed ideas are the building blocks of free enterprise and capitalism; an invisible hand laying each and every stone.

David Hume suggested that human history is naturally progressive in nature, at varying rates over time, showing steady improvement in the human condition. Hume seems to have been undeniably right if we look back at the time of Caesar Augustus and compare it to now. But what we have learned is that Hume's progression clearly has not been linear. It has had a disproportionate amount of steam gathered since the advent of the steam engine and the workings of free markets took hold. Julio needs the power of the free market. We all need the power of the free market.

Capitalism's greatest gift isn't the creativity or the imagination that it stirs in people. Its greatest gift is to allow the imagination and creativity that stirs in every human soul to be expressed and find fulfillment that benefits them, and everyone around them.

CHAPTER 6

THE FAIRNESS
OF FREE MARKETS

"Virtue is to be feared more than vice, because its excesses are not subject
to the regulation of conscience."

—Attributed to Scottish Philosopher ADAM SMITH

The longest four-letter word in the English language is "Capitalism."

I have traveled the country addressing every age group and every demographic and I never cease to be amazed by the baggage that the word "capitalism" carries with it wherever it goes. Back in 2012, focus-group guru Frank Luntz went so far as to tell Sean Hannity that conservatives should not be defending capitalism, they should be defending economic freedom. So capitalism has made us so rich as a nation that we have become rich enough to want to forget its name. Sadly, from a linguistic perspective, there is a real element of truth to what Luntz said and that is why at TPUSA we have spent so much time using the terms free markets and free enterprise.

The problem is, to most of the country the terms free markets and capitalism are interchangeable because, well, because they are interchangeable. They hear the objections to capitalism, including that it is unfair, it is exploitative, it is all about greed, it "trickles down," and it creates "One-Percenters." This is tragic because what people have come to believe about free enterprise has been taught to them using bad data and propaganda. Team Left has done an excellent job of demonizing capitalism, primarily by misidentifying the characteristics of big government and big business joining together as "capitalism."

On September 17, 2011, in New York's Zuccotti Park, the "Occupy Wall Street" movement was born. While it has moved over into the shadows as I write this in early 2016, the group is still around and still preaching against the inherent unfairness of capitalism (free enterprise). A posting on the OccupyWallStreet.org website in May of 2013 succinctly makes their argument:

> First of all: there seems to be some kind of misconception among some people of what capitalism actually is. There are some who believe that where there is a market economy, money and competition, then that's automatically capitalism. That's not true. In capitalism there is of course a market economy, but that can exist in other systems as well.
>
> What characterizes capitalism is that there is **private ownership of the means of production**. *That's* when you know you're dealing with a capitalist system. If this feature is absent, if it's not the case that some individuals privately own the means of production others are using, then (sic.) it's no longer capitalism. If it instead was a system in which, let's say, the workers themselves controlled and managed the means of production democratically at the place where they worked, and that these institutions were operating in a market system, then that would be some kind of market socialism etc. (sic.), not capitalism.
>
> And it is this **private ownership of the means of production** that's a huge part of the problem. Capitalism is tyrannical, exploitative and dehumanizing; it's intolerable.

A system that allows a few individuals to have undemocratic control and power, not only at the workplace, but in society in general, is unacceptable; a system that allows some individuals to exploit and profit on other people's misery is unacceptable; a system that allows more and more cash to be shuffled into the pockets of the owners and the wealthy, is unacceptable.

That is the message I, and every other defender of free markets, are up against when defending the virtue of capitalism/free markets/ free enterprise/private enterprise. What makes it even worse is that the message is being delivered not just by radicals on poorly written websites, but also by Ivy League-educated professors on campuses around the country.

If I'm going to paint a future for you that holds out free enterprise as one of the fundamental building blocks I need to convince you that it isn't just effective, it's just! America can never enthusiastically embrace free enterprise if our citizens can only get to the point of saying it's the lesser of many economic system evils. I want support for free enterprise, not tolerance.

To do that I'm going to need a little help, so I turn to the future Nobel Prize-winning economist and front-man for the rock group U2, Bono. During a speech at Georgetown University in 2013, Bono addressed suffering around the globe and the efforts he and others make to help. The news and entertainment world took notice when he said:

> Aid is just a stop-gap. Commerce [and] entrepreneurial capitalism takes more people out of poverty than aid…. In dealing with poverty here and around the world, welfare and foreign aid are a Band-Aid. Free enterprise is a cure…. Entrepreneurship is the most sure way of development.

If you're a celebrity, especially a rock star, in today's politically-correct climate, it usually means that you embrace the social democratic forms of political and economic systems; not capitalism. Why did Bono make such a bold statement and risk criticism from his peers?

For years Bono has been a champion of helping people throughout the world who have suffered from hunger, disease, and oppression. He has used his band, his friends, and his name to raise millions of dollars to alleviate suffering wherever he felt he could make a difference. What Bono came to learn over time was that just throwing money at any particular injustice wasn't enough. Unless there was a permanent economic system in place to provide for opportunity and wealth creation after the donated money ran out, real change couldn't take place.

Bono learned that only the harnessing of the powers of free enterprise can bring enough prosperity to a nation to create a tide that raises all ships. Instead of thinking, like many other rockers do, that free enterprise only makes the rich get richer, Bono has come to see that it can truly help the poor get richer.

I believe that if you examine the facts you will find that in every nation of the world where the people enjoy an overall standard of living superior to those of other countries, you will find that either they eagerly embrace the principles of free enterprise or they have done so in their not-so-distant past. The nations that have drifted away from free enterprise principles and still enjoy prosperity are those where they continue to live off the momentum that free enterprise generated for them.

There are many myths that have been crafted by politicians, educators, and pundits about the failings of free enterprise to address social justice concerns. While some of the people who perpetuate these myths are those who truly mean to do good works, others are people who simply attack free enterprise with a false sincerity. For those people, it is important to discredit free enterprise because they know that it places power in the hands of the individual, and makes it harder to keep people under the control of an all-powerful state. They are sophists. They want people to believe that free enterprise is inherently unfair and creates social injustice. They say that free enterprise is a disease that makes a nation morally sick.

Bono however, knows it is not a disease; it is the cure.

I feel it is important to address the common complaints and arguments brought against free enterprise that you might have heard from a professor, a pundit, or a politician, all of which suggest that the results it produces are unfair and are contrary to notions of social justice. These arguments get made both from religious organizations and secular concerns. I'm going to address each of these common arguments. I believe that letting individuals be free to make their own choices can produce, and has produced, the highest standard of living any nation can experience. If the world of Julio is going to arrive, Americans have to stop seeing capitalism as an evil to be fought at every turn. It is going to be necessary for every one of us to be able to say:

"I'm a good person. I care about others. I'm a capitalist!"

Let's start by addressing the most common and most general complaint against free enterprise. It is that some people are purely greedy and care nothing about others. In the 1987 motion picture Wall Street" Michael Douglas' Academy Award-winning character, Gordon Gecko, utters the famous line, "Greed is good." That single line from a movie has done as much harm to opinions about capitalism as any other statement from any person, real or fictitious, in the last 50 years. When Gecko utters that line, audience members think Gecko believes he's a capitalist and is just telling it like it is. The problem is that even if Gecko considered himself to be a good capitalist, his rationalizing defense of free enterprise is neither accurate nor necessary. There are very few people who truly think greed is good. Fortunately, free enterprise creates checks and balances to make certain that greed alone cannot prevail.

Imagine the greediest person you know, or simply think about Gordon Gecko. If Gordon carried a gun and there were no laws, he would rob everyone he came across in order to acquire all the wealth he could possibly amass. In an economic system where the government has control over how the economy operates, Gecko could form an alliance with government officials, who would then pass rules to force people, or entice people, to purchase items only from him.

He would be able to use force, with the help of government, to give himself an advantage over other citizens.

Now place Gecko into a free enterprise system where individuals are free to produce and consume as they choose and where private property rights are protected by law (Gecko can't use a gun!). In a free enterprise system, the government will not step in to help Gecko acquire his wealth by granting him an advantage over others. Since Gecko can't rob people to acquire wealth and since he can't have government officials move him to the front of the line, how will he satisfy his greedy impulses?

In a free enterprise system where the only exchanges are voluntary exchanges, Gecko can satisfy his greediness only one way, by finding something he can sell, that enough people want to buy, so that he can accrue his fortune. The beautiful part is that even though Gecko is rotten on the inside, every dollar he generates comes from someone buying something that they needed or wanted. His virtue, or lack of virtue, is irrelevant.

Now, if I replace Gecko with his complete opposite, Allen Altruist, watch what happens. Altruist cares nothing about himself. All he wants to do is to help other people. He wants to give them money, clothes, medicine, and everything else they can possibly need. How will Altruist satisfy his need to please others? Well, if he had a gun and there weren't laws, he could rob from those who have and give it to those who have not (and no, that *isn't* the Robin Hood story... Robin Hood was taking from the government and giving back to the citizens). If the government controlled the economy, he could turn to them and say, let's use our power to take things away from those we think shouldn't have and give it to those we think should have. What does Altruist have to do in a free enterprise system?

The question is almost rhetorical. He has to do the exact same thing that Gecko had to do, and he will do it with the exact same outcome. Imagine, two completely different men with two completely different sets of values and goals, both needing to behave the same way in order to accomplish their objectives; both of them benefiting others along the way. How can this be possible?

The answer reveals the self-correcting morality of free enterprise. The engine of free enterprise that creates wealth and opportunity for all is powered by the purpose of each and every individual. Some may be greedy, some may be altruists, some may be hedonists, and some may have no particular agenda at all. Whatever their motivations, whatever their purpose, in a free enterprise system the only way they can fulfill their purpose is to produce or provide something that someone else wants to have.

Greed is a word associated with evil or even sin. Is it possible to believe that we will ever eliminate evil or sin in all people? Again, rhetorical. What is the best way to put evil in check? It is by creating a system where an evil person cannot gain an advantage over a decent person.

Free enterprise is that system. With the government now controlling a larger and larger share of the economy, does anybody believe that none of the people working for the government is evil? Are none of them greedy? When people with bad intentions have the power of the law behind them they can take advantage of others. When people with bad intentions are forced to operate in a free enterprise system, they cannot gain advantage over anyone without producing something that somebody wants.

Put in Bono's terms, free enterprise neutralizes the disease of greed within a society by not permitting the greedy person to gain an advantage over decent, caring people.

Another common criticism of capitalism is that it allows, even encourages, employers to exploit workers by paying them slave wages while forcing them to work in unsafe or dangerous conditions. Critics of capitalism like to use terms like "sweat shops," "child labor exploitation," and "non-living wage" in order to make people believe that in a capitalist system workers are at a disadvantage and require big government stepping in to force business owners to treat them fairly. But it is precisely in countries where capitalism isn't present that those kinds of situations exist. As a general rule, the freer the market, the better off the workers.

Many of the arguments against free enterprise and the conditions of the worker still find their origin in stories about America back in the 1800s during the industrial revolution and the Gilded Age. There is no question that the life of the worker in the early days of molding steel and building railroads was filled with long hours and varying degrees of peril. But the harsh, often dangerous world of the worker in 19th century America existed because industries were so new and expanding so rapidly that those tough conditions were no different than the growing pains that every human experiences in their early years of life. They weren't being exploited by their employers; they were riding beside them on a free enterprise learning curve. You don't build anything using perfection as a tool. You build something with the tools you have while working toward perfection.

Millennials are very concerned with job mobility and not wanting to be stuck in a position that isn't to their liking. Only a free enterprise system provides the millennial with freedom to move from one job to another. Without big government managing the economy and telling people where they can work, or telling employers how many people they can employ, each individual is free to change jobs if they so desire and have the skills to make the move. If a steel worker feels that his job is too dangerous, he can apply to a less perilous manufacturer. In a true free enterprise system, where every worker has the right to work and every employer has the right to hire, each individual is protected by the very best method possible—they can leave if they want. There are still plenty of countries today that do not allow their workers the freedom to leave one position for another without any restriction.

In terms of wages, the competition for workers in a free economy is the best way to ensure that everyone gets paid the highest wage that the company can afford. If there are 20 companies competing in the cell phone industry, any one of those companies will quickly lose their best workers if they try to pay them significantly less than their competitors. In an economy where the government tries to manage the wages of the workers in order to make certain they are "fair," the business owners may not be able to afford those workers in their operations and may be forced to hire fewer people. Is there greater social justice when a company hires only one worker at $30 per hour or two workers at $15 per hour?

Critics of capitalism contend that business owners seek to keep costs down in order to make a profit and as a result, they will always try to pay their workers as little as possible. That statement is a half-truth. Business owners do try to keep their costs down to maximize profits, but in order to generate those profits they need to have quality workers. The competition for employees amongst employers will cause them to pay neither a high wage nor a low wage; it will cause them to pay the best wage they can while still maintaining profitability. They don't pay their workers as little as they need to. They pay them as much as they have to.

In a government-controlled economy, each time the government intervenes in the labor market it creates interference in the process of companies establishing the right level of wages for the right number of workers. This invariably leads to not enough jobs for all the people seeking them. The fair wage, the just wage, is the wage that the employer and the employee voluntarily come to agreement upon. Social justice cannot be served while some have a little bit extra while others have nothing at all. It can only be served when each and every person has the opportunity to earn as much as they can, by offering the skills and talents they possess to employers who need those skills and talents.

¢   ¢   ¢

In the 2016 presidential election cycle, Donald Trump has generated a lot of interest, and controversy, when he brings up companies like Coca Cola, CF Industries, or Terex who have moved their corporate headquarters overseas, to anywhere from Britain to Finland. He also rails against Ford for planning to invest $1.5 billion in Mexico to build a plant that will produce 350,000 cars per year. Many listeners to his speeches from across the political spectrum applaud his criticism of what they feel is an inherent flaw of capitalism: greedy companies concerned only with profits forsaking Americans.

It always makes headlines when U.S. companies lay off workers and send jobs overseas. China and Mexico are known for low-cost manufacturing, and India is becoming increasingly known for customer service-type positions. But when an American company closes its plant in Michigan and opens one in Mexico, is it a failure of capitalism? Is it a failure of something else? Is it a failure at all?

It is easy to say that a business owner is un-American and greedy when he outsources production to a foreign land. But businesses do this all the time and are doing it at an increasing rate. Are all business owners un-American? This overly simplistic notion is dangerous and doesn't take into account that decisions to outsource jobs aren't inherent in capitalism. They are often made necessary because of the government interfering with capitalism.

First, consider when it is a good idea for a capitalist business to move jobs to another country. We live in a global economy now where different nations have developed different strengths and capabilities in their economies. Some nations do some things better. When that is the case it makes good business sense to send work to those nations that do the work more efficiently. In a free market, that's ok, because while we send jobs to one nation, another nation is sending jobs to ours. In a free market it is not a winner and loser situation.

The problem in outsourcing gets created when the government interferes in the capitalist system and creates impediments to U.S. companies being able to keep jobs in the U.S. in a cost-effective manner. Each time the government issues a new environmental regulation, each time it raises the cost of labor (through union preferences, health care costs or other means), and each time it raises the corporate tax rate, the choice for the business owner to move operations elsewhere gets easier to make. Writing in the *National Review* in February of 2016, Jared Meyer notes:

Since 1988, the average corporate tax rate for 34 Organization for Economic Cooperation and Development countries has fallen from 44 percent to 25 percent. Over that time, the U.S. rate actually increased. Even the Nordic countries that Democratic presidential candidate Bernie Sanders so admires have lower corporate tax rates than America does. Finland has a corporate tax rate of 20 percent, Sweden's is 22 percent, and Denmark's is 24 percent.

Ask any business owners in the U.S. if they would prefer to have their operation in Malaysia or across town and they will always say "across town." So why do so many move? Because the capitalist system in the U.S. has been interfered with by the government, often in the name of social justice, to the point where the business owner can no longer make the same profit by keeping operations here at home. The cost of compliance with regulation, the corporate income tax rate, and now the newly imposed costs of Obamacare all tie directly or indirectly into social justice arguments, and all lead to fewer Americans having jobs to support themselves.

In a capitalist system, jobs go overseas, or come in from overseas, when it is calculated to be in the best interest of both parties. In an economy with big government interference, that calculation still takes place. Now that the U.S. government has grown so big and has imposed so many rules and costs upon business, that calculation has been artificially altered. Jobs that never would have gone overseas before go there now to escape big government. This isn't a failure of capitalism, it is capitalism trying to overcome obstacles and find a navigable path.

¢   ¢   ¢

Let me go back to that rich source of capitalism-bashing, the Occupy Wall Street movement. Since it started, members of the media and academia have been driving home the disparity between the 1 percent (meant to mean the people who have the most in America) and the 99 percent (the people who have the least). Their intention is to deliver a message that capitalism creates great income inequalities within a nation and, therefore, is inconsistent with notions of social justice. In just a few years we now have people on college campuses who don't know who the 16th president of the United States is but who can tell you instantly what the definition of a "One-Percenter" is.

This argument is designed exclusively to convince people that it is OK to take from people who have and give to people who have less. Capitalism, however, isn't about anybody taking anything from anybody else. Capitalism is about voluntary exchange and letting each individual attain whatever level of income or other satisfaction they wish to attain based on talent, skill and effort. Not everyone will make it to the top of the income scale. In fact, that isn't even possible, because if everyone is at the top, then there is no top! But in a capitalistic society everyone has a chance to get to where they want to be through hard work and self-reliance.

The notion of income unfairness and redistribution truly began to be worked into American policy during the Great Depression. In 1932, Franklin Delano Roosevelt gave an inspired speech some now credit for adjusting the trajectory of what's considered the legitimate role of American government to meddle in the financial lives of its citizens. In that speech he referred to "the forgotten man." Speaking in the early stage of the Great Depression, which his policies would ultimately extend, he said, in part, "These unhappy times call for the building of plans that rest upon the forgotten, the unorganized but the indispensable units of economic power, for plans...that build from the bottom up and not from the top down, that put their faith once more in the *forgotten man* at the bottom of the economic pyramid."

The problem with FDR's reference is that it was a deliberate corruption of an expression coined by Yale University professor (and the first in "Sociology") William Sumner back in the 1800s. Sumner, the proto-libertarian and antithesis of the collectivist FDR, had coined the term "Forgotten Man" in his pioneering discussion on the welfare state. He wrote:

As soon as A observes something which seems to him wrong, from which X is suffering, A talks it over with B, and A and B then propose to get a law passed to remedy the evil and help X. Their law always proposes to determine what C shall do for X, or, in better case, what A, B, and C shall do for X.... What I want to do is to look up C.... I call him the forgotten man.... He is the man who never is thought of. He is the victim of the reformer, the social speculator, and philanthropist, and...he deserves your notice both for his character and for the many burdens which are laid upon him.

Since FDR, the American government has been increasing its interference with the free market in order to help 'the forgotten man" and redistribute income. In the process, it has widened the gap between rich and poor and has slowed the growth in household incomes now to a near-zero or negative rate.

There is income inequality in every society. Whether in the former Soviet Union or today's China and Cuba, there are the very privileged and there are the masses oppressed by a government that intervenes in the marketplace. The only places that have close to equality of income are those nations where *everyone* is poor. No nation where the government controls the economy can maximize personal wealth, because the free market forces of capitalism are not unleashed to produce goods and services that provide productive jobs.

Much of the income inequality in the U.S. today is not because of capitalism but because capitalism has been corrupted by government policies that punish or deter people who want to produce. Starting a new business has never been harder than it is today. Barriers to entry, from education to banking, from energy production to farming, have made it difficult for enterprising citizens to follow their dreams, build a business, and increase wealth. Also, when those kinds of people build a new business, they need to hire workers and lift their income levels as well. So long as big government makes it difficult for people to build new businesses, thereby creating wealth and jobs, those who are at the top will remain at the top.

In a government-controlled economy driven by "'social justice" concerns, wealth is torn down and scattered. In a capitalistic system, wealth is built and benefits all. When leaders say that, in order to be "fair" we need to take from those who have more and give to those who have less, what they are counting on is that those who have acquired more will continue to do so even though they know it is going to be taken away. Think about it: Would you study hard in your college classes to earn an "A" even if you knew that once you earned it that the grade would be dropped to a "C" so that another student could receive a "C" instead of an "F"?

Income equality can never, and should never, be a goal. The goal should be to provide an opportunity for everyone to continue to receive a higher income through economic growth, jobs, and success. Only capitalism can provide the vehicle to permit that to happen. It can be the cure for the hopelessness felt by those at the lower end of the income ladder by giving them the steps to climb to the higher levels.

ɕ   ɕ   ɕ

One of the more notable oxymorons of the English language is the term "underprivileged." When it's used it is meant to describe people who, in simpler and less euphemistic times, used to be called "poor." The argument used against capitalism with regard to the "underprivileged" is that the system leaves them outside the economy, living lives filled with hopelessness, starvation, and despair. The problem is that the exact opposite is true. Free enterprise alone provides the resources for a compassionate society to help those who are truly needy

Imagine yourself as being down to your last dollar on a cold, winter day in the north. You are without a coat and are shivering as you walk down the street. As you look ahead you see a homeless person out in the street, also shivering, and without a jacket. You're a good soul and you want to help them but you have no money and you, yourself, have no jacket. Both of you are in for a frigid night out on the street. You can't help because you have nothing to give in order to help.

An economy is no different. In order to clothe those who can't clothe themselves, you first have to be able to produce coats. Capitalism is the vehicle by which those coats get produced. While maybe we haven't been doing it lately, it's the United States that is the nation that has most enthusiastically embraced the purest form of capitalism. Despite our increasing turn away from free markets, even today the U.S. remains the most willing and able nation on earth when it comes to helping others. When a tsunami strikes in Thailand, the U.S. delivers aid. When an earthquake levels Haiti, the U.S. leads the way for rescue and assistance. Here at home a typical member of the "poor" has a cell phone, a television, and often even a car. No other nation on earth has ever had the capability or the willingness to assist people in need as has the U.S.

Contrary to what many politicians and academics like to contend, capitalists do believe in charity. At our core, we are a profoundly compassionate and caring people who believe it is our privilege as decent members of the human race to help those who are truly in need. Whether it is at the mandate of our God, or the direction of our reason, we feel somehow completed when we can extend a hand to others.

The people of the United States are the most charitable, giving people on the planet, and research has shown that those who tend to associate themselves with capitalistic values are as giving, if not more so, than are the social justice critics of free markets. The big difference is that capitalists believe that charity is a personal calling, not a collective one. Those who feel God summons them to give, feel that He calls to them individually as members of His community. Others who, through reason alone, feel compelled to help others do so because of their own unique sense of inner purpose which drives their need to act.

Individual obligations for compassion aside, if a nation wants to help the poorest amongst them, if they want to give them winter coats, they must first have the wealth and means to produce and pay for those coats. Only capitalism can provide the abundance of surplus to properly care for those who cannot care for themselves.

Charity directed by people in power, forcibly taking from the citizens to address social justice and help who they decide to help and how they decide to help them, is not charity; it is theft. It erodes the intensity of individuals' call to help and can turn the virtue of charity in the giver into the curse of entitlement in the recipient. When someone in need benefits from an act of charity they usually feel gratitude and want to somehow "pay it forward" when they become able. When someone feels entitled, they lose their own sense of purpose and their desire to help themselves and others. They feel they are owed something. In a capitalistic system we believe in helping others not because we owe them, but because we love them as fellow individuals. Free enterprise is the only cure for helping lift the truly needy to a place of safety and comfort!

$$\mathcal{C} \qquad \mathcal{C} \qquad \mathcal{C}$$

Do you remember in 2015 when a privately owned business operating in a free market environment spilled millions of gallons of toxic heavy metal waste into the Animus River in Colorado? If that doesn't sound familiar, how about when a similar group of companies contaminated the water supply in Flint, Michigan, with high levels of lead pollutants? If you don't remember, it's OK because neither of those events was caused by greedy business owners exploiting the environment under the flag of free enterprise. Both of those significant, environmentally harmful and life-threatening events were caused exclusively by government. Despite the facts of these cases and numerous other examples, opponents of free markets would have you believe that our environment and natural resources are deliberately and constantly being damaged and exploited for economic gain. The truth, however, is that capitalism creates its own incentives for conservation and preservation.

Critics of capitalism often point to the exploitation of the environment as a reason that it cannot be allowed to operate as an economic system unchecked by government. They cite air pollution, water contamination, deforestation of rainforests and the endangerment of species as just some of many examples. Of course, the damage done in each area adversely impacts the quality of everyone's life, so social justice once again raises its head.

But the critics ignore the fact that today the cleanest and safest methods of production, and the nation most concerned with environmental safety, is the United States. In nations like China and India, where the government controls the direction of the economy, concerns for the environment are almost nonexistent and harmful pollutants fill the air and water supply. In Mexico, where the economy is overseen by a corrupt, often criminal government, it is not even safe for a tourist to drink the tap water.

The U.S., which has the longest running track record of embracing capitalist market solutions, also exhibits the cleanest and most environmentally-friendly means of production. Forests are not stripped bare in the United States to harvest lumber; tree farms are grown. Raw pollutants are not drained in water supplies; they are treated and cleansed before being recycled. Smoke stack emissions no longer make it dangerous to go outside on a summer day in metropolitan areas; technologies created in capitalist companies have been able to reduce sulfur content and other harmful burn off.

Critics of capitalism point to the damage caused by industry in the past as a reason to regulate it and make it "safer" in the present. But that argument ignores the fact that *everything* normally improves over time. We don't punish doctors today because of their past use of trepanning (the drilling of a hole in the patient's skull) to allow evil spirits to escape. In America's Industrial Revolution and through the 20th century, new production capabilities generated new problems that were previously unknown and often not understood or anticipated. Over time, private industry developed ways to solve those problems and reduce or eliminate harmful consequences for the environment.

In an economic system controlled by the government, resources are not purchased and replenished; they are taken and consumed. Only the government has the ability to seize a forest, defoliate it completely, and then simply seize another forest. In a capitalistic system, every resource used has to be paid for and then replenished, if possible, so that it might be used again.

In a capitalistic system, "waste" means "loss." As a general rule, everything that gets wasted in a capitalistic system translates into lost money or opportunity for a business. In a government-controlled system there is no real concept of loss because there is no true profit. It is the profit motive in capitalism that provides a built-in incentive for conservation.

Each and every business owner and manager has to breathe the air and drink the water that surrounds their business. Don't believe politicians when they tell you that the business owner doesn't care about the environment. A business owner who jeopardizes the health of himself, his family, his workers, and the consumers won't be in business very long.

The same holds true for matters of consumer product safety and food safety concerns. Horror stories about the early days of the meat-packing industry in the U.S., exaggerated to begin with, dealt with an industry in its infancy in terms of mass production and delivery of meat. Nobody had to tell a meat producer it was bad business to make his customer sick. The profit incentive and the need for self-preservation found only in capitalism ensured that meat producers and others would constantly search for better and safer ways to produce their product and bring it to market. If the government controlled the meatpacking industry, would they care if the customers got sick? Could the government suffer loss or go out of business?

¢   ¢   ¢

Every major industry in the United States today is experiencing rapid consolidation. Pick a sector; banking, energy, retail, everywhere we are getting fewer players with greater power. Opponents of free enterprise point to this and say that capitalism fosters too few companies controlling too much economic power. Again, more myths and bad data.

There is absolutely no question that the larger the company, the greater its potential and likely control over our daily lives. The problem with the argument against capitalism when it comes to the formation and growth of large companies is that this happens not because of capitalism, *but only when capitalism is interfered with by the government!*

Going back to the early days of the railroads and Teddy Roosevelt's "trust busting" activities, the companies that always welcome and embrace government regulation of their industry are the large ones. The large companies know they can withstand the cost of increased regulation and taxes, but those smaller companies, or new potential entrants into their industry, will not be able to afford the burden. Large companies have used their influence with the government over time to gain protection and advantage, thereby becoming even larger. The current joint nightmares of Dodd-Frank (embraced by the big bank groups) and Obamacare (embraced by the insurance industry) are very contemporary examples.

Consider the health care industry and the recent passing and implementation of Obamacare. Large companies did not object too strenuously to the law and made public statements either in support or to ask citizens to withhold judgment. Every large insurance company, pharmaceutical company, and medical provider group knew that the new requirements under the law would make it almost impossible for any new competitors to enter their respective industry. While they knew that Obamacare might marginally decrease percentage profits, even in the long term, they knew it would also protect them and allow them to grow larger.

In a capitalistic system where the government doesn't protect large companies with regulations, tariffs, or other barriers to entry, when a company starts to grow it means their market is expanding. That invites other companies to enter the market to gain from the opportunity. When new companies enter, the market grows in terms of numbers, and no single company can gain a dominating position.

Stop and consider why, so often, large business can be found partnering with big government. When either one tells you that they care about the "public interest" or "social justice," ask yourself why, if they really do care, do they not welcome new competitors to enter their market space? After all, wouldn't that create more jobs for more people and improve the overall conditions of the nation? Of course it would. But big business and big government aren't concerned about social justice. They are concerned about maintaining the power and privilege that comes with their enormous size and the power of law.

¢ ¢ ¢

When I propose to you that we need to embrace the fairness of free markets, I am doing so hoping that you can consider the arguments I've just made and then realize how much propaganda you've been fed over time about capitalism, greed, and its inherent injustice. When people criticize some identified flaw in capitalism in order to justify taking control over the economy, please look and listen carefully. I can assure you that in every single instance the supposed failures of free enterprise to which the detractors point are directly traceable to some form of government interference or manipulation.

I do have to give the social justice opponents of capitalism some credit. They have managed to interfere with the fairest and most productive method for organizing economic activity, disrupt and damage it with their interference, and then repeatedly and success-fully argue that in order to fix it they need to interfere with it some more.

Early in this chapter I quoted a contributor to the Occupy Wall Street Movement. Let me close by quoting someone of a bit more substance: Noble Prize-winning economist Milton Friedman. This is from a transcript of an interview Friedman did in 1979 while a guest on *The Phil Donahue Show*:

> **Phil**—When you see around the globe the maldistribution of wealth; the desperate plight of millions of people in underdeveloped coun-tries; when you see so few "haves" and so many "have nots"; when you see the greed and the concentration of power, did you ever have a moment of doubt about capitalism and whether greed is a good idea to run on?

Milton—Well, first of all, you tell me, is there some society that you know that doesn't run on greed? Do you think Russia doesn't run on greed? You think China doesn't run on greed? What is greed? Of course none of us are greedy...it's only the other fellow that's greedy. The world runs on individuals pursuing their separate interests. The great achievements of civilization have not come from government bureaus. Einstein didn't construct his theory under order from a bureaucrat. Henry Ford didn't revolutionize the automobile industry that way. In the only cases in which the masses have escaped from the kind of grinding poverty you are talking about, the only cases in recorded history are where they have had capitalism and largely free trade. If you want to know where the masses are worst off, it's exactly in the kinds of societies that depart from that. So that the record of history is absolutely crystal clear: That there is no alternative way so far discovered of improving the lot of the ordinary people that can hold a candle to the productive activities that are unleashed by a free enterprise system.

Phil—But it seems to reward, not virtue as much as ability to manipulate the system.

Milton—And what does reward virtue? You think that the communist commissar rewards virtue? You think a Hitler rewards virtue? You think, excuse me, if you'll pardon me, you think American presidents reward virtue? Do they choose their appointees on the basis of the virtue of the people appointed or on the basis of their political clout? Is it really true that political self-interest is nobler somehow than economic self-interest? You know, I think you're taking a lot of things for granted. And just tell me where in the world do you find these angels who are going to organize society for us? Well, I don't even trust you to do that.

To each and every bureaucrat, social engineer, and angel I say: Leave our market alone. Give it back to us. What you're doing isn't fair. We have work to do that only a free market can help us to complete.

PART THREE

FORCE EQUALS MASS TIMES ACCELERATION

CHAPTER 7

HARNESSING THE ENERGY OF YOUTH

"The secret message communicated to most young people today by the society around them is that they are not needed, that the society will run itself quite nicely until they—at some distant point in the future—will take over the reins. Yet the fact is that the society is not running itself nicely...because the rest of us need all the energy, brains, imagination and talent that young people can bring to bear down on our difficulties. For society to attempt to solve its desperate problems without the full participation of even very young people is imbecile."

—ALVIN TOFFLER

In late April of 2016, Texas television journalist, and fellow millennial, Alexis Bloomer, posted a video on YouTube that had more than 40 million views in just a handful of days. In slightly more than two minutes, Alexis articulated all that she saw that was wrong with the millennial generation and offered an apology to the rest of the country on their behalf. Here is a transcript of what she said:

> If you guys have anyone on your social media like I do that's over
> the age of 40, you've probably seen them post at some point about

how much our generation sucks. Well, as a millennial I took it upon myself to evaluate what's so wrong with our generation and why they're so mad at us. And then I pretty much realized that we're just existing. We aren't really contributing anything to society.

Our generation doesn't have the basic manners that include "no ma'am" and "yes ma'am." We don't even hold the door open for ladies, much less our elders, anymore. We listen to really obscene music that degrades women and pretty much glorifies drugs and crime. We start to cuss now to prove a point; we use words like "bae" to describe someone we love. And we idolize people like Kim Kardashian and then we shame people like Tim Tebow.

We're lazy, we're really entitled, and we want to make a lot of money and have a free education when we're not really willing to put in the work. We spend more time online making friends and actually less time building relationships; and our relationship appearance on Facebook is more valuable than the foundation that it's actually built on. Our idea of standing up for something we believe in means going on Facebook and posting a status with your opinion. And we believe that the number of followers we have reflects who we are as a person.

We don't respect our elders; we don't even respect our country. We're stepping on our flag instead of stepping up to volunteer. And we mock the men and women that are fighting for us, but we praise the men and women that are fighting each other guys [*sic.*]. We're more divided as a country than ever before and I think our generation actually has a lot to do with that. Everything that used to be frowned upon is now celebrated. Nothing has value in our generation because we take advantage of everything. We have more opportunities to succeed than any of those before us, yet we don't appreciate the opportunities we have now.

Now I guess I see why people call us "Generation Y." Like why are we so entitled, because we don't deserve to be and we were raised better than this. I think that our generation...I always wonder what we're going to be remembered by and I for one want to break that stereotype and prove that my parents raised me better...don't you? To all of our elders, I'm sorry, and I do know that we were raised better. Thank you from this millennial for putting up with those and those that do not see wrong in their actions. I hope we start pulling our pants up and actually contributing to the society that we love and maybe make a difference in 2016 so we can make a difference in the future.

The reason that I included the entire transcript is that it is actually a concise way to present what I commonly hear about today's young people. I am frequently being asked to make an appearance on one radio or television show or another to discuss the latest article, survey, or research piece on why millennials are so lazy, disrespectful, and disruptive. Unfortunately, it is a gross oversimplification of the generation and it issuing very imprecise and sloppy language to create a completely unnecessary division within America; this time, not by race or gender, but by an arbitrary definition of "generations."

If Turning Point is going to be successful in turning around anything in America, it is going to have to make it happen through American youth. Long-term change requires a long-term lifespan to see it through. While we need the support of American "baby boomers" and those who are older, we need the lifelong commitment and work from those who are younger. We need the incredible mass that is youth; we then need to accelerate that mass with information and messaging and direct them towards free markets and limited government. Then and only then can we turn them into an unstoppable force.

It doesn't help to start out by universally insulting them.

Let me start by clearly identifying a couple of terms and time frames. First of all, the people we call "millennials" are also referred to by sociologists as "Generation Y." So subjective is all of this that if you spend just a few minutes googling the start date of this generation you will actually find different dates cited by different authorities. I always think it is interesting when people are speaking in absolutes and using objective-type terms about things, and then you later find out that the concepts about which they speak are actually subjective and without universal agreement.

For my purpose I will use one common definition that categorizes millennials as those people born between the years 1981 and 1995. That places them, at the time of this writing, between the ages of 21–35. That places me at the very south end of the millennial group. My associate writer is in a similar circumstance, but from a different period in time. He was born in 1962, placing him at the tail end of the baby boomer category (1946–64). He often relates that he does not feel he shares much in common with the vast majority of people who are considered baby boomers, but who were born earlier in the period, especially the 1940s through the mid-1950s.

In the 2010 census, the U.S. Government reported that there were 146 million people under the age of 35. That number is now dated but it is a good approximation. Of that number, 106 million were reported as "white," equating to 73 percent. For the nation as a whole, 78 percent are white. This means that in the younger group we are being joined by more people of differing races, and the numbers and percentages will continue to grow. This will impact how we deliver messages about freedom and free markets to "next" generations, and I will discuss that in another chapter.

Even beyond racial composition, this millennial group is not monolithic. When you consider that at the youngest end we have people who are still in college today, while at the upper end we have people who have been out of school for 10 years or more, anybody who has lived longer than that knows how much people change in that time frame. In addition, given the rapidly changing nature of today's society, driven by changes in technology and communication, I would argue that we are almost producing a new group to be "named" by experts every four to five years.

So while I am technically a millennial, and while I am frequently asked to comment on the activities of millennials, I really see the critical identification as being that of "American Youth." In defining it this way, it helps me, and Turning Point, recognize that every single day more members are added to the group. Our work is in reaching them as they emerge from the cocoon of childhood innocence and begin to become politically cognitive. We need to be standing right there, ready to provide them with facts and messages that support First Principles.

Millennials matter not because of their label, but because of their age. At 35 and younger they are going to be around a long time. That means that turning them towards our vision of America and getting them to share it can make a long-term impact. Further, since many of them are already in the workforce earning wages, they can become financial supporters of our efforts right now. It is important to understand them and connect with them.

In terms of their not being a monolithic block, I have made an observation since starting Turning Point that is not based on scientific research, but on anecdotal experiences that have been had over several years and all across the country. The observation is this: For those millennials who came to political awareness between 2008 and 2016, they have been, for the most part, lost to the seduction of victimization, entitlement, and the need for big government to address both. Let me explain what I mean.

Before I start, please keep in mind that the human experience is lived, for the most part, under the bell curve. This is not the only time in this book I will make reference to this point. This means that when I speak in generalities, *I am speaking in generalities on purpose.* I'm not suggesting there are not exceptions, either in terms of people or events being 10 standard deviations from the mean, or in terms of pure outlying data points. I am simply addressing what I see and experience overall and in general.

If you were anywhere from around 14 to 22 years old during the 2008 economic collapse, you were, by definition, at a time in life when you were easily influenced by external societal events. Somewhere in this age range is where young people start to get really interested in the world around them from an issue and policy perspective. When the financial markets collapsed during the 2008 presidential campaign, the message everywhere was that capitalism and free markets had failed and had destroyed the life savings of families across the country, indeed throughout the world.

It didn't matter that there wasn't even a shred of truth in the contention; the opportunity was presented for people who were opponents to free markets (many professors, mainstream media members, then-candidate Obama) to shout at the top of their lungs, or mumble somberly in front of a classroom, that capitalism had failed. For young people building awareness at that time, they could look in their own homes and see the economic misery; and then everywhere they turned for an explanation of what happened, they heard free markets blamed. In the next sentence they heard that only the federal government could come in and clean up the carnage. Big government programs and oversight were needed so this never happened again.

Now, combine that general theme with the charismatic nature of the big government candidate Barack Obama. Obama spoke in broad and sweeping terms, hopeful terms. He talked of a "fundamental transformation" of America. He told us that "we were the change we had been waiting for." He spoke of his rise signifying the moment "where this rise of the oceans began to slow, and the planet began to heal."

He spoke as if he were an evangelist telling an America in ruins to rise up. The messaging has taken a toll on young people, especially those young people who were most susceptible to being influenced by it during the right moment and time in their life. I have experienced this in my own life and have watched many friends and classmates be seduced by the call to collectivism. It had an opposite effect on me.

I remember being in high school during Obama's 2008 presidential campaign. I remember the energy bouncing off the walls as we neared Election Day. I remember random students holding up the signs "Hope" and "Change" as people drove into school. Walking through the parking lot, all the "cool" kids had Obama bumper stickers pasted on their cars.

I was asked numerous times to go and make calls and knock on doors for then Senator Obama. My teachers were unapologetic in wearing Obama shirts and giving out Obama stickers. Our own student council made posters saying "Vote OBAMA!" The enthusiasm was unparalleled and the energy unmatched. My generation elevated Obama to celebrity-rock star-superman status. He was the embodiment of all the hope my generation had, and the manifestation of the person who would fix the problems we faced.

In 2008, Senator Obama's following within the ranks of mostly college students and young Americans was legion. His energetic and charismatic vision for America was bought wholeheartedly by our nation's youth. The Iraq war was unpopular, and the Republican Party brand severely wounded. Come election time it was not a surprise that younger voters turned a cold shoulder to the GOP in 2008. I mentioned earlier in the book how, even four years later, the Romney campaign would show complete ineptitude in reaching out to college-age voters.

Heading into the 2012 election cycle I had reason to hope for an awakening within my own age demographic. Things had to be different. The commonly accepted belief was that that Obama had overpromised and underdelivered in his first term for younger Americans. Surely younger voters would wake up to Obama's disastrous policies? Or so we thought.

On October 5, 2012, I had friends on campus at the University of Wisconsin. It was the day after the first presidential debate and President Obama was licking his wounds from getting whooped by Governor Romney. He decided to play a home game and hit the campaign trail at the bastion of liberalism in Madison. I can still hear the chants from the tens of thousands of college students bleeding through my friend's cell phone when President Obama came to speak. I was told of the overflow of students flooding the streets afterwards proudly chanting "OBAMA! OBAMA!" There was the blissful ignorance of the students, locked in mob-mentality unison, as they danced the night away and celebrated a "historic" visit from the president. Despite what I was hearing from my friends bearing witness, I still thought the youth, my peers, would come to their senses and "wake up" in the voting booth come election day.

And like so many others, I was wrong again. I could not comprehend how an entire generation could vote for policies that are designed to isolate and do them harm. At the time, I could not believe that millions of young people would willfully siphon off their own personal and overall freedom in exchange for "micro" freedoms like taxpayer-funded contraception and gay marriage. Now today, young people are starting to experience and live through the suffering that is a result and by-product of their own ill-fated vote.

Never before in modern political history has a segment of the population been so negatively and so quickly affected by the repercussion of their own political activism and decisions. Millennials are being suffocated by the growth of government. The freedoms they thought they were going to be able to enjoy have vanished under the veil of liberalism. They can't find jobs, and they are compelled to buy health care they don't need or want and with money they can't earn. They are paying the wages of sin for not understanding the implications of their votes. We need to get them to understand cause and effect.

These young people can now be viewed as political prisoners of liberalism. They are shackled with the ankle bracelet of a crippled economy that cannot and will not absorb them. In every metric, poll, and measure young Americans are suffering miserably. Their "rock star" has given them high student loan debt (he said those would go away), an impossible job market (he spent a trillion dollars so they'd have work), and skyrocketing health care premiums (so they could have affordable coverage). The bright future we were anticipating in 2008 and again in 2012 is looking more and more like the backdrop for a Tim Burton movie.

Despite all this failure, millennials remain generally supportive of President Obama. In addition, the new generation of young people entering college is experiencing the trailing impact of their predecessors' support. Even with the folly of big government policies under Obama, the young people who were cheering in 2008 and 2012 were so indoctrinated by almost every angle of their surrounding culture that they remain supportive.

This doesn't mean we should give up on those middle millennials, but it does mean we should focus most of our efforts elsewhere. Sun Tzu taught us a very long time ago not to launch attacks into your enemy's strongest points of defense. That is why at Turning Point we are going completely outside and underneath the millennial category and getting our message into high schools.

$$\zeta \qquad \zeta \qquad \zeta$$

A couple of years ago when I was speaking at the Western Conservative Summit, fellow speaker and radio talk show host Warren Smith created a term that grabbed the attention of many in attendance. In the context of discussing American voting patterns he coined the term "moveable millennials." Smith was making the argument that young people, long a captured voting block for Democrats, are now beginning to awaken to the perils and pitfalls of big government gone wild and are ripe to be taken by candidates who make a compelling and contrary argument.

The best part about Smith's argument is that on-campus inter-action with students all across the nation indicates that he's right. For decades since the '60 s, and only interrupted by the conservative enthusiasm generated amongst youth by Ronald Reagan in 1980, the young vote has been equated with liberal vote. They have been reflex-ively voting liberal before the Obama folks launched their Facebook page and long before they began using their parents' credit card to buy a "Hope & Change" T-shirt.

As a general rule, and with exceptions rare enough that they attract "what just happened" analysis by the media, Democrats could count on young people to be a solid majority block for Team Left candidates in each election and at every level. The reasons for this are numerous but can be summed up by the fact that young people who are not yet experienced in matters of the "real world" become seduced by the traditional burp-solidifying, progressive arguments, such as: Conservatives think the "Hunger Games" means starving the poor; the polar ice caps are becoming bottled water because of free enterprise; religious people want to call up the National Guard to make certain girls never ingest needed medication, and so on. But as is often the case, whether in relationships, politics, or when assuming the garage door is open, if you take something for granted, interesting things can happen.

Without addressing the issue itself here, the scandals of 2013 involving government surveillance of cell phone records and emails, coupled with the revelations of Edward Snowden, were a callout to youth screaming, "Is there anybody alive out there?" Nobody anticipated their reaction. When college seniors started hearing NSA crosstalk through their headphones instead of Maroon 5, they hit the "pause" button on their taken-for-granted political assumptions and let out a loud and collective "what the hell's going on?" This is especially true of younger people falling just at the bottom of, or outside of, the millennial age group.

So now, American youth are doing some "listening-in" of their own. They are becoming more engaged in the political process, and not in the old-fashioned "let's just wear our underwear and sit in at the Dean's office" kind of way. They are listening to arguments and starting to ask questions about what they've been told about the evils of capitalism, the righteousness of redistributive income programs, and what "social justice" really means. They are open, more than at any time in the past 30 years, to hear the compelling argument for American First Principles. Somebody has to step up and make the argument.

Every candidate who considers himself or herself a "conservative" (in quotes because of the now near-mutilated characterization of the term in today's political discourse) needs to recognize that the young American mind, along with its attendant vote, is in play. They need to realize that young voters are not truly ideologically opposed to free market ideas; they have just been on "Team Left" for a very long time. They can make the transition to "Team Right" if somebody can just make them feel welcome when they get there. Just like strangers at a large party, they need to be introduced, to be shown around, to be made to feel like your friends are their friends.

Going back to when Barack Obama was first elected in 2008 and including the three national elections we've had since then, consider the following as to how Republicans and Democrats have fared over that time period:

	2008	2010	2012	2014
Senate	Dems +7	Repub +5	Dems +2	Repub +7
House	Dems +20	Repub +63	Dems +9	Repub +12

Attempting to draw a regression line through that data would be more dangerous to your eyesight than Ralphie's Red Ryder BB Gun. In 2012, just two years after America had rejected the president and Obamacare in the midterm elections, the same voters delivered unto the president 26 states and 5 million more votes than they cast for Mitt Romney. More shocking is the fact that with small gains for Democrats in both the House and Senate in 2012, you could argue that the president had coattails.

Looking at millennials' votes in 2014 enters more confusing facts into evidence. First of all, they still aren't turning out to vote in the numbers you'd hope to see for people supposedly shaping America's future. With a little over 20% of those eligible actually voting (approximately 9.9 million), it remained comparable to the midterm election numbers for the same age group in 2010. Did *anything* change? Actually it did, and in that change burns the faint but undeniable flame of hope.

While a majority of millennials did vote Democrat in the 2014 midterms, their numbers are shifting. Polling suggested that young people ages 18 to 29 voted for Democratic candidates by a 13-point margin. That number could seem discouraging but not when compared to the 22-point margin in 2012 and the 17-point margin in 2010 for the same measure. The gap is closing.

But the closing gap is not indicative of some movement of young people trending from labor union Democrats to country club

Republicans. The gap is closing because young people are embracing and channeling their inner-libertarian selves. In an era when the abuse of big government has become clearer than ever, young people are tiring quickly of a leviathan that is cramping their style while it's listening in on their cell phones. They are looking for a way to express that frustration at the polls. This is what we are tapping into at Turning Point

The Democratic Party's idea of individual freedom is to make sure that a woman can hop on a light rail train, while smoking a marijuana cigarette, in order to get to Planned Parenthood and pick up her taxpayer-provided birth control. In every other way, Democrats favor state control and collective decision-making over individual liberty and free market solutions. Republicans at least *try* to convey a message of individual freedom. They do it poorly. If they could do it better they would find more success, more immediately.

If today's generically-labeled "conservatives" and "Republicans" want to attract young people and retain them through their golden voting years, they need to kick out their political consultants and start doing what two rival, but complimentary, businesses do: They need a merger. Traditional Republicans and emerging libertarians need to realize that they have more in common than in opposition and they need to unite themselves against the people and the party that stand for collective control and a diminished America (read Democrats & Progressives). This is the same kind of "merger" I will call for later between campus-based groups like Turning Point.

If it were theater, this struggle for America is best likened to an "epic," which involves great challenges faced over some always lengthy, never specified, period of time, usually including some sort of "journey." In the epic, there is that moment in the film where something happens that forces the protagonist to choose a path. Much later in the film, the wisdom or folly of that choice is revealed to the characters and to the audience. The struggle to unite Americans who still believe in individual freedom, but who find themselves intellectually and spiritually dispersed, is an epic journey. Republican Party leaders and their running-for-office representatives need to choose very wisely at this particular juncture of the story. If Republicans can't figure it out, then they will find, when the youth of today's Turning Point arrive en masse into the voting world, they will be looking for a home elsewhere.

There is at work in all of this a politically fascinating paradox. For years the Democrats have taken getting the majority of the youth vote for granted. At the same time, the Republicans have taken losing the youth vote for granted. As of this moment, neither political party has seemingly noticed the current nature of the dangers and opportunities they simultaneously face. What is clear is that the "moveable millennials" are no longer taking themselves for granted.

The youth vote and its support of the Democratic Party and big government promises is so taken for granted it is even sometimes mocked by the same ruling class members who appeal to them and court their vote. Big government politicians are conning young voters. In the Academy Award-nominated movie *American Hustle* we get a literary-licensed version of the real life grifters Mel Weinberg and his muse Sydney Prosser. The story is of how they used their con-artist capabilities to assist the FBI in the 1978 ABSCAM sting operation involving bribes and U.S. congressmen. During the film we get moments where it is clear that the two protagonists don't always trust each other. After all, if you're a con man, how can you trust and respect someone who trusts you? The con man has contempt for the person they have conned.

Millennials should have figured out the ruling class, big government con, and the contempt they really have for their youthful "mark," when in 2014, while a guest on *The Tonight Show with Jimmy Fallon*, Michelle Obama was asked about the challenge Obamacare was facing in not attracting the requisite number of young enrollees. Her response was, "A lot of young people think they're invincible, but the truth is *young people are knuckleheads*." She went on to add that young people often cut themselves while cooking or injure themselves by dancing on bar stools.

Apparently, young people need Obamacare if for no other reason than to replace missing digits and treat bruised tailbones. Now Michelle was chuckling as she made this statement, which is of course designed to provide nonverbal cover to an otherwise outrageous verbal remark. But I won't provide quarter to the First Lady behind her smile. Her remarks were incredibly telling and should have generated outrage from the demographic she so flippantly dissed.

In 2008 and again in 2012, Barack Obama made reaching out to millennials one of the main weight-bearing pillars upon which he erected his campaign. In 2008 millennials chose Obama over John McCain by a greater than 2:1 margin (66% vs. 32%). Their unified support, combined with their high turnout, made the Millennial Generation the decisive force in his victory. Young voters accounted for more than 70% of Obama's almost 9 million popular vote margin over McCain. In 2012, while his numbers were down, Obama still beat Romney 60–36 in the same age group.

It is said that people in an unguarded moment say things that they don't really mean. That isn't true. What they do is say things they didn't mean to say. That is what Michele Obama did with Jimmy Fallon. Webster's lists synonyms for "knucklehead" to include *ignoramus*, *imbecile*, and *moron*. Did the First Lady not understand what the word meant? Can't be; the mainstream media has repeatedly attested as to her superior acumen. It is very safe to assume she didn't mean to call young people knuckleheads but it is equally safe to assume she meant it.

How can a millennial be an intelligent voter one minute and a knucklehead the next? If they are knuckleheads over health care, then they were knuckleheads before when they cast a vote for Obama. The First Lady can't have it both ways. The same group of people whose votes were bought with millions of dollars has just been told they were dupes; that their votes mattered deeply but were cast in ignorance

This is an age-old occurrence; when any individual or group of people seeks to attain power and control over others, they will seduce them in order to gain their trust and support. They will make every necessary promise and give lip service to every grievance from a given constituency. Once they have power, however, they treat that very same group with contempt. It has happened throughout human history and it is happening here.

During the Cold War, the term "useful idiots" was coined to label those who defended the Soviet Union. Millennials and young people need to understand history, but more importantly, they need to understand the present. Big government politicians see young people today as a means to an end. There is no question that people like the Obamas, the Clintons, and Bernie Sanders see young people as the 21st century American version of "useful idiots." They are conning us with promises of programs that pander to the notion of victimization and entitlement. All the while, when we aren't around, they sit in their comfortable chambers and speak of more ways to corner the "knucklehead" vote.

ᏨᏨᏨᏨᏨ

The anti-capitalism feeling in youth is strong and one that requires constant rebuttal. A Harvard University poll conducted in the spring of 2016 found that 51% of people age 18-29 do not support capitalism and only 42% do think of it positively. The same poll had 33% supporting socialism.

It might be easy to say that the gap isn't wide enough to be concerning, but consider this: the free enterprise system is at the very core of what it means to be a free people. There is no human freedom without economic freedom, and a majority of young people polled say that we shouldn't have it.

Of course, that isn't what they are really saying. What is taking place is that we are seeing the evidence of the damaged brand of capitalism talked about in preceding chapters. If you were to have a poll that asked these same young people, "Do you want the federal government to tell you what you can and cannot do in every aspect of your life?" you would not get 51% saying "yes." You should get identical percentages for those who reject capitalism and those who support complete governmental control, at least if they understood what they were talking about. The alternative to capitalism is a government-controlled economy where they tell you everything you can and cannot do. Why the disconnect?

The disconnect exists because young people only know that they have been told capitalism is bad. There is no dialectical process in place. These enemies of free enterprise know only that it is supposed to be evil. They aren't in support of any particular economic alternative, they are only against capitalism. The good news is that we don't have to win them back from some thoughtfully selected alternative. We just have to educate them that what they have come to learn about free markets are lies. I will show in a subsequent chapter how they're open to that message.

The rise of Bernie Sanders is something that I predicted to people around me from the moment he declared his candidacy. This was not hard at all to see coming unless, of course, you were a Washington insider who views every circumstance as if it has a corresponding predecessor. Sanders did not. What Sanders did have was years of classroom and societal training of young people to make them ready to receive his message of big government dependency. Professors and the media softened the earth for him with a bombardment of messages that make it seem OK to people to think without contemplation, that perfect strangers should be forced to pay for their education.

Messaging to young people about the benefits of big government doesn't just come from classrooms or the media; the government, itself, messages to them. Remember Pajama Boy, the 2014 latte-sipping figure used by the Obama Administration to encourage health care sign up? Then they had Adam Levine using his sexiest-man-alive swag to encourage enrollment. In another ad, an Obama impersonator croons in a lyrically enhanced version of *Drop It Like It's Hot*. There's the college son whose parents tell him they have "something really important to talk to him about" when he arrives for the holidays. On the drive, his mind envisions parental horrors but he's then pleasantly surprised to learn they only wanted to tell him to sign up for health insurance.

It doesn't have to be an Internet or television video production to show that advertisers for Obamacare think our youth are easily persuadable. The Colorado print ads showing a coy young girl hip-hugging her birth control pills while ogling a Ryan Gosling-type infer that signing up with a health care exchange is a ticket to a good time without the fear of consequences. Other messages came from Lady Gaga, Taye Diggs, Sarah Silverman, Jennifer Hudson and others who were featured in a wide variety of endorsement spots. Bottom line, when big government starts using taxpayer money to advertise for big government, and against free enterprise, if you are promoting capitalism you are officially betting against the house. Not easy to overcome.

¢   ¢   ¢

My associate writer likes to tell of growing up in a small community up north where people were cautious about change. Because his father was 19 years older than his mother, the debate in his house between his parents was who had actually ruined young people: Elvis or the Beatles? Every generation thinks the one coming up is destined to not be as good as they were and that the end of the world might just arrive with and through them. And yet the world keeps marching on, generation to generation. I spend too much time on my iPhone, but to the reader older than 45, how much time did you spend with your Sony Walkman?

That said, it doesn't mean that changes don't matter and that they don't signify something. I find myself a guest on programs where an always older host will grill me about the poor work habits and social interactions between millennials and other young people. They will want me to explain why my generation is such a mess. My first thought always is that we can't all be as responsible and upstanding as were the attendees at Woodstock. Of course, cynicism doesn't solve anything. The truth is that there are some things about youth today that are good and some things that are not so good. That hasn't changed from the beginning of time. What has changed are the particulars. It is the particulars that require some attention.

As a nation we are raising young people, and have been for a while now, to feel as though they are victims. Victims of what? Anything; it doesn't matter. Whether it is because of your race, or your religion, your sexual orientation, your weight, your sensitivity, your attention deficit disorder, you're being bullied, whatever it is, there is a way to figure out how to get yourself described as being a victim of something. It is like a business finding its Standard Industry Classification (SIC) code. For every business type there is a code created to describe it by type to the rest of the business world. Each young person is being taught to search for and find their SVC (Standard Victimization Code).

Once you can identify as a victim, then you are able to become entitled to something to address your victim status. I could list a thousand programs or groups that would fit into this category but I don't even have to name one. Every reader has a couple in mind right away. Now, once you become entitled to something, there are two ways to get it. The first lands you in jail because you just go out and take it forcibly without permission or sanction. While we see plenty of that, it isn't the worst form of the problem.

What is worse is when you turn to big government and ask it to pass a law to take something away from someone else and give it to you because you are a victim. That is the Forgotten Man of Sumner talked about earlier. This is the model in Europe in general, and so prevalent in particular in countries like France, Portugal, and Spain. Increasingly, young people are being taught that the European model should be our model because it is the only one under which they seek redress for grievances.

Countries in Europe have some excuse for their misplaced belief placed into a nanny state arrangement. All of this started in earnest after WWII, when the entire continent had been ravaged by a war fought on its soil. After the incredible loss of life and treasure, you can almost forgive the people of a nation for huddling together, looking toward the "throne" and saying "please take care of me." Americans have no such excuse.

Given my description of what we are producing in terms of entitled victims, why don't we just go to educators, politicians, and the media, point out the problem, and ask them to stop? The reason is that they are complicit. This is deliberate. A victimized populace becomes an entitled populace. An entitled populace becomes a dependent populace. And a dependent populace votes people into office forever who will promise them "free stuff." At Turning Point, we teach young people that it is better to have "freedom" than it is to have "free stuff." Nothing is ever free.

American youth is soft; not just physically but emotionally. Think of the 18-19-20-year-olds in 1944 who stepped off the landing craft in Normandy. Do you think that we are still those people? Do you think that American youth could still (again think bell curve) step from those boats? In the classic Spielberg movie *Saving Private Ryan*, a small detachment is sent out to find the last surviving son from a family that has already lost all of its other boys to combat. In the process of saving Private Ryan, the group suffers numerous casualties, including Tom Hanks' lead character. As Hanks lies dying, after seeing all the sacrifice, he looks into the eyes of the young private and says to him simply, "Earn this." I can't help feel like we aren't earning the sacrifice of American youth made just a few generations ago.

As opposed to courage and sacrifice, now we have a new enemy for young people to fight. It is the enemy of being given offense. We are now to the point where we are teaching young people something like this:

- ▶ If you disagree with someone, you might offend them.
- ▶ If they are offended, they have a right to be sheltered or protected.
- ▶ People shouldn't have to be sheltered or protected.
- ▶ So, don't ever say or do anything disagreeable that might cause offense.

Of course, this has led to a nation of Barack Obama's "pajama boys," who have heightened sensitivities and lowered thresholds and capabilities for problem solving. We have succeeded in producing the softest generation in American history. Unfortunately for us, much of the world itself is still like a very bad neighborhood at about 2:30 in the morning. This weakness makes it hard for us to show the fortitude to persevere and be successful in a free market where competition is required. That makes it harder to get young people to support the free market because they tend to be afraid of the possibility of failure.

The implications of our weakness on the global stage will wait for another book.

Regarding this "softness" and other attributes in these millennials that the prior generation likes to complain and worry about, let me offer a thought. To the extent that millennials seem to be spoiled, pampered, and petulant, they are what they have been taught to be. Helicopter parents who protect and spoil their children, along with institutions that reward participation as an end in itself instead of encouraging victory, have so insulated us from adversity and sheltered us from failure that we don't understand how to contend with either. For the proud parent of the child who just finally connected after 10 swings in t-ball, remember, if you taught us how to hit, you also taught us how to sit! We aren't inherently lazy. We've been trained.

Political correctness has also taken firm hold inside this generation. As I said at the beginning, political correctness is nothing more than voluntary self-censorship. My greatest fear is if Turning Point and others who are like-minded aren't successful. As this generation takes over the positions of our nation's lawmakers, will they turn the voluntary censorship into state-mandated censorship? There are already significant steps underway on the part of the Obama Administration to make it a crime under the RICO Act for companies and think tanks to express disagreement over global warming. Keep your eye on those efforts because, if successful, the First Amendment is completely in play and Turning Point might not be able to reach out to millennials or anybody else.

Where do I see the greatest hope with our youth? First, because the true commitment of the entrepreneur to risk-taking, hard work, and sacrifice seems to be less ingrained in young people as an overall percentage of the group, the rewards will be great for those who do. The price you pay for success hasn't changed. There may just be fewer people willing to stand in line. Turning Point is trying to fill that line back up.

Another great hope I see is in the students still in high school and in those who will come behind them. They do not yet have the taint of the Obama transformation and they can be reached with the messages of free markets and limited government. I am finding them to be very politically independent. They don't like Republicans, they don't like Democrats, and they don't like politicians in general. They are distrusting of all.

All we need to do is get them to not like big government either and the battle tips in our favor. To do that, we have to take back our campuses and then spread the right messages. In the next two chapters, I will show you how we are doing both.

CHAPTER 8

TAKING BACK OUR CAMPUSES

"The smallest minority on earth is the individual. Those who deny individual rights cannot claim to be defenders of minorities."

—AYN RAND

In the spring of 2013 I went to visit a friend of mine who was attending an Ivy League college I will intentionally not name (he is still a student and I don't wish reprisals). He asked me to sit in on his principles of macroeconomics course. I was happy to do so, having heard from him that his professor was an aggressive advocate of so-called "progressive" economic policies. My friend had one request of me before we entered the large lecture hall: please don't get into an argument with the professor. I assured him I'd be on my best behavior.

You can probably guess where this was heading. I sat in the back of the lecture hall, one of maybe 120–130 students, listening quietly. Eventually the professor started on an anti-capitalism rant. My friend, who was sitting rows in front of me, turned to look at me at put a finger to his lips to give the "shh" signal. Unfortunately, I hadn't spent my high school graduation money to start Turning Point for the purpose of remaining silent in a classroom.

I raised my hand and engaged the professor. We had a spirited back and forth which involved a good deal of me asking him questions to explain and defend his position, and him getting increasingly agitated. He told me that capitalism was inherently evil and its distribution of wealth always was unfair. Our debate continued until he finally got around to asking me if I was actually a student at the college. I was forced to recede into the shadows.

After the lecture, I was astonished at the response. Student after student (please remember they were/are my own age) came up to me and thanked me for my remarks. They said that nobody had been willing to stand up to the professor for fear of their grade being negatively impacted. Many said they believed in free markets but knew they had to keep those opinions to themselves or face academic punishment.

So went my first in-classroom encounter with the anti-capitalism, pro big government environment that is so prevalent on college campuses today. It would be the first of many and I've been joined by thousands to fight back against it ever since.

People hear reports in the media about what is politely called a "liberal bias" on college campuses, but that doesn't mean they truly understand the depth and breadth of the problem. In 2014, a survey by the Higher Education Research Institute at UCLA showed that 60 percent of professors identified themselves as either liberal or "far left." That compares to 42% for the same measure in 1990. Clearly, the trend is in the wrong direction.

What is interesting is that the gap in students, according to the same research, isn't as wide. There is only about a 10 percent gap between students who identify themselves as liberal and those who identify themselves as conservative. Almost half the students consider themselves moderate. Despite that, we see incredible and disproportionate power being exercised on college campuses by Team Left students. Why that is happening will get addressed near the end of the chapter.

The shift in professors is not just a coincidence or some sort of sign of the times. In a study published in 2012 in the *Journal of Perspectives on Psychological Science*, psychologists Yoel Inbar and Joris Lammers from Tilburg University in the Netherlands reported that more than one-third of responding professors indicated that they would vote for the more liberal candidate of two equally qualified job candidates. One respondent wrote in that if people in the department could figure out who was a conservative they would be sure not to hire them. Relatedly, Jonathan Haidt, professor at the NYU Stern School of Business, has likened being a conservative graduate student on campus as similar to being a closeted gay student in the 1980s.

The problem isn't just the professors, but they are a very big part of the problem.

Team Left student groups have become notorious for chasing conservative speakers from the stage and forcing them to cancel events in advance or duck for cover during a speech. In May of 2014, former Secretary of State Condoleezza Rice backed out of an invitation to give the commencement address at Rutgers University because faculty and students protested her involvement in the Iraq War. Ann Coulter has had pies thrown at her on the University of Arizona campus and has been shouted off the stage at Loyola University in Chicago. The list goes on.

Students have now demanded that many universities create "safe zones" where students can be protected from being made to feel uncomfortable by free speech. These are physically set-aside areas where expression is so sterilized that only someone who is offended by not being offended could actually be offended. This doesn't just create a problem insofar as students are being taught that it's ok to be insulated infants, it also limits free speech on campus, because if you have a safe zone in the first place, it becomes reflexive to try to avoid ever having any discussion that might drive a student into the safe zone.

In contrast to the "safe zone," approximately one in six campuses now have what are called "free speech zones." This is a set-aside area on campus where students can actually engage in free speech, as opposed to other parts of the campus where they may be limited by a campus speech code. In some instances, the students need to get a permit to use the free speech zone; obviously a preemptive censoring of speech just by the definition of a permitting process.

At Creighton University, Turing Point and our ROTC campus enthusiast Justin Carrizales has been locked in a battle to have a chapter formally recognized since 2014. We have been battling with the administration, faculty, and students. As I'm writing this in May 2016, there is still no resolution. Having been denied campus approval for Turning Point to be officially recognized as a campus-sanctioned organization, we continued to support student members at Creighton who wanted to be part of Turning Point. In other words, the students were so committed to our message of free markets and limited government that they wanted to embrace Turning Point even if it wasn't officially recognized by the university.

The problem became exacerbated when Creighton officials wanted Turning Point to not list *on its own website* that it had student members at Creighton. That contention is so preposterous it is hard to take seriously and even devote word-count to addressing. That said, it has led to cease and desist letters being sent to our organization by university lawyers. Here is the full content of the letter. Note that they argue that Turning Point is not being permitted on campus because it is too similar to other groups:

To Whom It May Concern:

It has come to my attention that your organization's website inaccurately identifies Creighton University as sponsoring a Turning Point USA chapter (http://turningpointusa.net/chapter-directory). Recently, some members of our student body submitted an application to our Student Organization Review Committee to have TPUSA registered and recognized as a new student organization at Creighton. At the conclusion of the application and interview process, the TPUSA application was denied because the organization was unable to distinguish itself from existing organizations with similar mission statements. Furthermore, the decision to deny the application was also supported by Creighton's Vice Provost for Student Life, who thoroughly reviewed TPUSA's application. In light of this decision, TPUSA is not currently recognized as an authorized Creighton student organization. Your website implies that Creighton has sanctioned and approved TPUSA as an authorized student organization, and is therefore misleading.

In order to avoid any further misrepresentation of TPUSA's status on Creighton's campus, we are requesting that you modify your website by removing any reference to Creighton University as having an authorized TPUSA chapter.

Sincerely,

A professor at Creighton was so disturbed by Turning Point being associated with the university that he wrote a letter to the administration detailing reasons why it was worth fighting to have us excluded. This is the same professor who made national news by asking the following extra credit question on a test:

Donald Trump is:
    a. A fool
    b. Already in hell
    c. A clown
    d. An evil man
    e. The Anti-Christ
    f. All of the answers are correct

While removing his name, I am reprinting the letter in full and without edits. Please note the grammar. He is an English professor:

I'm attaching additional materials illustrating some of the operations of Turning Point USA on our campus in 2015. I wonder whether perhaps the Faculty Council might want to consider some of the following questions:

    —How can a student group that supposedly was denied official status openly operate on our campus, list a CU official address as its own, and freely use University buildings, furniture, and other facilities for well over a year?

—How can a group that has engaged in open and blatant viola-
tions of the most elementary expectations of student conduct
act with perfect impurity and even find vocal supporters
among certain faculty?

—How can a group without official recognition incite acts of
political persecution and racist, threatening harassment
against a faculty member and get away with it without even a
reprimand from the administration?

—How can the office of the President acknowledge and politely
answer the communications of the partisans of such a group
and systematically ignore and leave unanswered communications from those objecting to the operations of that group?

—How can the University tolerate the activities on our campus
of a group that promotes the ownership and use of guns,
especially at a time when campus massacres are becoming
common at schools in our country?

I am particularly concerned that a student group can be denied
explicit recognition and yet act with tacit, de facto approval and
fully enjoy the access to our community of any legitimate student
organization.

I am also concerned that the political agendas of Turning Point
USA (free markets, limited government, guns, no taxes, no welfare
or help for the poor) happen to correspond with absolute precision
to those of the "philanthropists" who have recently transformed our
University into their private "think tank" and tool of their business
and political interests. Turning Point USA in fact partners not only
with the NRA with various other organizations, including Heritage
Action for America, the Heartland Institute, the Ayn Rand Institute,
the Leadership Institute and others which are directly or indirectly
financed by the same "philanthropists." Essential reading in these
respects: Jane Mayer, *Dark Money: The Hidden History of the Billionaires
Behind the Rise of the Radical Right (2016)*.

Many thanks for your attention and consideration of these
questions and concerns.

From the Turning Point perspective, we have three criteria to consider a chapter having been formed by students:

1. Complete a TPUSA registration form.
2. Have at least five active members.
3. Organize at least one campus activist event per semester.

We are well within our rights, within our constitutional rights, to establish any criteria for membership we wish. We will continue to fight this matter as necessary and appropriate and we will not turn our backs on our student members.

¢　¢　¢

The challenge with trying to spread a message of free markets and limited government on campuses is threefold. First, the students have literally been brainwashed into thoughtlessly believing that capitalism is unfair and discriminating, and without the government stepping in everywhere, all would be lost. Second, the professors who are part of the brainwashing process believe within their academic minds and hearts that the United States is built on principles of individualism that are oppressive and exploitative by their very nature and must be struck down. The third problem, perhaps the greatest problem, is the university administration is financially tied into big government and won't risk biting the hand that feeds it. The third problem will be addressed in greater detail later in the book.

The stories cited above are all indicative of this collectivist triad. In starting Turning Point, I knew that it was going to be a challenge; otherwise, it would not have been needed in the first place. I will admit that I underestimated just how challenging it would be. One of the things that I learned quickly is the strategy of student groups, professors, and administrations in suppressing "libertarian" type ideas. Each of the groups, in their own way, is counting on students seeing the task of spreading their message to be so formidable that they will give up almost immediately.

Consider the risks as perceived by the students: If you engage in disagreement with a professor, they can hurt you through the grading process. If you anger the student government, they can make you a campus outcast. If you fail to conform to the administration's rules and edicts, you can find yourself dismissed from the university. It is easy to trivialize these risks as being remote when you are on the outside. I can assure you these risks are real. It is also easy to suggest that if something really matters, then a student should be willing to fight for it to the full extent of their abilities.

The problem with the latter line of reasoning is that it leads to the assembly line production of 18-22-year-old political martyrs. It is easy to speak of the nobility of sacrifice when it is the sacrifice of someone else. Most students don't show up on a college campus planning to offer themselves up as fodder for a cause. Most students show up, at least they should, for the purpose of getting an education to prepare them for the rest of their lives. Once they realize that their future can be jeopardized by speaking up, they quickly, and you can argue prudently, retreat into the shadows. It is especially easy to make that choice when you are without support.

Enter Turning Point. Our group is providing support in terms of numbers of people and outside resources to help students fight back. We have made it possible for students with innate courage and commitment to become willing and able to challenge the status quo and fight back against oppressive political correctness and outright censorship on campus. I will share a couple of stories about our successful experiences on campus to give a glimpse into the resistance we are facing, and our unwillingness to yield to the better funded collectivist campus machine.

Moriah DeMartino was starting the second year of her Associate Degree program in Political Science at Hagerstown Community College in Maryland when she attempted to start a campus-recognized Turning Point USA chapter. In August of 2015 she wanted to file an application with the Student Director of Activities Office as was campus protocol. There was no reason to suspect that her application would be denied as it appeared to clearly meet the required criteria.

In advance of filing, Moriah went to the director and asked if there would be any problem for Turning Point. She indicated that they had the required faculty oversight and the minimum of three active student members. The director told Moriah she would talk to the dean and get back to her.

A week or more went by and Moriah followed up with the director to inquire as to the status. She wrote back the following e-mail. Please note the enthusiasm of the response as indicated by exclamation marks:

> Hi Moriah! I was able to talk to the dean and also to the director of public information and government relations…. You and I can talk about the club tomorrow, but the highpoints are:
>
> a. We can start a Republican Club, but not a Turning Point USA Club, though club members can belong to that national organization.
>
> b. We can start a Republican Club as long as we also start a Democrat Club at the same time.
>
> c. Clubs can set up displays and distribute information about candidates, but candidates will not be allowed on campus to campaign.
>
> d. Clubs will need to work in conjunction to hold candidate debates—all candidates must be invited to all debates/forums, as appropriate.
>
> See you tomorrow!

This is the kind of situation where in the past a student might have just taken that "no" as an answer and figured "what else can I do?" Because of the inertia of Turning Point, and because of Moriah's own resolve, the story doesn't end here.

Moriah went into the director's office in person to appeal her case. She made clear that Turning Point is nonpartisan in nature and not attempting to promote political candidates. In that case, the director suggested, she should simply join the political science club on campus as that group would cover the same sort of issues and topics as Turning Point. The very fact that the campus was rejecting our chapter was almost de facto proof that the campus's poli-sci group wasn't going to cover the same ground as would Turning Point.

Moriah met in a campus coffee shop with the political science professor who oversaw the organization to see if Turning Point could operate within the political science club. The professor indicated that Turning Point had a definite bias in its literature and it could not be incorporated into the group. Feeling as though her constitutional rights were now being violated, Moriah took to Twitter.

The regional director of Turning Point then contacted the Foundation for Individual Rights for Education (FIRE). The mission of FIRE is to "...defend and sustain individual rights at America's colleges and universities..." FIRE reached out to Hagerstown officials asking them to reconsider or face legal action. The Leadership Institute also got involved, both with attorneys and with their student journalism network, and contacted the school. The dean actually responded in writing to a reporter from Campus Reform, the student journalist arm of the Leadership Institute. Here is that letter, reprinted in its actual grammatical form:

> As you know, Moriah DeMartino inquired about the possibility of establishing a Turning Point USA club on the campus of Hagerstown Community College. Upon review of her inquiry, I determined that this request does not meet the necessary requirements to allow my approval for the club's formation. The reason for my decision is based on several things, including the first statement listed under "Starting a Club" on page two of HCC's Club Guide. It states the following:

The first step to create a new club on campus is to research existing clubs to be sure the mission and purpose are not duplicated.

HCC continues to have an active Political Science Club, under the advisement of (name redacted), instructor of political science at HCC. The purpose of the club is to further educate and expose its members to the principles of political science in a true objective manner with respect to all student rights.

The objectives of the Political Science Club are quite broad and include nonpartisan, but inclusive, political engagement, political learning, and political instruction. Student learning outcomes have been established to engage students in a collaborative learning environment to develop and deepen their knowledge of political structures. Furthermore, they will develop a normative appreciation of elements that characterize politics in the United States, elements such as democracy, freedom of speech, human rights, market distribution of goods and services, provision of public goods, collective action dilemmas, and free rider problems.

After further review of the mission, purpose, and activities of the Political Science Club, I have determined that both Republicans and Democrats, as well as any other political parties, are able to be fairly represented as members of the currently existing club, without the creation of any additional clubs. This decision is further supported by board-approved policies that guide student services and student life on campus. As such, I encourage Moriah to seek active participation in HCC's Political Science Club.

Sincerely,

Moriah took to the campus with a petition to garner student support. The question on the petition was along the lines of "should the administration have the final say on what clubs/groups are started on campus if the student body wants the group?" Within the first two hours of commencing, Moriah had collected 200 signatures. Campus police then arrived and then shut down the petition process. The police said the students were soliciting and needed to stop or they would be removed from campus. When it was pointed out that they were only gathering signatures, the police presented the incoherent argument that any collection of information was solicitation.

Ultimately, the Alliance for Defending Freedom (ADF) got involved. ADF is an association of attorneys from around the country who contribute their time to efforts to prevent just the sort of injustice that was taking place in Hagerstown. Through their exertion of legal pressure, Hagerstown was forced to revisit the issue. Finally, in late April of 2016, the Turning Point USA chapter was approved by the college. The very next day registrations commenced and overnight it became one of the largest groups organized on campus.

ↄ   ↄ   ↄ

In 2015, The College of DuPage found itself under federal investigation for suspected criminal activity in areas related to administrators' expenses, contracts with the college's fundraising foundation, and credits that were awarded to police recruits at a law enforcement academy on the Glen Ellyn, Illinois, campus.

Given the depth and breadth of the scandal, a zealous advocate of law enforcement might make the argument that the officials of the campus should have been simply whisked away in the middle of the night, locked up in a remote area, and never heard from again. Fortunately for all of the accused, the Constitution of the United States protected them from meeting such a fate. That protection will seem ironic in light of the following story evidencing more campus hostility towards First Principles and the students who support them.

Joe Enders was beginning his third year at that school in September of 2015 when he found himself in the middle of controversy over copies of the Constitution and their distribution on a college campus. On September 18, 2015, one day after Constitution Day, a couple of members of Turning Point visited the DuPage College campus to pass out pocket-size copies of the U.S. Constitution. They set up a small table and with one of them wearing a "Big Government Sucks" T-shirt, they commenced. Joe was in class at the time.

The Turning Point representatives were told by campus police they would have to stop passing out the Constitution because they weren't actual students at the school. Remember, mind you, these interlopers were just passing out copies of the Constitution, not "Support Che Guevara for President" buttons (although that might not have landed them in trouble). They decided to wait for Joe, who was joining them after class, because he would allow them to satisfy the requirement of student enrollment. Joe is also a fighter. If you tell him to sit down, he stands up.

When Joe emerged they told him the story and they decided to change campus venues and to protest what had just happened. They started passing out fliers titled "America—the real free speech zone." They also put together a petition to support free speech on campus.

They immediately started getting positive responses from students who were accepting materials and signing the petition. Some professors walking by did some eye rolling, especially at the American flag Joe had draped over his back. Eventually, these three scofflaws were approached by campus police.

The officer told them they were going to have to stop their activity because if they didn't, soon everybody would be doing it. Joe suggested that all they were doing was exercising free speech, to which the officer countered that it wasn't free speech, it was soliciting (apparently some campus police officers need to spend a little time on Sunset Boulevard to understand the difference between free speech and soliciting). When they queried the officer as to what it was exactly that they were soliciting, he responded that they were soliciting their own opinion.

I am going to permit you at this point to set the book down, get up and stretch, and grab a glass of water before resuming, because I'm certain that last line gave your brain a cramp.

After being threatened with arrest, the Three Constitutioneers went to head inside to the main campus building. Joe had one last question and asked if it would be OK to bring the American flag into the building with him. The officer told him it would not be OK and the flag would have to remain outside.

Much of this encounter was captured on video. The Turning Point people and Joe decided it should be posted on the web for people to see. When it was viewed by the people at The Drudge Report, they decided it should be exploited. The battle was on. The ADF stepped up and offered to represent our side for free. The College hid behind their free speech policy, which did not permit cover for the kind of activity in which Joe and Turning Point were engaged that day. Joe attended a college meeting and made his case publicly. He argued that constitutional principles should be the number one priority on any campus.

ADA drafted language for the college to incorporate into their free speech policy. The process dragged on. During the delay, Joe received comments from students along the lines of, "I like prohibitions on speech because then I don't get bothered." He also heard, "You shouldn't have the right to make me feel uncomfortable." One political science professor went so far as to say that since the institution was only semipublic, the Constitution wasn't fully binding. Obviously, that professor got a job teaching political science because all of the jobs in the astrology department were filled with tenured professors.

Ultimately, the policy was amended and now includes protections for the kind of raucous activity that is passing out copies of the U.S. Constitution on or about Constitution Day. Joe Enders is a fighter but he would not have been able to have been successful without the joined forces of legal assistance, social media, and a campus-based group committed to the fight.

ç   ç   ç

One of the almost completely unknown stories regarding the spread of collectivist, Team Left intolerance on college campuses is the role played by student government and the control being exerted upon it by outside influencers. Parents tend to think of student government as a sort of popularity contest for young people and the way to pad your thin resume heading out of college into the workforce.

The activities are thought to include such pressing matters as planning Greek Week and having commemorative oak trees planted on campus. There is a lot more to student government than most people think.

Student governments control incredibly large budgets. As examples, the University of Central Florida has a budget of more than $17 million. The University of Colorado and the University of Florida both have student government budgets of more than $20 million. The University of California Los Angeles (UCLA) has a student government budget of more than $30 million. The majority of American businesses do not have revenue streams as large as the dollars that are being controlled by student governments.

As tuition rates have increased (discussed later in the book), student fees and charges have tracked in the same upward direction. These student fees have a similar feel, as does the union dues paid by labor members. The fees are simply part of their tuition statement (like a union worker having them withheld from their paycheck); the student pays them, and then has little say over how the fees are ultimately utilized, just like the local UAW member.

Remember the numbers cited above regarding the lack of universal agreement among students as to their political persuasion. It isn't as though 90 percent of students fashion themselves to be Bernie Sanders supporters (although the media would like you to think they are).

While the student governments are in charge of funding traditional campus activities, they also are given tremendous discretionary control over how the dollars are spent. In addition, while university officials are technically exercising the final say over the spending, they are generally unwilling to give a firm "no" to student government requests.

This has led to spending on various campus groups, speakers, and events that are contrary to First Principles, free markets, and limited government. After spending on required events, students at the 300 largest universities may each have discretionary spending dollars left over, ranging anywhere from $1 million to $2 million.

The student governments have been greatly influenced by off-campus Team Left organizations, each working closely with students to help them get elected and then to coordinate activities. This allows for the spreading of certain messages and the suppression of others. One such group exerting influence is the United States Student Association (USSA) and its local satellite affiliates.

The USSA ostensibly represents itself as a not-for-profit organization dedicated to helping student governments create activities and campaigns on campus. They charge a per student fee in order for a campus to join. The fee is paid for by the student government. If you're a tuition-paying parent reading this, part of your check to the university is going indirectly to fund this organization. Here is a description from their own website about their first annual "National Student Power Summit" held in March of 2016:

> "From Free Higher Education to increasing recruitment and retention of students of color, from Socially Responsible Endowments to the for Movement Black Lives[sic], from Ending Sexual Violence to the Robin Hood Tax, from Ensuring Voter Protections to Supporting Workers Right to Unionize, we are standing at the forefront of change and we are demanding Education Justice."

Not the kind of conference Julio would have attended while in school.

The two major themes that are in evidence today on college campuses and funded by student governments are attacks on United States "nationalism" and attacks on capitalism, with a special focus on fossil fuels. These two have derivatives and they come together into a unified, singular attack. That attack can easily be described as wanting to eliminate the notion of American exceptionalism, and to replace First Principles with ideas that are more collectivist and global in nature.

The attack on the United States and nationalism translates into an attack on our allies, in particular on Israel. The Students for Justice in Palestine (SJP) is a very active presence on campuses across the country spreading an anti-Semitic message and tying United States funding to their fictional descriptions of Israeli atrocities.

I said at the start of this book I wasn't going to venture into foreign affairs or "social" issues. I'm not. While the discussion of Israel and the Middle East turmoil will have to wait for a future edition, it is relevant in this context, because what SJP is doing is creating a syllogism, albeit an invalid one, for students:

Israel is evil and gets money from the United Sates.
The United States economic system is capitalism.
Therefore, capitalism is evil.

If it weren't for the fact that the logic professors at many American universities are likely to agree with the above statement, the students would all get an F in their studies of Aristotle.

On the University of Southern California campus there is an active chapter of SJP, and its influence is felt through events and attempts at censorship. On March 22, 2016, a column appeared in the USC student newspaper, *The Daily Trojan*. The column was defending the attempts of students to force conservative speaker and writer David Horowitz to withdraw from an event being hosted by College Republicans that week. The topic was the hatred of Jews on college campuses.

In the editorial, an excerpt of which appears below, the writer is justifying the attempt to have Horowitz blocked from appearing by insinuating that disagreeable speech can be called "hateful" and therefore should not be permitted. In reading the piece below, please pay careful attention to the chilling logic used in the second paragraph:

There is very little respect for those who disagree with the Zionist cause. I find this ironic, coming from a campus organization that constantly recycles the same two arguments when faced with a difference of opinion—that the opposition to inflammatory rhetoric is an attack on freedom of speech and that students who enjoy left-wing privilege do not make room for intellectual diversity on campus. This said, why is an opinion different from traditional conservatism met with degradation? It seems as though the argument for intellectual diversity is only valid when it backs the conservative cause.

What the College Republicans need to understand is that criticizing Horowitz is not an attack on freedom of speech but rather on hate speech [italics added]. According to the American Bar Association, hate speech is "speech that offends, threatens or insults groups, based on race, color, religion, national origin, sexual orientation, disability or other trait."

When you read the entirety of the column, you can see the writer's own form of "hateful" speech in her construct of the differences between being Jewish, being Israeli, and being a "Zionist." To the best of my knowledge, nobody protested her right to have published her hateful column.

The fossil fuels campaign is a bit similar in that the message is created that the world is being destroyed because of fossil fuels and that the destruction is a result of American capitalism. Students walk away from events saying, "Wow, the U.S. capitalist system allows the genocide of Palestinians and the destruction of the earth's climate. Capitalism is evil, toxic, and immoral."

The buzzword being used throughout all campus activities that relate to anti-American, anti-free market and First Principles messages is "divest." Divest from [FILL IN THE BLANK] is the message of the day. Not troubled by the notion that you have to invest before you can divest, the anti-American movements have effectively copywritten the word, and it is taken to mean, "Get out America. Get out American business." Because these messages are spread by outside groups coming into campuses and forming alliances with student government that possess extraordinary discretionary budgets, they are a formidable opponent.

¢ ¢ ¢

Crystal Clanton, who has been integral to the success of Turning Point while effectively serving as its chief operating officer, deals each day with the difficulties of successfully establishing a presence on campuses. She is the one who oversees completion of all the necessary procedural steps to have Turning Point formally recognized by a university as a legitimate group.

Crystal told me at the point of this writing that so far in the 2015–16 academic year we have had 24 denials of applications, and three to four dozen "tabled" by universities until next year. This is the campus equivalent of a president's pocket veto. When a university denies us an application while on their best behavior, they will cite some vague reason such as there is already another group similar to ours on campus. When they are aggressively puffing out their chest with arrogance, they will go so far as to look into my own personal Twitter account to cite "conservative" Tweets which are, to them, the same as hate speech.

Please, rest assured, I am not hateful. More to the point, what does my personal Twitter account have to do with granting status to a 501(C)(3) on campus?

Crystal is not going to give up because she believes the fight is one that has to be fought and that every time we win it makes it all worthwhile. Turning Point needs more Crystals; so does America.

In order to fight back against the forces at work on our campuses to change America into something that it was never intended to be, it is going to take a relentless commitment on the part of all freedom-loving advocates, and coordination among the various groups involved in the fight. It will also require the use of the technology of our times to spread the message. Here are some of the things that we need to do in order to reverse the momentum.

Give students something to do: The front line in this battle is going to be the students themselves, on campus. The problem up until this point is that they have been largely unorganized by free market and limited government groups. While Team Left has been zealous in terms of creating campus activities, freedom-loving students have been mostly relegated to the op-ed page in the campus newspaper and consider it a victory just to get their letter published.

It isn't enough just to have them join a group. We need to focus on activities that are compelling and persuasive in nature. We need to counter-message what is being said and done by groups like USSA, SJP, and MoveOn.org. The student body is where this will have to happen. I will specifically address the kind of messaging that resonates with young people and how to deliver it in a separate chapter.

Relentlessly use social media: There is YouTube, there is Twitter, there is Facebook, there is Hypeline (more on that later), and there are so many other outlets to get out video content and descriptions of university discrimination and suppression that our students have to be willing to use them in almost every instance. In a real sense, this battle in which we are engaged is a public relations battle. We are trying to give good press to First Principles and bad press to those who don't support them. The other side is trying to do the same thing.

My guess is that almost anyone reading this chapter, regardless of age or education, learned some things that really surprised them. We need to spread the word of incidents and events that are contrary to our interests so that nobody is surprised by anything anymore. You can't fight back against something if you aren't aware of its existence. General awareness is helpful, but it isn't enough. What is required is specific knowledge of specific circumstances so that concerned citizens can rally to support students whenever it is required. That awareness can be instantly created at a marginal cost of zero through the use of social media.

Unity of campus-based "First Principles" organizations: Avengers, assemble. There are a number of different groups that espouse messages related to free markets, limited government, and "conservatism." A list of some of the major players:

- ▸ Intercollegiate Studies Institute
- ▸ Students for Israel
- ▸ Young American Foundation

- ▸ College Republicans
- ▸ Young Americans for Liberty
- ▸ Leadership Institute

Each one of these groups, including Turing Point, needs to come to a common understanding that the enemy is collectivism and not each other. While we are united on general vision and our hopes for America, we do all compete on some level for the same donor dollars. That means that it is easy for any of us, if we aren't vigilant, to not always come across as being supportive of one another. Add to that our constituency, college students who can be competitive by nature, and we sometimes find ourselves butting heads with one another.

We simply can't allow that to happen. It is imperative that we unite and try to coordinate efforts wherever and whenever possible. When we can't act in unison, we have to abide by the rule of "do no harm" with regard to each other's activities. Team Left does a much better job of not interfering with one another and even collaborating.

I will make a pledge on behalf of Turning Point that we will do whatever we can do in support of other First Principle organizations. Make no mistake, we are activists. We are committed to taking and holding ground in the fight to restore liberty. There is no reason, however, for anyone to suffer from friendly fire in the process.

Bring strong cases to legal firms offering to defend liberty: I mentioned earlier that Turning Point has received assistance from different law firms specializing in defending the rights of conservative students on campus. These groups of professionals have to be saluted because we live in such a litigious society that, if you do not have access to the courts with competent representation, your ability to affect change is limited. Without the threat of a lawsuit, and without that threat being delivered from a credible source, the power of the university system is simply too great to be successfully combated by the simple protests of students.

A key to the success of these firms is the quality of the cases they are given. People involved in fighting discrimination and censorship from campus collectivists need to be vigilant in documenting their case and organizing their facts. Here is where the use of video, e-mails and other forms of permanent and verifiable records become critical. In the stories I've mentioned where Turning Point has had success fighting back, it would have been unlikely that we would have prevailed if we had just been relying on word of mouth and "he said-she said" accusations. In order for the lawyers to help us, we have to help the lawyers. Every First Principles group needs to be training their members on how to document discrimination.

In addition to FIRE, some of the other groups are The Center for Individual Rights, the Alliance for Defending Freedom, the American Center for Law and Justice, and the Liberty Institute. Parents should get acquainted with these groups and their works before sending the kids off to college. Understanding the kinds of cases they pursue and their areas of specialization will make you more aware and informed should your student run into adversity.

Inform and persuade private university funding sources to demand change: In addition to the big government trough that is the student loan funding mechanism (as promised, more on that later), universities get large amounts of money from private donors, corporations, and foundations. These donors usually give money out of a sense of pride and public service. Perhaps they have an alumni connection, perhaps they believe in the research efforts of the school, or maybe they just want to help young people in their state or community. Regardless of their motive, they are not always in touch with specific activities on campus that limit freedom. They need to be.

We are accustomed to seeing on the news frequent boycotts and protests by Team Left of various groups and organizations that are connected, even if remotely, to some politically incorrect cause. While I am not suggesting we start a "Divest from Duke" campaign, I am suggesting that we need to forcefully and coherently send a message to donors about just exactly what is happening on their favorite campuses and gain the power of their purse to help impact change. We don't need to behave like a mob in approaching these people. We can use reason in appealing to their sense of fairness and to their likely-held beliefs in First Principles.

In the spring of 2016 the students at Stanford University were asked to vote on whether the school should require a course to be taken in Western Civilization as part of general education requirements. Up until the 1980s such a course had been required. The proposal was defeated by a vote of 1,992 to 347. The vote so bothered my friend and political commentator Dennis Prager that he felt compelled to write a column about it. Here is part of what he wrote:

> ...So, the Big Question is, why? Why is the left hostile toward Western civilization? After decades of considering this question, I have concluded the answer is this: standards. The left hates standards—moral standards, artistic standards, cultural standards. The West is built on all three, and it has excelled in all three.
>
> Why does the left hate standards? It hates standards because when there are standards, there is judgment. And leftists don't want to be judged. Thus, Michelangelo is no better than any contemporary artist, and Rembrandt is no greater than any non-Western artist. So, too, street graffiti—which is essentially the defacing of public and private property, and thus serves to undermine civilization—is "art."....
>
> ...And finally, we come to the left's loathing of the religions of Western civilization—the Judeo-Christian religions, which have clear standards of right and wrong.

Bible-based religions affirm a morally judging God. For the left, that is anathema. For the left, the only judging allowed is leftists' judging of others. No one judges the left—neither man nor God.

We all need to understand and accept that my friend is right. What we are seeing on college campuses today reflects a deep and abiding hatred of all that we have been and all that we are. The university culture is one that suggests that they are transcendent. They are moving away from the flawed past of the West and opening a new pathway to enlightenment and truth.

The truth as they see it.

I prefer the truth of our founders. It is going to be hard for any of us, and impossible for Julio, to live it if the schools aren't teaching it. At this juncture I'd almost be willing to settle for them at least permitting it to be discussed openly without being actually taught.

I said *almost* willing. We are not going to let this fight go. We will take back our campus culture and restore it to the free-speaking, free-thinking model that wasn't just intended by our founders, but as far back as the Greek masters themselves. The future depends on it.

There is a dismissive argument often made by apologists for the excesses which are taking place on the universities today. It is made by people sympathetic to the Team Left cause, but who feel uncomfortable with the extremes evidenced by administrators, faculty, and students. The apologists say, "There is no real harm being done here. After all, it is a university. All they are doing is exchanging ideas." Those apologists, and all of us, would do well to remember the words of Scottish essayist Thomas Carlyle, who, when being chided at a dinner party about always carrying on about concerns over books and ideas, replied, "There once was a man called Rousseau who wrote a book containing nothing but ideas. The second edition was bound in the skins of those who laughed at the first."

Having been on college campuses all over the country, I can assure you Team Left is getting ready to go to press. There is no moral equivalency here. Our ideas are better than their ideas. Ours promote freedom, theirs promote slavery. I hope this chapter, and this book, has clearly presented that idea.

CHAPTER 9

THE POWER OF BANDWIDTH: DELIVERING MESSAGES

"I don't know the rules of grammar. If you're trying to persuade people to do something, or buy something, it seems to me you should use their language."

—DAVID OGILVY, the "father" of advertising

In the early spring of 2014, Turning Point was beginning to hit its stride. We had successfully established a presence on a few hundred campuses, we had created a key contingent of influential supporters, and we were beginning to get media attention for our efforts. As we approached the end of the spring semester, it was time to turn our attention to the fall and decide what we would do heading into a midterm election season that would culminate the first week of November.

Our donors were of course preoccupied with the upcoming election. I had my own personal hopes for it, as well. After all, what good was it for me to support and advocate for free markets and limited government if I didn't occasionally get to see the election of people who supported those goals? On the other hand, from the perspective of Turning Point, I was interested in mobilizing students and getting them excited about our ideals for now and for the rest of their lives. I was thinking about the long game.

As a team we started to consider what could we do in the fall that would be an inspirational campaign, address all of our themes, get young people tuned in and motivated, and maybe get them interested in joining the political process as part of their daily lives? Ultimately, we decided upon a 10-week campaign of activities and information that would include differing themes and issues each week. The name we chose for the overall program was "Big Government Sucks!"

Now, when I first began to share this title with donors you can guess that I met with a healthy degree of skepticism. One of the areas where members of Team Right pride themselves over members of Team Left is that they often consider themselves to be a little above the gutter tactics used by the other side. "Big Government Sucks" seemed to many to lack, well, decorum. One at a time I convinced them, some begrudgingly, that we were trying to create a message that would resonate with, and energize, youth, not upper-middle class, 50-year-old, suburbanites. The idea was ultimately approved by all necessary parties.

The concept was to have a 10-week program, consistent on all campuses across the country, with a different theme each week, every theme somehow relating to the excesses of big government and its direct impact on student freedom, and liberty. It was an election season so there was an acute level of interest. At that time our not-for-profit status was still pending approval from the IRS but we were conducting ourselves in a way that would make us compliant as if we had already obtained it. That meant we could not support individual candidates or parties. We would insist on holding our members to that requirement.

We did have a hope that if a student decided to get involved in the political process because of our program and our messages they would not be registering to support their local collectivist candidate. In other words, if they had a spiritual awakening about limited government because of Turning Point, and then decided to vote, they were not terribly likely to go punch the ticket for a Bernie Sanders type. Imagine us as a post-hypnotic voting suggestion.

The campaign as conceived had the following week-by-week themes that were consistent at all campuses across the country wherever Turning Point had a presence. All that has been changed is the tense from present to past. This is our actual set of themes and goals:

- ▶ **Week One: Student Activism Week** To recruit students for future activism initiatives, and get them involved with Turning Point USA.

- ▶ **Week Two: Capitalism Cures** To make the moral argument for capitalism. Many young people don't realize that capitalism has improved living wages and social conditions more than any government system or welfare program.

- ▶ **Week Three: National Debt Awareness Week** To educate students about how the national debt is impacting the future for the next generation.

- ▶ **Week Four: Constitution/Free Speech Week** To educate students about the significance of the U.S. Constitution, the importance of adhering to it, and the ways in which the Obama administration has repeatedly ignored it. We focused on the right to free speech.

- ▶ **Week Five: Keep More Stuff** To educate students about the fact that the next generation is being forced to give away more and more of what they earn and own. Everyone wants to keep more stuff, especially when it belongs to them.

- ▶ **Week Six: They're Listening** To educate students about how the NSA is invading American citizens' privacy, and how young people don't like it.

- ▶ **Week Seven: No Free Lunch** To educate students about the fact that there is no free lunch.

- ▶ **Week Eight: The Great Youth Depression** To educate students about how Obama's unemployment rate is creating a great "youth" depression.

- ▶ **Week Nine: The Truth about Obamacare** To educate the students about the ways Obamacare is having a negative impact on everyone, especially the next generation.

- ▶ **Week Ten: Big Government Sucks** To educate students about why big government sucks, with an emphasis on Obamacare's negative impact on the next generation.

Note that none of these titles would be found on the brochure promoting a symposium at Oxford or Cambridge. But we weren't promoting a symposium at either of those places. We were trying to connect with 18-22-year-old students on American university campuses.

Each one of these weeks had associated with it specific activities and materials to be engaged in and handed out. There was a kit that each school received that was organized by weekly theme. It would be tedious to go through them all, but I thought taking one representative week and exploring it in detail would be worthwhile. Let me take you a bit deeper into *Week Nine—The Truth about Obamacare*.

Every campus had a Turning Point display table set up in as prominent, and as high-traffic, an area as the campus would permit us to occupy. The table for this week displayed banners and signage noting "Big Government Sucks," and "Say No to Obamacare." As an enticement to get students to come to the table, we actually included candy in the activism kits. That might seem a little childish at first pass, but think about it—how many students will simply walk past a free sweet treat and not bother to stop and grab one? When they stopped, we grabbed them.

At our tables we would have a variety of materials for wearing or displaying. These included Big Government Sucks dorm posters, buttons, and stickers. We also had Turning Point brochures that described the organization in general. There were e-mail sign-up sheets, Obamacare disaster booklets, and books from the think-tank Heartland Institute, a key strategic partner of Turning Point. Each of our field people would engage students who stopped, asking them awareness questions about Obamacare. This created an opportunity to inform and correct misperceptions.

As a side note to the 10-week campaign, but relevant to Obamacare, one of the key elements used by Turning Point in delivering compelling messages is to embrace pop-culture as a vehicle to get attention. In late November of 2014, just after the conclusion of the campus campaign, we released a booklet entitled *The Healthcare Games*. The release of the booklet coincided with the release of the then most current entrant in the *Hunger Games* motion picture series. It was also the start of the next open enrollment period for Obamacare.

The booklet used artwork that called the movie images to mind to grab someone's attention visually. Once they started to read, they found a combination of satirical fiction, based on *The Hunger Games* storyline, mixed with pure factual sections talking about what Obamacare was, how it was damaging to America, and how it could be repealed and replaced. The fictional story was based on the dilemma of the heroine "Welniss" (as opposed to her Hunger Games counterpoint Katniss), who was about to turn 75 years old (the age at which meaningful life ended according to Obama health care architect Ezekiel Emanuel, also parodied in the book) and found herself in a competition that would allow the victor to continue life and have access to health care. Losers would meet with a less fortunate fate.

These books were taken by students to theaters all over the country, where they used Twitter and other social media to post pictures of themselves holding a copy of the book up against the theatrical movie poster or up against the movie screen while the film was playing. We had succeeded in inserting a free market message into a popular culture delivery vehicle, and getting students enthused about promoting it publically. That is a win.

Prior to the start of the Big Government Sucks campus campaign, our student activist leaders were all brought to Chicago for training. We taught them the themes to hit, the way to engage in discussion and questioning with other students, and we got them informed with facts. The background preparation is critical. Absent thoughtful arguments and accurate facts, people quickly become belligerent. When you arm someone with information they are more likely to hold level-headed conversations and not let themselves devolve into one of the many rants so easily found on YouTube these days.

The campaign was a huge success. Donors who had been worried or skeptical by the edgy theme were won over based on the media attention received and the social media responses from students. In addition, Turning Point signed up tens of thousands of new members and, I believe, led to young people that November searching for, and making, small government choices wherever they could be found (and unfortunately they are not easy to find in either political party). Territory that had previously been surrendered to Team Left was being challenged and taken. We were doing exactly what I had promised Foster Friess we would do. We were becoming the counterpoint to MoveOn.org.

During the 2016 presidential primary season, candidates Ted Cruz, Rand Paul, and Carly Fiorina all could be heard using the terms "big government." Cruz and Paul both could be heard to say "Big Government Sucks." We introduced a phrase into the nation's lexicon that was "sticky." We have placed the phrase Big Government Sucks on the minds, at the lips and in the hearts of people at all levels of political interest and activity. Now I want to discuss why messaging is so important in the context of what Turning Point is trying to accomplish and how our messaging can be considered contextually with other moments in American history.

¢   ¢   ¢

Properly understood, Turning Point USA is a movement. The campus-based organization that we have created is nothing more than a vehicle through which that movement can grow and express itself. Every movement in American history has had an objective. The objective of our movement is to restore free markets and limited government to American life and revive a deep and abiding belief in First Principles (in case the reader hadn't figured all that out yet by this point in the book).

Some of the more significant movements since just before and then after the turn of the 20th century are the Women's Suffrage movement, which culminated with the 19th Amendment to the Constitution ratified in 1920, giving women the right to vote; the Labor movement, which saw its greatest success evidenced with the passage of The National Labor Relations Act and The Fair Labor Standards Act during FDR's administration; the Civil Rights movement of the 1950s and 1960s, which led to the passage of the Civil Rights Act in 1964; and the current LGBT movement, which is in-progress but has already achieved victories with regards to same-sex marriage and having the federal government sue state government over public restrooms and gender identification.

I have no interest in this context in commenting on the merits of any of the above mentioned movements. What does interest me greatly is how each of them messaged its membership in the particular time period of history. What I have learned is that messaging is both simple and complex. Some elements remain consistent, such as simplicity, repetition, diffusing, etc. The delivery mechanisms available over time have changed (newspaper vs. Internet for example), but it is not just as simple as saying that you deliver the same message through different means. The nature of delivery mechanisms actually impacts the messages. There are things you can do today because of the speed of the Internet that never could have been contemplated in previous times.

The Women's Suffrage movement, which you could say started as far back as 1776 when Abigail Adams wrote to her husband John asking him to "remember the ladies," officially commenced in 1848 when, at a conference in Seneca Falls, New York, under the leadership of Elizabeth Cady Stanton, the attendees adopted a position calling for equal suffrage for women. It would take 70 years but they would ulti-mately prevail. Messaging in the early portion of their movement was limited to locally organized groups deciding upon actions to be taken (like the Susan B. Anthony organized "vote" in 1872 that landed her and other women in jail for voting) and the passing out of brochures. Mass communication didn't exist. This was truly grassroots.

As the movement progressed over time, the use of posters and political cartoons became important. The simple three-word phrase "Votes for Women" became the rallying cry for the movement. It was simple, direct, and didn't create any "fat" to be attacked by dissent-ers. There would then be other compelling phrases, including: "She's good enough to be your baby's mother—and she's good enough to vote with you"; "Women bring all voters into the world—let them vote"; "A woman's place is everywhere." One cartoon showed a group of women sitting atop a steamroller with the word "Progress" written across the front of the roller.

The Labor movement had a key three-word phrase that appeared in much of its media and printed content. They rallied around "Agitate-Educate-Organize." As their movement truly gathered strength and momentum after the turn of the 20th century, news-paper circulation was broader than it had ever been and literacy rates were extremely high. This presented Labor with more message delivery capability, and with the capability to deliver more detailed messages where appropriate. The Agitate phrase was also used by the Women's Suffrage movement as they were kindred spirits with labor and sometimes worked together, sometimes moved alongside.

The Civil Rights movement ultimately circled around the phrase "We Shall Overcome." That song is believed to have had its origins in a 1948 issue of *People's Songs Bulletin*. This was a publication of which the late folk music legend Pete Seeger was a director. Somewhere around 1958 the song became adopted by the movement and then the simple title became its three-word theme. From Martin Luther King Jr. to Lyndon Johnson, and hundreds of thousands of protesters in between, they turned "We Shall Overcome" into "We *Did* Overcome."

The Dr. King "I have a dream" speech would add another poignant phrase to the cause.

The LGBT movement is a contemporary of Turning Point. We are using the same message delivery methods and many of the same organizing tactics. They use social media, rallies, and pop-culture messaging, just like we do. Despite our very different agendas, there is no question we have adapted our movements into the times in which we live.

I am intrigued by what we are doing at Turning Point and how it shares so much in common with other famous American movements. Because I started Turning Point at such a young age, I simply hadn't had the time in life to have studied in detail various historical movements and how they created traction and gathered support. As I can continue to learn, I realize that the fact that we are doing so many things in a similar way means there are likely some universal truths and principles surrounding what makes a movement successful. Even our slogan, "Identify-Empower-Organize," ought to sound familiar.

In his 2012 book *Uprising: How to Build a Brand—and Change the World—by Sparking Cultural Movements*, author Scott Goodson birthed the concept of "movement marketing." Here are five key insights from his work:

1. Discerning what people care about is far more valuable than trying to influence them.

2. The Internet and social media enable collective action, changing the way movements form and develop.

3. As traditional marketing becomes less effective, "movement marketing" provides a powerful connection with consumers.

4. "Restlessness"—a "sense of dissatisfaction" with an aspect of the social environment—spawns movements and uprisings.

5. Early advocates form the core of an emerging movement by backing an "alternative idea" to resolve an existing problem. Help shape that idea and provide resources to facilitate connections and action. Interact with people not as individuals but as parts of an interrelated group."

At Turning Point, we are incorporating all of these elements into our efforts on campuses and through social media. As I walk through our approach to messaging, refer back to these five key elements from Goodson's work and see how they interconnect.

I am a strong believer that messages don't just harness a movement; the messages can actually create the movement. This is a little like supply side economics, wherein the argument is made by economists that supply can create its own demand. This doesn't mean that the ideals of the Turning Point movement didn't exist before we began to promote them, but it does mean that they hadn't necessarily crystalized or taken on urgency in the minds of young people before they heard some articulation of them.

Young "conservatives" have had a hard time articulating their beliefs for a long time. It could be the case that the last time young people were thoughtfully organized and aware around those ideas goes back to my associate writer's first election vote, which was Reagan in 1980. I noticed this lack of clear articulation while still in high school. I also noticed the power of condensed messages.

Take, for example, the Obama campaign's use of the phrases "Hope & Change" and "Forward." These phrases are very open-ended and allow the listener to interpret them into whatever they want them to be. This provided Obama with a chance to attract followers who might have completely different belief systems in terms of government's role, or in terms of economic policy, but who did believe in "hope," "change," and moving "forward." The contrast to this was Republican messages like "Trusted Leadership," and "Believe in America." These are sterile compared to the Obama messages. There is nothing fresh or image-invoking about them. They sound old; and old doesn't typically appeal to young.

I believe that there are several keys to messaging. It is important that messages be memorable. Once they are heard they need to be retained. "We Shall Overcome" is a perfect example. It was easy to hear that once as a protester for civil rights and never forget it. Another key element is that the message needs to be broad-based in its appeal.

Nearly every person, regardless of their situation, could be attracted to the concept of "overcoming." The message should be able to mean something to different people. That might seem counterintuitive to you at first but let me elaborate.

When people heard the Obama message of "Hope & Change" there was no possibility, nor was there need, to control what people might be hoping to change in their minds. Through the consistency of his public speeches, interviews, and campaign ads, everybody had a general idea of what kind of politician Barack Obama was. In addition, he was running as a Democrat so that gave some sort of brand identification just by itself. But within the context of having a general idea of Obama's directionality, the voters could sit back, close their eyes, and imagine the change they wanted.

Maybe Obama would change the medical system so they could get covered. Maybe Obama would change the disability system so they could find a way not to work. Maybe Obama could change the threat from the Middle East so their grandchild would grow up in a safe world. Maybe, maybe, maybe. Whatever their desired change might have been, Obama gave them a reason to hope for that change.

Messages have to come from a trusted source. This is a particular challenge for a group like Turning Point because those who oppose us lead into their attack by saying we cannot be trusted. There is a reason why they say that. They know that if they can make people question their trust for us then they will be less receptive to the message. One of the key reasons for the ultimate success of the Civil Rights movement is that Baptist minister Martin Luther King Jr., to all but the most hateful of racists, came across as someone who was very credible and trustworthy. Once he became the face of the movement, its likelihood of success increased, because reaching white Americans became easier. White Americans tended to trust the messenger. It is interesting to conjecture what might have happened if Malcolm X had been the perceived leader of the movement instead of Dr. King.

Another factor of successful messaging is that it has to create energy and conversation. There is no better example of this in Turning

Point's brief history than "Big Government Sucks." This phrasing was so blunt, and so disinterested in conformity, that it got attention in every venue where it was seen or heard. Septuagenarians in health clubs could see one of our T-shirts on a fellow club member many years their junior and approach them to say, "I love your shirt." When we rolled out this campaign to our campus activists, they couldn't wait to hit the ground with it and start to talk about it. They thought Big Government Sucks was just plain cool.

When I say that messages create movements it is because messages need to generate in the listener or reader the energy to participate and the willingness to attend. Today, everyone is overwhelmed with messages of all sorts, from virtually every direction. If somebody goes to a fine restaurant where they are served a flight of wines, they can sip from a number of different glasses. Even if they find all pleasant and agreeable, there usually comes a moment in time where they take a sip and say "Ooh. That one." Then they request a bottle for the table. That is what Turning Point is trying to do. We are trying to become the message they request for everybody to share in and enjoy.

One of the most important business books ever written, and one of the most influential books for me, was *The Tipping Point*, written by Malcolm Gladwell in 2002. The term "tipping point" refers to that moment when the growth path of something as measured along a curve hits an inflection point and starts to grow at a pace less linear and more logarithmic. The term is often used in the area of infectious diseases to denote when something turns from an outbreak to an epidemic. Gladwell's book, technically not written as a business book, was intended to show how social and cultural phenomenon can hit that tipping point and be turned into an epidemic.

This is what we wanted to accomplish in starting Turning Point. We wanted to take the ideas of free markets and limited government and turn them into a social epidemic. Notice that I do consider Gladwell's book to be a business book. There is a reason for that. From the moment I envisioned Turning Point I saw it as an organization that would be run as a business and not as a "think tank." I have absolutely no problem with the think tank model. The Heart-land Institute is a very trusted and valued partner of Turning Point and has supported us with intellectual muscle and publications since our inception. For them, the model works. For us, we wanted to do something different. Gladwell's book helped me think like a businessman.

If you are going to start a business, you need to start by answering some very basic questions:

- ▶ What am I selling?
- ▶ Who is my customer?
- ▶ How will I produce what I'm selling?
- ▶ What will it cost to produce it?
- ▶ Through what channel(s) will I get my product or service into the customer's hands?
- ▶ How will I price it?
- ▶ How will I promote it?

The idea here is not to generate a debate over what I may have left out of the above formulation. It is essentially complete. It is also not the way that groups like Turning Point typically "go to market."

What we are selling are conversions to the belief in First Princi-ples, capitalism, and small government. Our primary customer is a young person from high school age through college, who will hope-fully become a customer during that time and then remain a customer throughout the remainder of their life. We are producing those conversions through campaigns that combine literature, apparel, educational meetings, media appearances, and activism programs. Our production costs are a function of our geographic and campus coverage and can be lumped into the primary categories of materials, conferences, and staff.

From a distribution standpoint, initially we focused on creating campus activism and information "kits" that contained compelling messages and materials that could spread our message. We sought out groups that were already on campuses that had similar missions to our own, certainly groups that supported First Principles. By choosing this route we greatly increased our speed to market and reduced our overhead expense. We did not need to have a fully funded "sales staff" on every campus overnight. We took advantage of "salespeople" already in place pushing similar "lines" to ours. We were applying the principle of leverage in order to get presence on as many campuses as possible as quickly as possible.

From a pricing perspective, the cost to our customer was time and engagement. For every student who we would encounter, we would not just ask for them to listen, we would ask for them to help. We collected every piece of personal contact information they would share and then asked them how they would like to participate with Turning Point.

In terms of promoting, we moved on several fronts. Again, relating to Gladwell's work, we sought to develop messages that were "sticky:" meaning, ones that would remain with the student well after the first encounter. Once we had those kinds of messages, we would insist that our campus activist would stick to the sticky messages. In other words, while we encourage free expression and enthusiasm, we also knew that the materials we were developing would connect, so we made sure they were used.

We employed an aggressive use of social media. If you don't tell the world you are engaged in social activism, and what it's about, then nothing happens. This is more than just sending out "tweets" about topics, it is about using social media in a way that Gladwell surely would have included in his book if it had existed in 2002.

Gladwell identified three types of people useful in creating a tipping point for social phenomena. First there are salespeople. These are the people who will go out and try to convince everyone they know that they simply have to buy the new product or service they are using. They are persuasive. These are people who evangelize and convert directly. We wanted salespeople to spread the word about our product.

The next type of person is a connector. These are people who know many other people and who take deep personal satisfaction in making introductions and watching good things happen as a result. Connectors were important in order for us to get onto the next campus or into the next event.

Finally, there are mavens. Mavens are recognized as subject matter experts by their peers on any particular topic. If we could find people who were considered mavens with regard to political, social, and economic science matters to support what Turning Point was selling, then other students would listen.

We began the monitoring of social media in order to identify young people who were expressing ideas and commentary that would indicate them to be either likely customers of Turning Point, or perhaps members of one of the three key categories of salespeople, connectors, or mavens. As soon as a Turning Point staffer would find a message that resonated, we would reach out to that student and ask them to join our group. We would then ascertain their strengths and put them to use. This process allowed us to grow from my graduation money in 2012 to where we are today on more than 1,000 campuses, in just under four years.

In order to continue to promote, we launched a new product line, which was the actual production of salespeople and mavens. We were vertically integrating. By finding people who had the innate talent and drive to sell, we gave them the skills and the tools to step onto campuses and start selling. For others who were extremely intellectually curious and already respected by peers, we gave them enough access to information about free markets and First Principles to become mavens.

We have made use of the Internet in so many ways. In addition to Facebook, Twitter, and our own website, we have now established a news site called Hypeline. Hypeline is our answer to BuzzFeed, which is where primarily young people go to break and report on stories usually involving celebrities or Team Left agenda items. Hypeline was intended to counterattack and give students the chance to post stories that support all of the freedom-driven issues that matter to Turning Point. Since its inception it has broken several national stories, and with its usage now increasing at a near tipping point rate, it can be expected to break many more. It ties into the things I discussed in the preceding chapter on taking back our campuses.

So we are building a business. Sales are up. Profitability is solid. Our future projected growth rate is excellent. We have our cost structure under control and mostly variable in nature so that it moves in accordance with sales. Our marketing program is effective, low cost, and guerrilla in nature. We will continue to seek additional capital raises, but to facilitate new growth, not to refinance past mistakes.

Our business model of selling conversions is, perhaps, deserving of being taught at the Harvard Business School. Sadly, Harvard isn't likely to be inserting free markets into its curriculum any time soon.

¢   ¢   ¢

All of these great ideas being messaged, and the energy being created, need to have something to focus upon and do.

Earlier in the book I mentioned Uber when discussing the power and capability of free markets. Uber has become of particular importance to Turning Point in terms of what we teach and how we teach it. We have used Uber to combine activism with education, making the point that if students like the results of the free market, then they have to be willing to go to bat for the free market when it becomes necessary.

When we were discussing the "Big Government Sucks" campaign in the summer of 2014, one of our student activists pointed out that there were serious students on campuses who wanted examples of why and how free markets worked so well and why big government sucked. This was an issue taken seriously inside our walls when it was raised. We realized that we didn't just want to make theoretical arguments. We needed to be able to point to something that students grasped and that meant something to them.

During the discussion, the same activist asked the people in the room if they knew about Uber. To my surprise, about half our people actually weren't yet familiar with the new entrant into the world of public transportation. After the room was filled in on the Uber story, a decision was made that when we dispersed out to the campuses for the fall campaign we would look into the Uber phenomenon and report back afterwards.

In January 2015, when we reconvened for a recap of the fall activities, we brought up the Uber topic. Our people reported that college students were big fans of the company. They loved the flexibility, the technology, the all-inclusive pricing; all of it. We made a decision that Turning Point was going to embrace Uber as an ongoing project in the applied engineering of free markets. We were doing this not because of some vested interest in Uber the company, but because of what Uber could represent to our members. Uber was a tangible example of the fight between free markets and crony capitalism, the partnership between big government and big, institutionalized, business interests.

So Uber became part of the Turning Point "pitch" to students on campuses when discussing free markets. We would explain to students how this new car service that they found to be clean, reliable, convenient, and safe was being attacked by government at every level. In fact, Uber is great to hold up as an example of both macro and micro level economic interference on the part of government.

At the federal level, the National Labor Relations Board under President Obama has gone after Uber by trying to have their drivers classified as employees instead of independent contractors as the company contends. If the feds are successful, that will give them an entrée to exercise control over Uber in numerous ways. At the local level, city councils everywhere are holding hearings to find reasons to either outright deny Uber access to their market or to so restrict their access that it makes it untenable from a cost-benefit perspective. All of this is done to protect the taxi cab industry, long a sacred partner of government in a rigged transportation system.

Uber is the perfect contrast of free market capitalism to crony capitalism. Everything about their system involves voluntary exchange without government interference. This is anathema to the taxi cab industry, typically relying on a "medallion" system where the cost of entry is high and the number of entrants regulated by the locality. Prices are artificially set and competition is nonexistent. Students love Uber, but they tend to act as though it just "appeared" instead of being the byproduct of innovation, investment, and sweat. We point that out to them.

As we began to spread the Uber story on college campuses we began to create pockets of activism around Uber with motivated students. Turning Point members from Broward Community College in Broward County, Florida, on their own, petitioned and addressed the city council in an effort to have Uber service restored to the area. They were ultimately successful. In Iowa City, more than 30 students worked for months to get that municipality to reinstate Uber and were ultimately successful. These are both instances of college students fighting for free market capitalism over government-controlled markets. At the University of Southern California, however, they took support of Uber in a different direction.

With the help of Turning Point USA activists, the USC student government reached an agreement with local Uber drivers that between the hours of 10 p.m. and 3 a.m., students could call Uber and get a ride at no charge to the passenger. The student government used money from the student activities budget to pay for the rides. This addressed concerns over student safety late at night and also over students drinking and driving. Having Uber partner with the university protects students from possible sexual assault and keeps non-sober drivers to a minimum.

Messaging around Uber has led to action from students. They know that Uber's car door might be open but the ride isn't free. They have to work to protect it. They are now taking actions that call to mind the invisible hand of Adam Smith, insofar as Turning Point is not directing the students to do what they are doing. We are sending them a message that resonates and then they are taking action on their own. This is how we intend to create a return to free market values. This is how we intend to help pave the way for Julio.

As an aside, I have not met Uber founder Travis Kalanick. I don't even know if he has heard of Turning Point USA. Uber keeps to a fairly hands-off approach with activist groups. They know that being connected to any of them could simply come back to harm them in their battles with government at every level. So we are not getting sponsored by them, nor are we receiving key introductions to donors from them. We are simply using them to get a ride. That ride isn't taking us just to a geographic destination; it's taking us into the hearts and minds of young people.

What happens with students when we put all of this together? During the 2016 campaign, as we all have heard, the socialist candidate Bernie Sanders experienced great popularity with college students. "Feel the Bern" shirts and stickers could be found almost everywhere you look. When he speaks at a college, the crowds are large and boisterous. How on earth do you reach students with a free market and limited government message when they are supporting a candidate who wants the government to control every aspect of economic activity and who is promising to send kids to college for free?

There is a recurring event that is being experienced by Turning Point activists across the country after they set up a Turning Point table on a campus, complete with our banners and our "sticky" messages. A group of students, wearing "Feel the Bern" T-shirts, will walk by our table and see a sign that says "Big Government Sucks." Those students, supporting a socialist candidate, will see our sign and say "Big Government Sucks! Cool! Good stuff!" Our students will then engage them and ask why they are supporting Bernie Sanders? Do they realize that socialism is all about government control? Usually, the answer is that they really don't understand what socialism means. We even had one student tell us that socialism means that Bernie is in favor of social media (I'm not making that up). Our students will then discuss free markets and limited government with them. Sometimes we generate conversions (close a sale). Always, we generate thought.

The above example shows how to bring two opposing sides together. We have found a way to use the old Dick Morris idea of triangulation. We are taking two completely different sets of students based upon their belief systems, well-formed or otherwise, and finding a way to get them to agree on something. If you ask a student, "Do you want the government making decisions about what you can or can't do or about how much of your own money you can keep?" their answer is almost categorically "No." We are reframing. We are also planting seeds. Even if those same students end up voting in 2016 for Bernie, if they like the Big Government Sucks message it will stick with them and it will be brought back to mind at some future moment in their lives when they encounter a big government obstacle.

As I've said, we are playing a long game.

Of the two political parties, it is the Republican Party that tends to associate itself with free markets. Unfortunately, they do a lousy job of messaging to young people. Our newest theme at Turning Point is "Free Markets–Free People." It is open-ended, subject to students interpretation, and hopeful. It is so simple but we got there by listening to students for four years and crafting this particular message. We are confident it will be "sticky".

We have done other things that are similar. We have tackled the student loan crisis by calling it the "Game of Loans" based on the popular novels and HBO series *Game of Thrones*. We have used Kevin Spacey's image from *House of Cards* to send a message about the power and corruption of big government. We keep in mind the truism that if doesn't fit on a bumper sticker, it doesn't stick.

Republicans have been negligent in reaching out to Latinos. Our conference for Young Latino Leadership, started in 2015 and growing in 2016, is built on the idea of reaching out to them and talking about free markets and limited government helping their families find jobs and grow in prosperity. Our successful publication, *Capitalism Cures*, making the social justice argument for capitalism, has been translated into Spanish and reaches thousands. The Republican Party has made no such efforts.

The Young Women's Leadership Conference in 2016 will have 500 college ladies from around the country being taught that the Obama campaign's life of Julia is not the alpha and omega of the life they should want to live. They will leave our conference filled with facts, motivation, and plans for action. Team Left likes to talk about a war on women. Turning Point is teaching women how to wage war.

Our high school conference will be much the same. No conservative youth-based group has ever conducted this kind of outreach to students between the ages of 14–18. When I was in high school fighting against the teachers' union attacking Scott Walker, I had nowhere to turn for support or for education on the issues. We are giving high school students that outlet. Teachers are going to find a collection of students increasingly informed and skeptical about collectivist teachings and globalization arguments.

Earlier I made mention of some very famous historical movements in U.S. history. Some might argue that I am being a little pretentious by including what we are doing with Turning Point alongside such notable events as women getting the right to vote, or African-Americans being fully recognized as equal citizens. I will counterargue that in a very real sense our movement is even more important. Without liberty, what good does it do a woman to have a vote? Without a respected and observed Constitution, what liberties do African-Americans, the LGBT members, or any other minority group have to protect? At a minimum, we stand deservedly side by side with every necessary movement that has taken place in America since 1776.

In addition to the historical importance of our movement, there is something else that is special and unique about it. Every other significant movement in American history has been about people asking the government to *do* something. Our movement which calls for a return to free markets, limited government, and First Principles is asking for the government to *undo* a great many things. We want it to remove the restrictions and limitations it has placed upon individual liberty. Modern historical experience suggests that getting government to reverse its actions and cede its power is a very difficult task.

I'm now known in many circles as the "Big Government Sucks guy." I couldn't be prouder. If it sticks to me it will rub off when I, or Turning Point, bump into you. Even though we planned this approach when we started, I have to say I am surprised by the breadth and depth of its success. We will continue to persevere and keep our sights set on selling more products, which means getting more conversions to a way of life that Julio will be able to join about 20–25 years down the road.

There are a couple of big obstacles that stand in our way. We need your help to dismantle them. Both will be discussed next.

PART FOUR

OBSTACLES
WE NEED
TO OVERCOME

CHAPTER 10

ENDING THE GAME OF LOANS

"The most dramatic instances of directed behavior change and 'mind control' are not the consequence of exotic Forms of influence, such as hypnosis, psychotropic drugs, or 'brainwashing,' but rather the systematic manipulation of the most mundane aspects of human nature over time in confining settings."

—PHILIP ZIMBARDO, *The Lucifer Effect*

In March of 2015 I was a guest on Neil Cavuto's program on the Fox Business Network. The topic of discussion was the student loan debt crisis. In answering one of the questions, I pointed out that the federal government was involved in more than 90 percent of the student loans outstanding. Neil politely challenged me on the issue and I politely reasserted. After the interview was over, a producer from his show did some fact-checking because they were certain that I'd spoken in error. It turned out I was right; they just hadn't been aware.

I don't mention this for the purpose of embarrassing Neil Cavuto. Neil has been extremely good to me and to Turning Point, opening doors for us and providing a media outlet that we would not otherwise have had. I am mentioning this because as informed as Neil and his staff are, even they weren't aware of what is really happening behind, or not-so-behind, the scenes with government control of higher education.

In a previous chapter I discussed the size of big government. It would seem appropriate that its intrusion into higher education would be appropriately placed into the context of that chapter. Instead, I'm placing it under the heading of "What's Stopping Us?" I'm treating this as an obstacle to success instead of just a problem to be solved, because the unholy alliance between big government, universities, and professors is creating a fortress around which, or through which, our message has to be able to gain access. All three groups have a vested interest in keeping the current system in place and as-is.

This is an American debt crisis. It is being felt now by more than 40 million young Americans, the people who will be responsible for the future of the nation. It is the crisis of student loan debt. Over the past several decades the cost of higher education had been soaring, far outpacing the rate of inflation as measured by the increase in prices of other goods and services. While the cost of education has been rising dramatically, young people more than ever have been told that they must have a college education in order to be successful in a competitive global economy. Activists, politicians, and sociologists have told us that the disparity between whites and minority groups is a direct result of whites having greater access to higher education, and the gap can only be closed by getting more students of all colors into college.

But a college education has been getting so expensive, so fast, how could it be possible to fulfill the dream of more students getting easier access to the coveted four-year diploma? The answer has been to lend them the money to get their education and to lend it in the most simplified manner possible.

The current student loan cycle, in very simple terms, works like this: Tuition is expensive. Students and their parents borrow. Universities get paid. Universities then raise their tuition. Students and their parents have to borrow more. Universities again raise their tuition. If you read no further you can see where this has been and to where it is heading.

There are two compelling reasons why this *Game of Loans* persists. The first is that the university system, in perfect lockstep with government and financial institutions, has crafted and nurtured this mechanism to increase their largesse and increase their levels of power, prestige, and profit. This profit is not of the free market kind that comes through voluntary exchange, but rather, the profit that is had at the true expense of others, created only through interfering with the free market. Just like the hospitals and the mortgage lenders before them, the universities have harnessed the power of government as a third-party payer to line their pockets and expand their sphere of influence.

The second reason is more sinister than the first. By creating graduating class after graduating class hopelessly, and increasingly, buried in federally subsidized debt, government officials are creating a permanent dependent class. While the government has done this with other segments of society (topics covered in other Turning Point USA publications), this turning of youth into debtors is particularly odious because they are the educated—the ones who are supposed to be successful and free. Through the proliferation of debt, the government has made the very people who were promised prosperity before entering college into nothing more than overextended borrowers. To say that this was an accident provides far too much benefit of the doubt to those who constructed the system.

This is a story about money, about prestige, and about influence. It has all of the elements (save for the "red wedding") of the novels and HBO series *Game of Thrones*. The problem is it isn't fiction set in make-believe time and land. It is right here, right now. If we can't end this story it is going to be difficult for Julio's world to develop. We will continue to graduate students who are deeply in debt, looking to the federal government for relief, and who have been indoctrinated to believe that capitalism is bad and big government is good. It is as if a message-proof vest is being placed over young people during their most formative years in terms of their political consciousness.

To start, I'm going to share how we got to this point, how deep the financial hole is, and explain the interrelationship between the universities and the government. At the end of this chapter I will share some specific changes and reforms that could be enacted to help end the Game of Loans.

ϛ   ϛ   ϛ

The student loan debt crisis has reached a critical point. But it is even more important than that. It would be one thing if students were contracting large amounts of debt and then being able to earn so much from their education that they could easily pay it back in a few years. That isn't the case. They are getting less for their dollars. What follows is a list of some of the very concerning facts regarding the state of higher education in terms of cost, debt, and employment.

According to the College Board here is a current table of college average tuition costs and room and board charges for the 2015–16 school year for different types of universities:

	Public Two-Year In-District	Public Four-Year In-State	Public Four-Year Out-of-State	Private Nonprofit Four-Year	For-Profit
Tuition and Fees					
2015–16	$3,435	$9,410	$23,893	$32,405	$15,610
2014–15	$3,336	$9,145	$23,107	$31,283	$15,160
$ Change	$99	$265	$786	$1,122	$450
% Change	3.0%	2.9%	3.4%	3.6%	3.0%
Room and Board					
2015–16	$8,003	$10,138	$10,138	$11,516	–
2014–15	$7,856	$9,786	$9,786	$11,162	–
$ Change	$147	$352	$352	$354	–
% Change	1.9%	3.6%	3.6%	3.2%	–
Tuition and Fees + Room and Board					
2015–16	$11,438	$19,548	$34,031	$43,921	–
2014–15	$11,192	$18,931	$32,893	$42,445	–
$ Change	$246	$617	$1,138	$1,476	–
% Change	2.2%	3.3%	3.5%	3.5%	–

The inflation rate for 2015 was 0.1%. This means that college costs increased 20 to 35 times more than other costs. In fact, this is a historical trend. The March 18, 2016, issue of *Advisor Perspectives* put together the following comparative chart using data from the Bureau of Labor Statistics:

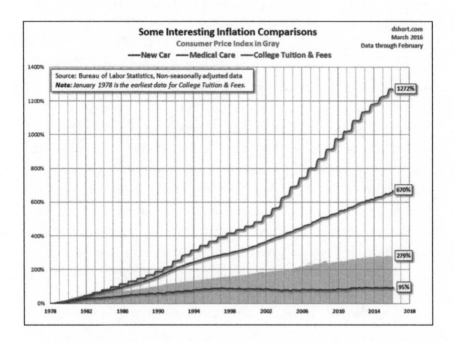

Since 1978, when such statistics started being kept, the cost of college has increased an incredible 1,272% compared with the Consumer Price Index climbing only 279%. The national "scandal" of soaring health care costs that justified the government takeover of the medical industry pale in comparison.

Debt is increasing along the lines of tuition charges. The education data site www.StartClass.com uses public data from government loans and estimates of private college loans to put the total amount of student debt at $1.3 trillion as of January 2016. They further estimate that the number is growing by $2,726 *every second*. According to a study by the New York Federal Reserve in 2015, estimates for delinquency on that debt are as high as 21 percent. In round numbers, that means that there could be more than $260 billion worth of debt that is in some stage of default. It is important to note that when the Fed released those numbers they were revising the estimate up from 10 percent delinquency. Depending upon the type of university (public, private nonprofit, private for-profit), anywhere from 66–88% of graduates leave school with debt. That is according to the Institute for College Access and Success.

The delinquency numbers are masked by changes that the Obama Administration put in place that delay initial payments upon leaving college and change the definition of "distressed borrower" to avoid delinquency status. All of this means there is a really big bubble.

In May of 2015 the "Millennials Jobs Report" created by the not-for-profit organization Generation Opportunity showed unemployment numbers for millennials between the ages of 18-29 to be at 13.8 percent compared to a general unemployment rate of 5.4 percent for the same period. You can't say that attending a university caused this difference. You can't even say that it partially caused the difference. What you can point to is that young people are not attracting jobs at some incredibly favorable rate after graduation.

What kind of "learning" are college students receiving for this incredibly high price tag? I know it is cherry-picking to look at ridiculous courses to point to waste at our universities. On the other hand, it is instructive because these kinds of courses should not exist at all. I can't resist. Allow me to name some for you, courtesy of www. OnLineUniversities.com:

- ▶ The Adultery Novel In and Out of Russia: University of Pennsylvania
- ▶ Those Sexy Victorians: Ole' Miss
- ▶ Sex, Rugs, Salt & Coal: Cornell
- ▶ The Science of Superheroes: UC-Irvine
- ▶ Joy of Garbage: UC Berkley

Of course, those are only isolated courses. *Forbes* went the additional step to point out the "10 Worst College Majors" and included their unemployment rates. Some might surprise you:

1. Anthropology (unemployment rate 10.5 percent)
2. Video & Photographic Arts (12.9 percent)
3. Fine Arts (12.6 percent)
4. Philosophy & Religious Studies (10.8 percent)
5. Liberal Arts (9.2 percent)
6. Music (9.2 percent)
7. Physical Fitness & Parks & Recreation (great show but 8.3% unemployment)
8. Commercial Art & Graphic Design (11.8 percent)
9. History (10.2 percent)
10. English Language & Literature (9.2 percent)

The unemployment numbers would actually be worse if you were looking at whether they landed a job in their field of study. These numbers simply reflect whether they have a job, not whether they are working in a field they may have paid $160,000 to enter. According to *Forbes*, a full 60 percent of college graduates do not get a job in their chosen field of study. Further, these numbers are for those who matriculate. Imagine the rates if they included those who failed to graduate.

You can see that we are ringing up a lot of debt, in a system with spiraling costs, and not getting satisfactory results for all of the financial hardship. Something is obviously wrong. So obviously wrong that you have to wonder why nobody in a position of authority is stepping forward to solve the problem.

Maybe they don't want the problem solved? Maybe they don't consider it a problem at all? Perhaps, for those involved in the political, financial, and educational systems, this is nothing more than an opportunity to exploit, control, and profit? For any of you reading this who are millennials, you are exactly the ones they are exploiting.

ᘓ   ᘓ   ᘓ

In February of 2012, President Barack Obama said:

> When kids graduate, I want them to be able to afford to go to
> college. If they've been working hard, if they've gotten the grades to
> go to college, I don't want them to cut their dreams short because
> they don't think they can afford it.

That statement sounds very appealing. After all, who wouldn't
want to see every child receive an education if they truly desire one?
What's worse, what if the only thing standing in their way of getting
that education was an unaffordable price tag? You can almost hear
the chords on the social justice Stratocaster beginning to sound. We
know the federal government is here inside the world of university
funding and student debt, but how did they get here in the first place?
Like so many other big government interventions into our lives and
liberties, it started small and with good intentions and grew into an
enterprise unto itself. One which has long since lost track of its altru-
istic roots and has evolved into a metastasizing economic cancer that
right now has the nation's educational system at about Stage Three.

The 1950s were the Eisenhower years in America, famous now for
their uneventful times, an interstate highway system, and perhaps
that military escapade into Korea. It was under Eisenhower, however,
that a low interest college loan program was established through the
National Defense Education Act of 1958. Under this initial program,
the loan dollars were advanced directly by the government.

The next development came during the presidency of Lyndon
Johnson and his "War on Poverty" and "Great Society" programs. The
Higher Education Act (HEA) of 1965 was part of that big government
stew, and, among other things, expanded the government's low interest loan program.

HEA changed the way the federal loan program was funded.
State and national banks would fund the loans instead of the government funding them directly. The government would "guaranty" the

loan (meaning if the student defaulted and the bank lost money, the federal government would step in and make them whole). The government now was able to take the direct cost of the student loan program off their books as an expenditure and/or debt obligation because they were only liable to pay if the borrower defaulted (this should sound familiar to anyone who has studied the collapse of the mortgage market in 2008). The government looked better, the banks got cut in on the interest-earning game, and the universities had more money and students. All this was done ostensibly to give more poor students access to college. Again, a noble sounding endeavor, but nobody was stopping to think about the consequences of subsidizing college education with easy to obtain debt.

Or were they?

The Student Loan Marketing Association (Sallie Mae) was created under the watch of President Richard Nixon in 1972. Everyone thinks of Nixon and the damage he did to America because of the Watergate scandal. Sallie Mae was likely worse in its long-term deleterious impact on the nation. Operating exactly like "Fannie Mae" and "Freddie Mac" did in the mortgage market, Sallie Mae, with the help of the U.S. Treasury Department, pumped liquidity into the guaranteed student loan market by having those individual loans made by banks "pooled" and "securitized" for sale to investors. This meant that if a bank made $1 million of student loans it could sell those loans through Sallie Mae, get a check, and then make more student loans.

The floodgates were now opened. In this new system the bankers could take risks that were essentially "risk-free" while the American taxpayer was left to cover the defaults of the student/parent borrower. The free market mechanism of failure leading to a company going out of business was replaced with "failure insurance" from the federal government. If you failed, you would get a check and you could lend again.

In the 1990s, then President Clinton recognized that the federal bailout system for banks was more expensive to taxpayers than was simply having the government make direct loans as it had under

Eisenhower, so he sought to restore the old system. Some lawmakers were rightly skeptical of a pure government takeover of lending, so a compromise was struck that can only be struck within a leviathan state: Direct loans by the government were phased back in while keeping the guarantees in place for the banks!

This system stayed in place right up until the financial market collapse in 2008. With the banks in crisis, Congress gave the Department of Education the ability to buy loans from the troubled bank lenders. The banks began exiting the *Game of Loans* and they were systematically replaced by the federal government.

In 2010 President Obama, while participating in the "health care games," packaged legislation inside of Obamacare to remove the commercial banks from the guaranteed student loan program. Now, the federal government had regained complete control over student loan funding. Banks can still make student loans but they do so without the guaranty of the government.

Learning this history, you might think that despite a drunkard's walk evolution in the world of student lending, order has finally been restored to the universe. The program started simply enough under Eisenhower as a direct loan program to enable more young people to be able to afford college. Despite the irresponsibility of the banks and Sallie Mae, President Obama has returned the program to its rightful spot and now a simple, reasonable set of standards for the programs can be put in place and they will be responsibly administered. But if you think that then you don't understand the true nature of the *Game of Loans*.

¢   ¢   ¢

Today there are several different types of student loan programs. First, there is the Federal Perkins Loan. This is for undergraduate or graduate students and eligibility is based upon need. The school itself is the lender, with the federal government kicking in money as well as the school. There is the Direct Subsidized Loan for undergraduate students enrolled at least half-time and demonstrating financial need. The U.S. Department of Education is the lender. Finally, there is the direct Unsubsidized Loan available to undergraduate and graduate students who are enrolled at least half-time. There is no financial needs test for this loan. The USDE is the lender.

Note that the loan programs, when taken together, cover essentially everyone. You can get a loan if you can't afford to pay for school any other way (or even pay the loan back unless things go really well once out of school), and you can get a loan if you don't need one at all (mom and dad are rich but just decide not to use their cash or sell some investments from their portfolio). And if you are in between (where perhaps a combination of smaller college choice, part-time work, and part-time class load could get you by without borrowing), well, there's a loan waiting for you, too!

The problem with all of this is the seductive nature of debt due to its deferring of the pain of paying. Decisions to commit to spend money are made very differently when the payment has to be made on the spot versus when the payment can be made later but the enjoyment can begin immediately. Many an American consumer has been financially wounded when the 12-month "no payments required" bill finally comes due for their $5,000 3D smart TV. By their nature, people will attempt to delay pain and expedite gratification. In the case of student loan debt, this not only leads to parents and students potentially borrowing too much money, it also leads to more dollars being more quickly fed into the university system.

The price of anything is determined by the amount of money chasing it and the velocity with which that money is traveling. The more money there is and the faster that money is spent, the higher the cost of, in this case, tuition. This is how an inflated money supply impacts the price levels in the economy. Since we've already shown that college tuition rates are increasing at a much higher rate than other prices in general, that must mean that a lot of money is coming into the system at a very high rate of speed. In the *Game of Loans* this tips the balance of purchasing power away from the student and towards the government and the universities.

The first thing every college student learns in a basic economics course is the law of supply and demand. Refresh your memory by glancing below:

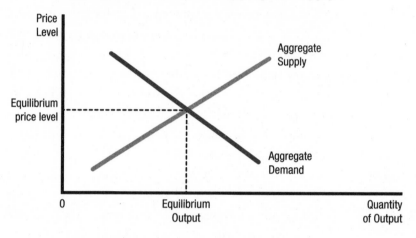

Aggregate Demand and Aggregate Supply

In short, it tells us that the higher the price for something, the more of it a supplier will want to supply and the less a consumer will be willing to purchase. A free market brings these two contrary forces together and finds the right price where buyers want to buy and sellers want to sell. That price is called "equilibrium." And in real life it is just as good as it sounds. Markets are stable and goods and services experience neither a shortage nor a surplus.

The problem with the current student loan situation in America is that it creates too many dollars chasing a college education. Students are willing to pay more not because they want to but because they can! The universities are then able to raise their tuition accordingly. Once they raise it, ironically, they can raise it again because they know the federal government will provide the liquidity through loans (and Pell Grants, which don't have to be paid back but contribute to higher tuition costs) that students need to pay the still-higher tuition. There is no inevitable end to this process. It can continue as long as students can borrow more money.

Unfortunately, upon their exit from college, once the university has already been paid, that is where students may well come to find their own financial end.

Remember the delinquency percentages estimated by the New York Federal Reserve? Their 21 percent delinquency rate translates into more than $200 billion of nonperforming loans. This is not sustainable. Graduating students are becoming desperate. But don't worry, big government is coming to the rescue. Never is there a better time to remember Ronald Reagan's famous quote, "The nine most terrifying words in the English language are I'm from the government, and I'm here to help."

₵   ₵   ₵

Whether it is President Obama, Bernie Sanders, Hillary Clinton, or other big government proponents, there are ideas and proposals circulating to change the rules of *Game of Loans*. They range from allowing students to go bankrupt to discharge their student loans (paid for by taxpayers who did not receive the education), having the students soften their loan burden by participating in public service (big government indoctrination), and even having the first two, or all four, years of college be "free" (free, of course, to the student, not to the taxpayer). These and other similar proposals are efforts to make students more dependent upon big government and educational institutions even more controlled by big government.

If big government undertakes any sort of one-time loan forgiveness program, nothing in the current system will change. The day after the graduates' books are wiped to zero they still won't have a better set of job prospects, and nothing will be done about changing the borrowing patterns for the next semester's set of students. If big government extends student loan payments, then the debt will simply be less painful to accumulate and there will be *more* upward pressure on tuition rates. If big government creates a "public works for debt forgiveness" program, then the participants will become slaves to the culture of a bloated state and won't develop the skills required to be productive members of the private sector.

Proposals to reduce the level of student debt by making the first two years, or all four years, of college free are perhaps the most nefarious of all the pleasant-sounding ideas. People like to debate these types of proposals by saying, "It's a great idea but how are we going to pay for it?" That argument is intellectually lazy and misses the point. It isn't a great idea no matter how you are going to pay for it because it will give the federal government complete control over the school that is receiving the payment! Government money, invariably, comes with a price!

There is no quick fix or government bailout that can solve this problem. Consider that the entire current funding system for higher education is nothing more than a government bailout program with lipstick. So many dollars have already been thrown into the system that simply rearranging them or throwing more won't help. Government isn't the solution to the higher education funding problem, government is the problem.

There are two dramatic events in recent political and economic history that are having a significant impact in American daily life. The first was the collapse of the mortgage market in 2007–08 that destroyed the value of homes, caused banks to fail, and caused a radical change in the structure of the economy. The second was Obamacare, which saw the federal government take control of more than one-sixth of the nation's economy and install a system where access to doctors and medical procedures would be rationed and controlled by heartless bureaucrats instead of doctors and patients.

The current problem with student loan debt, the skyrocketing cost of college, and the inability of graduates to get jobs in their field are the result of the government and the educational system employing both of the key factors that led to the collapse of the mortgage market and the seizure of the health care system. The first is that artificial liquidity has been pumped into the system (just like the mortgage market), and the other is third-party payments have disconnected the buyer of education from the seller of education (just like the health care industry).

The residential mortgage market saw an explosion in the 1990s through the mid 2000s because of the aggressive funding and the attendant junk bond market created by Fannie Mae, Freddie Mac (government supported agencies that operated exactly like Sallie Mae), and large financial institutions. At the instruction of politicians and/or with the tacit blessing of regulators, these groups encouraged lenders to relax lending standards and make as many loans as possible to be packaged and sold as investment securities. This endless source of easy liquidity into the residential housing market caused prices to soar and homeowners to borrow far more money than they could ever hope to pay back. When the debt level could no longer be sustained, the entire system collapsed like a house of cards.

The argument for government intervention in the mortgage finance market was that house prices were too high, so the government had to provide liquidity so people could afford them. The problem was it was that extra liquidity that was causing the prices to increase. The more-loans-higher cost-more loans cycle was a perfect circle, with no beginning or end point.

The student loan debt crisis is tracking along the same pattern as did the mortgage debt crisis. Students are taking on more and more debt as tuition costs keep climbing. Eventually, the system has to collapse. Any financial circumstance created through artificial stimulation and intervention cannot stand forever. Just like Pompeii, the walls will come tumbling down at the universities we love.

Everyone knows about the problems in health care and how costs had dramatically risen throughout the 1990s and the first decade of this century. Hospitals and doctors would say it was because of the cost of innovation on the positive side and the cost of malpractice coverage on the negative. Politicians claimed it was simply because insurance companies and hospitals were greedy and that doctors ordered all sorts of unnecessary tests and procedures on purpose in order to afford more exclusive country club memberships.

While there are grains of truth and reality found in all of those contentions, none of it would have gotten so out of hand if we had not had a third-party payer system for medical bills.

When you go to the doctor you don't ask what anything is going to cost if you have medical insurance. You visit the doctor in his office, go through all of the doctor-ordered tests, and then go and fill your prescription. After that, you wait. You wait about 30 days for a bill to come in the mail to tell you what all of your medical procedures cost, how much your insurance company paid, and how much is left for you to pay. If you are like most people, opening that envelope will be the first time you even have a clue as to what sort of bill was being run up. That's because payment was being made between the insurance company and the doctor, and you only had to pay what was left. At the time of services, you didn't even ask about the bill.

Government's intrusion into education has created the effect of a third-party payer. Because of the myriad of funding sources available to parents and students, they end up focusing only on that part of the cost of school that they will have to directly and immediately come up with out of pocket. In medical parlance, they are focusing on their deductible and their copay. In the meantime, the government and the universities are in collusion to keep the bill increasing and lengthen the graduate's period of indentured servitude.

College education is becoming the modern day version of *Jack and the Beanstalk*. Remember the English fable from when you were child? Jack and his mother are so poor that she sends him into town to trade their milking cow for something of value. Instead, he trades it for some magical beans. Suffice to say mom wasn't happy, and we know what happened with the beans. Unfortunately, the way college is being sold to young people today, for many of them upon graduation they might have been better off with magic beans instead of a diploma.

A great myth has been created in this country that without a four-year college degree you are simply not as employable as someone who has one. There has been an element of self-fulfilling prophecy to that, as people who go to college do fare better than those who don't. That can be explained fairly simply by noting that if so many people are able to go to college, why wouldn't they be employed before someone who did not attend?

The truth is that much of what people are learning in college is not directly translatable into relevant job skills in today's employment market. While there is nothing immoral about studying public relations, British literature, or multiculturalism, if you expect that to translate into employment after graduation you are mistaken. The high tech world in which we live, and the complexities of science and engineering, suggest that *Beowulf* won't take you as far as it once did. What is worse is that hundreds of thousands of students every year are spending more and more money on these degrees of no value they've been told they must have.

Consider this list of the top jobs and their average income as compiled by *U.S. News & World Report* for 2016:

Best Health Care Jobs
1. Dentist: $108K–$187K
2. Nurse Practitioner: $83K–$114K
3. Physician: $125K–$187K
4. Dental Hygienist: $60K–$85K
5. Physical Therapist: $69K–96K

Best Technology Jobs
1. Software Developer: $74K–$121K
2. Computer Systems Analyst: $65K–105K
3. Information Security Analyst: $67K–$114K
4. Web Developer: $45K–$87K

Best Business Jobs
1. Market Research Analyst: $44K–$86K
2. Marketing Manager: $91K–$171K
3. Accountant: $56K–$88K
4. Operations Research Analyst: $56K – $102K

Best Social Services Jobs

1. School Psychologist: $52K–$90K
2. Speech-Language Pathologist: $56K–$90K
3. Elementary School Teacher: $43K–$68K
4. High School Teacher: $45K–$72K
5. Middle School Teacher: $44K–$69K

Best Construction Jobs

1. Cost Estimator: $45K–$79K
2. Construction Manager: $65K–$114K
3. Plumber: $38K–$68K
4. Sheet Metal Worker: $33K–$60K

Best Creative Jobs

1. Public Relations Specialist: $41K–$77K
2. Architect: $57K–$95K
3. Art Director: $61K–$122K

In viewing the list, you can see that some require an advanced college degree, some do not require a degree, but most of them require a skill that could be taught in a setting that did not contain all of the frills and costs associated with a four-year university! What the youth of this country are being told about the value of a four-year college education is a lie, an expensive lie. It isn't just expensive in terms of the financial cost. It is even more expensive in terms of the time and energy it drains from many young people who end up buying (borrowing) into the lie.

The problem couldn't really be any worse. Universities are charging too much money for a degree that everyone tells an 18-year-old they have to have. The government then buries them in debt to get the degree. Once they have it, many can't use it to get a job, but they still are indebted to big government, which has exploited this arrangement to gain control of the majority of citizens throughout their 20s. Government and universities are selling junk bonds in the form of a college education. That is part metaphor and part literal as I'll show you at the end of the chapter.

This problem has not been created overnight and the solutions will not be easy, immediate, or painless. That said, if America doesn't decide soon to make some significant changes there will be a collapse and a takeover like we've seen in the housing market and health care. Only this time it will be our youth who are collapsing and losing their liberty, not home values and medical practitioners.

In the early 1980s when Ronald Regan became president of the United States, the country was experiencing a crisis of inflation. Under President Carter the money supply had so drastically increased that prices for everything had risen faster than incomes, and interest rates were so high they made a loan from Tony Soprano appear underpriced. The nation had become strung out, just like a drug addict, on the ever-increasing money supply. Reagan knew the solution would not be easy.

Enter Federal Reserve Chairman Paul Volker. He, with Reagan's support, steadily contracted the money supply and wrung the inflation out of the American financial system. It was painful but once they were done, America went on to experience one of the greatest eras of prosperity in its 200-year history. Solving the current student loan debt problem will be just as difficult and painful as was the reversal of inflation in the 1980s. However, just like that experience, if Americans can work their way through some difficult upheavals, the result will be an educational system that is reasonably priced and delivers practical knowledge instead of raised-letter diploma wallpaper.

To this point, what I've presented can be summed up as follows:

- ▶ The absolute cost of higher education is too high and has risen at a rate far exceeding that of other goods and services offered within the economy.
- ▶ Government intrusion into the financing element of higher education has provided it with greater control over the process and has left students buried in more than $1 trillion in debt.

▶ The degree that students are receiving from four-year programs that is leaving them saddled with debt is increasingly worth less in terms of finding employment relevant to the degree.

If the problems were only found in those three areas it would be bad enough, and it would have merited coverage in the "Big Government Sucks" chapter. Unfortunately, while this problem contains elements that could place it in that chapter, it also contains elements that place it into "Taking Back Our Campuses." While students are enrolled in theses colleges, incurring significant amounts of debt and earning degrees that can't get them employed, they are also being indoctrinated. The big government message is everywhere. There are few chimes of freedom to be heard among the school bells.

I've already spent considerable time in this book showing what takes place on college campuses to force conformance and impose a collectivist, big government ideology on students. When you overlay that reality with a mechanism that has been created to impose financial servitude, you end up getting graduates who are experiencing a form of personal and financial slavery and who have been taught that the very system that created their problem is the only system that can solve their problem. This situation has to change in order for our message to be heard. Students are in such a state of cognitive dissonance it makes it harder to get them to open their minds long enough to look for a better way.

I'm not just going to identify a problem and ask you as a reader to figure it out. Here are some straightforward but significant steps that can be taken to change the system and end the Game of Loans:

▶ To address the absolute cost of education being so high, I propose converting the traditional four-year degree into a three-year degree: This idea has received support from Scotland to the *New York Times* and points in between. Condensing the time required to receive a degree of higher learning by one year reduces the overall cost of education by 25 percent right off the top. It will also force colleges and universities to focus course offerings in areas that actually benefit the students once they graduate. Facts will replace fluff. Students who want to attend school for more than three years can do so, but not at the expense of others.

▶ To address the government forcing the students into debt, driving up costs, and taking over control of university operations and students' lives, I propose a gradual phaseout of government-provided (or guaranteed) loans and replacement with purely private transactions between banks/lending institutions and students/families. If loan transactions take place purely on a voluntary basis between private parties, then the level and pricing of those loans will adjust to market forces instead of artificial stimulation from the government.

Without subsidy or taxpayer support, the amount of loans will initially decrease and the price of loans will initially increase. Both of these adjustments are necessary to get the price inflation out of the system. Universities will be forced to address their bloated budgets because they won't have government-guaranteed dollars coming in to support them. The only support the government should give to the program is having its regulators treat these loans favorably when examining a bank's capital structure. If the government is off their back, banks will be a bit more inclined to lend.

▶ In order to provide students with an educational outcome that gives them a greater opportunity to find employment in their chosen field of study, I propose the aggressive use of business tax credits to encourage the creation of "skill schools." These schools, created freely by interested businesses needing a trained workforce, would have no government intervention of any sort and would be exclusively devoted to educating students with the skills needed to compete in the workforce. These schools cannot be created by the government because nobody in government knows anything about what it means to work in the private economy. This program would allow businesses of all sizes to contribute and would move away from large gifts to large university endowment funds, and would move toward a market and results-driven "crowd funding" atmosphere. Instantly, students would be getting an education not just that they chose, but an education they could use.

These ideas may be considered radical by some and not aggressive enough by others. I believe they are easy to understand, easy to implement, and will have near-immediate positive impact. Input from all Americans is needed and welcomed but in addressing the problem, two things are of critical importance for all participants to keep in mind. First, the situation as it exists cannot stand, as it is placing the financial markets of the United States in peril and it is leading American students into individual financial ruin. Second, the solutions to the problem need to be found within the framework of private transactions and free markets. Turning to government to solve this problem ignorantly disregards the fact that government caused this problem.

ᚳ   ᚳ   ᚳ

One of the top movies of 2015 was *The Big Short*. The movie told the story of several unrelated financial industry players who, separate from one another, anticipated the mortgage market collapse of 2008 that led to a devastating worldwide recession. The title of the movie referred to a popular investment tactic known as a "short sale." In simple terms, selling short means that you agree to sell a security today at whatever price it currently has in the market, with an agreement to buy it later at the new market price. You sell before you buy because you are convinced the price is going to drop. The protagonists in *The Big Short* all, in various forms, sold short on mortgagees because they saw the collapse coming.

An October 2015 article written by Baily McCann and published in *Institutional Investor* indicated that hedge funds were beginning to smell blood in the water. There is evidence that, based on growing delinquencies, some investors are beginning to take short positions in and around the student loan market. In the movie, the key delinquency rate they talked about for mortgages collapsing the system was an overall 8 percent. Student loan debt is delinquent at a rate of approximately 20 percent.

If we don't take steps to end this Game of Loans, it is going to end itself. I don't want to wait for the movie.

CHAPTER 11

ENDING THE GAME BETWEEN TEAM RIGHT & TEAM LEFT

"The ignorance of one voter in a democracy impairs the security of all."

—JOHN F. KENNEDY

On August 9, 2014, Michael Brown, an 18-year-old African-American teenager in Ferguson, Missouri, was shot and killed by Darren Wilson, an on-duty, 28-year-old white police officer. Brown had just been involved in the robbery of a convenience store but Wilson was not aware of that fact (he was aware there had been a robbery). As Wilson was responding to the incident he encountered Brown and a friend walking down the middle of the street, blocking traffic. After stopping to instruct them to move, he then realized they matched the description of the robbery suspects. What ensued was a confrontation that led to the shooting death of Brown and polarized the nation. He was unarmed at the time. A grand jury investigation concluded that Wilson was justified in the shooting incident and no charges or disciplinary action would be brought against the officer.

Two years earlier, on August 5, 2012, Wade Michael Page, a former military veteran and a member in a white supremacist rock band, walked into a Sikh temple in Oak Creek, Wisconsin, and murdered six temple members before taking his own life after he was wounded by police. It is speculated that Page thought he was killing Muslims but didn't study religious geography very well. The error only compounded the senselessness of the tragedy.

What did these two seemingly unrelated criminal events have in common with one another? On their face they would seem to just be stand-alone incidents, each with its own set of facts and preceding series of events that are always fascinating to criminologists. What they weren't, under any reasonable interpretation, were political events. Or were they?

Immediately after each of these events, media members, political and social commentators, and politicians began making statements. In the Ferguson case, on one side there were people defending the police officer for the shooting, even though the teenager was unarmed. On the other side, political hucksters like Al Sharpton were screaming racism before they even learned Brown had just committed a crime. In the Oak Creek case, because of Page's affiliation with white supremacist groups, and his devotion to the racist 1978 William Pierce novel *The Turner Diaries*, which revolves around the overthrow of the U.S. government, commentators called him a "right wing extremist." Eager journalists searched unsuccessfully to see if they could find a connection to the Tea Party.

Why did people jump to make a political firestorm out of law enforcement matters? More importantly, why did people automatically, reflexively, come to the defense of one side or the other and render judgment before any semblance of a complete representation of the facts were even known? The answer lies at the heart of the current deep division found in American society. This division is often referred to as the battle between the "right wing" and the "left wing".

I can tell you from the time I've spent in political activist circles, from the Silent Generation to millennials, that the battle can be better described as "Team Right" vs. "Team Left."

¢   ¢   ¢

The country is incredibly divided. If you're reading this book it might be because you're aware of that and wonder what can be done about it. In previous chapters, I've shared how Turning Point uses messages that have a cross-sectional appeal. The problem is that there is so much animosity and blind rage out there that getting people to close their mouths and open their ears is a real challenge.

We are operating in a world filled with labels: Left-Right; Conservative-Liberal; Fascist-Communist, to name a few. These phrases are used so casually in today's America that people just assume that everyone knows what they are talking about when they use them. When these phrases are used by politicians, news people, or "experts" (also known as talking heads, as they appear on so many different shows), the people *hearing* them assume that the people using them must know what they are talking about.

However, the truth is that nobody knows what anybody is talking about anymore. The terms we are using are used as pejoratives and what one person means by using them isn't necessarily what another person would mean if they used them. When I travel around the country I find that if I ask five people what it means to be a conservative or a right-winger I will get five different answers. I shouldn't. If the terms have real definitional meaning, then everybody should mean the same thing when they use them. Instead, the way they are used is almost always just to insult people they don't agree with and create an "us-them" mentality.

If we are going to be effective in creating Julio's future, we need to get people to stop insulting each other and unite on common ground. I've discovered that the same people who support Bernie Sanders cheer out loud when they see a "Big Government Sucks" sign on a college campus. Yet those same people will tell you they don't like conservatives or "right wingers." We have to get these people to come together and realize just how much they have in common. While we are fighting amongst ourselves, big government collectivists are busy doing their best imitation of Chicago Mayor Rahm Emmanuel and not letting the crisis go to waste. They are taking away our freedom.

During the NSA surveillance scandal, Fox News commentator Britt Hume was on Bill O'Reilly's program discussing the matter. O'Reilly was pointing out that people on both the far left and the far right were objecting to the NSA. Hume responded by explaining that at the extremes the far right and far left actually touch each other.

Really? Exactly how does that work? People who are diametrically opposed to one another suddenly do complete reversals, all of their profound differences go away, and they agree on everything? Does that mean that fascists and communists become one? Libertarians and progressives? Republicans and Democrats? If you drew that sort of a political continuum it would turn it into an ellipse and there wouldn't, or couldn't, be any extremes.

So, there is at best inconsistent and at worst contradictory use of the terms left wing and right wing when describing events and political positions. In general, however, it seems that people tend to be referring to "Republican types" when saying right wing and to "Democrat types" when saying left wing. The confusion would be OK if everyone gets to the same place anyway, but they aren't. The terms "right wing" and "left wing" can mean very different things to people and what's worse, they might not even mean the same thing consistently to the same person.

This team mentality in America today has become a cultural disease. The only way to eradicate a disease is to understand its fundamental elements and where it came from. I want to take you through the history of right wing-left wing in America and show you how we got to where we are now. I believe if everyone could come to understand how we've become so politically sick, America would be ready to open itself up to a heavy dose of freedom as a cure almost overnight.

ᘓ   ᘓ   ᘓ

When I was in high school and we were studying basic political science theory, here is the political continuum that was presented to me. It is the classic model that has communism at the far left and fascism at the far right. A moderate is found at the midpoint.

L------------------X------------------M------------------Y------------------R
Communist   Moderate   Fascist

Variations and deviations from this model have been formulated for the past 50-plus years. They have taken many shapes and forms, some even being represented as a quadrant diagram or a 3D rendering. These elaborate models look more like a personality profile than anything having to do with a political thought movement, but that's indicative of the struggle to clearly show the dichotomies and progressions of political positions.

While there are numerous problems with this continuum, perhaps the most obvious is that of characterizing points X and Y marked above. Who are those people? What do they, and what don't they, believe in? Don't bother trying to figure it out. You can't. The problem with this political continuum and the representation of right and left is that it attempts to depict a continuous data pattern in a directional path that doesn't exist.

How we got to this simple, inaccurate, and functionally useless line is a knowable story that, once I explain it, will allow you to discard this dysfunctional paradigm and replace it with one that can predict patterns and show opportunities for coming together and solving problems. The continuum shown above is at the very core of the division in America today, and virtually nobody is aware of it.

ᘓ   ᘓ   ᘓ

Everything comes from something. It is easy to hear the casual terms "right and left" and assume that they have been around since the beginning of man and have always held the same universal meaning. That's never the case with language and it is especially not the case here. The terms have no universally agreed-upon meaning. How we got to this point explains a lot of this ambiguity. More importantly, understanding how we got here provides insight into how to change the way we use language, define terms, and have discussions. It provides light along the path to healing. I'm going to quickly lead you through a historical timeline that will help explain the evolution of the terms and how we have come to use them to categorize people today.

The birth of "Right Wing and Left Wing" took place at the beginning of the French Revolution. The Assemblée Nationale (National Assembly) was convened in June of 1789 in prerevolutionary France. It was led by the Third Estate (the commoners or "people"), who then offered participation to the members of the First Estate (the clergy in its entirety) and Second Estate (French nobility, excluding the monarch, who was outside the "estate" system). These were the very people in support of King Louis XVI, (the monarch), the man and institution the Revolution would ultimately overthrow.

The Third Estate had the members of the First and Second sit on the right side of the chamber, because in French culture it was considered proper etiquette to have your guests sit to the right of the host (as most people are right-handed). As a result of the seating arrangement, the people sitting on the right side were the supporters of the French monarchy (right wing) and the people sitting on the left side were the commoners supporting what can very loosely be called democracy (left wing). It is this time and place where the terms "right wing" and "left wing" originated. While the French Revolution went on to become notoriously violent, temporarily victorious, and wiped away by Napoleon, the terms "right wing" and "left wing" would survive.

There was no political continuum yet that had a left and right end point. There were just two sides; the monarchists on the right and the social democrats on the left. So the terms that divide America today, and have us talking past each other instead of to each other, came about because of French table manners and furniture arrangements.

¢   ¢   ¢

The next critical event in American right-left evolution again took place off our own shores. Everyone knows about the Bolshevik Revolution and the beginnings of "Communist" Russia in 1917. What isn't as widely known is the impact that revolution would have on how Americans would ultimately come to describe themselves politically.

Vladimir Lenin was an admirer of the instigators of the French Revolution. He admired their spirit, studied their ability to foment a mob, and learned from their failures in terms of not being able to solidify and hold power on a long-term basis. He spoke and wrote about the French Revolution, always extolling its virtues and warning against its failures. As Lenin positioned his revolution as that of the workers, the common people, uniting against the czar (the monarchy), the world took notice of the similarities to the French experience and came to see the Russian Revolution as essentially the second French Revolution. One of the offshoots of that was that the term "communist" was a contemporary and intellectually trendy fit for the "left wing" heading created almost a century and a half earlier. "Communism" took a seat in the left wing of casual political language.

So with communism positioning itself as the new left, it would be left to Mussolini, Hitler, fascism, and Nazism to come along and build out the right side of the new political continuum. Europe was a dangerous and rapidly changing place after the end of WWI. Mussolini brought fascism to Italy, making the trains run on time and opponents just run. Lenin, and then Stalin, consolidated what they were calling communism inside of Russia and neighboring countries like Ukraine, where Stalin systematically starved to death 11 million people. Franco brought totalitarianism to Spain in 1939 with the help of Mussolini and the increasingly powerful corporal from Germany, Adolph Hitler. On the other side of the world, imperial Japan was dusting off samurai swords and fueling "Zeros."

The United States watched carefully and nervously as events unfolded across two oceans, hoping to stay out of the war raging around them. December 7, 1941, made that hope disappear. Once America was attacked by Japan, a member of the Axis Powers with Italy and Germany, there was no keeping it out of the world conflict. Despite official problems with the communist government of Russia, the U.S. now found itself an uncomfortable ally with the murderer Stalin in taking on the Axis. While it is difficult to argue the choice to throw in with the Soviets, there was an unintended consequence that has had a lasting impact on American domestic politics to this day.

Hitler and Stalin were the same guys. They were bloodthirsty, totalitarian monsters who sought power through conquest and had no reservations about murdering anyone necessary in order to attain and retain it. Their economic systems and political structures differed in specifics but were essentially the same in results: they controlled everything and their people lived in fear and slavery.

In order to side with one against the other, we needed—the world needed—to make them different. Politically, that meant placing Nazism and fascism as the polar opposites of communism. Remember, communism had already claimed the "left wing" position before the war. Now, at last, the dated concept of "monarchists" could be replaced with something more contemporary seated in the "right wing." Fascism and Nazism would hereafter lay claim to the "right."

ℭ ℭ ℭ

By the end of WWII, we had the current structure of communists on the left and fascists on the right. What happened next is the domestication of the terms into the American lexicon and then using them in the context of a series of events to help divide the nation into two competitive teams.

ℭ ℭ ℭ

The first of these events was what has come to be called the "McCarthy Era." After WW II, and in what seemed an effort to cleanse its palate of the aftertaste of cozying up to the Soviets, American political leaders turned their attention to looking for communists right here in the United States. They went looking in two general categories: political/public servants and citizens in positions of influence within the general population. Chief amongst the latter category were members of the Hollywood film industry.

While the era and events in question have come under the general historical heading "McCarthyism," the truth is that Wisconsin Senator Joe McCarthy sat on a committee that primarily looked for communists inside the Truman administration, especially the State Department. It was the House Un-American Activities Committee (HUAC) that went after Hollywood. HUAC was established in 1938 and lasted until 1975. Despite its long run, its truly impactful years were those immediately following WWII.

An examination of HUAC membership during the committee's existence, and from the mid-1940s to the mid-1950s, shows back and forth control between Republicans and Democrats. This was a bipartisan affair. That said, the Republicans were seen as being more zealous in their pursuit of communists while the Democrats were more "reserved" in their approach. Democrats did not want to appear too extreme in either direction with regard to the matter because of the following slightly confusing reasoning:

- Democrats did not want to appear to support communists and, by extension, the Soviet Union.
- The Russian Revolution had ostensibly been a workers' revolution.
- Organized labor generally favored the preferences preached (not practiced) by Communist Party members.
- Democrats were political partners with organized labor.

So the Republicans were seen as being "more" anti-communist, in part for real reasons and in part because Republican Joe McCarthy was the poster child for what the press called a "witch hunt."

When HUAC went after the group that came to be known as the "Hollywood Ten," writers and producers who were called to testify in

October of 1947, the nation in general, and Hollywood in particular, took notice. These people were all suspected of being members of, or associating with, the Communist Party. In their testimony they were asked to affirm or deny, for the record, their affiliation with communists. They were also asked to name other Hollywood members they knew, or believed to be, communists. They refused to cooperate. All of the Ten were cited for contempt, sent to prison, and blacklisted from working in Hollywood when they were let out.

So this period in American history had two very significant impacts on the formation of "Team Right" and "Team Left." The first was in Hollywood, where once it licked its wounds and stopped trembling from the HUAC hearings, the film industry (ultimately spreading to entertainment in general) would assert itself against the "right wing" and would stand strongly against the side that persecuted it. This would come to be reflected in both the attitudes of its stars and the ideas expressed in its films. (Compare the kind of movies Hollywood made about America before 1950 to those it made after 1960; there was a transitional decade.) The other impact it had was to label Republicans as anti-communist and, therefore, "right wing." The formulation goes like this:

- ▶ Republicans presented themselves as strong anti-communists.
- ▶ We just fought alongside the communists against the fascists/ Nazis.
- ▶ Communists are left wing (and since Democrats were on the softer side of the hearings, they became associated as being sympathetic to communists and, therefore, "left wing).
- ▶ Republicans are right wing, the opposite of communists, and now are to be associated with fascists/Nazis in terms of their points of view.

There was another "team-building" and divisive development that came out of the "McCarthy Era." The House and Senate investigations hit their height in the early 1950s in the dawn of television and television journalism. Then CBS News reporter, and now industry icon, Edward R. Murrow ruled the airwaves as the original investigative television journalist. Murrow had become famous as a war correspondent for CBS, where he covered live the Nazi invasion of Austria, the bombing of London, and other major WWII events. After the War, Murrow eventually started an investigative TV show called *See It Now*. It was on that show that he relentlessly attacked Joe McCarthy, ultimately leading to McCarthy making an appearance on the show to explain and defend himself. It did not go well. McCarthy ultimately disappeared in shame and Murrow would go down in journalistic history as the man who slayed the witch hunter.

Murrow's ascendancy to the pinnacle of the investigative journalist platform has led him to be revered both directly and indirectly for the last three generations of journalists. There is almost a biblical lineage that can be traced (Murrow begat Cronkite; Cronkite begat Rather and Brokaw; Brokaw begat Williams, etc.). These big celebrity names and faces of journalism are representative of the Murrow-inspired core of the Fourth Estate which today finds itself securely part of Team Left, planted there by Murrow over a half century ago.

ℂ   ℂ   ℂ

Now I will move into the 1960s and the profound divisions which took place because of the Johnson Administration. The Civil Rights movement started in the 1950s' segregated South and culminated with President Kennedy's proposal of the Civil Rights Act (CRA) in 1963, which became law, after his death, in 1964. Ironically enough, President Kennedy had been slow to embrace civil rights legislation and required a great deal of persuading from his brother, Attorney General Robert Kennedy. Perhaps it is less ironic when you consider that the South was largely governed by Democrats! That's right. The party that today is associated with protecting minority interests was, in very recent history, the party in charge of suppressing those interests.

So how could it possibly become the case that African-Americans would come to join "Team Left" and become such captured members of the very party that had suppressed them for decades? The answer is complex but clear and has impacted American politics for more than 50 years.

After the assassination of Kennedy, Democrats and Republicans alike sought to honor his memory by passing the bill which Kennedy had supported. That said, the Southern Democrats did not support it and that is reflected in the final vote tallies, which show them voting overwhelmingly against it. However, there were enough Democrats in the North to combine with strong Republican support (the Republican Party House and Senate members were far more receptive to the CRA) to get the legislation through.

Immediately after the CRA became law, the next string of legislation all related to Lyndon Johnson's "Great Society" programs. This was the beginning of the modern day welfare state. Johnson had received enormous support in the wake of Kennedy's assassination, and when the 89th Congress was elected in 1964, Democrats outnumbered Republicans by a margin of 68-32 in the Senate and 295-140 in the House. Lyndon Johnson and the Democrats could do whatever they wanted to do. What they did with that power was create a whole series of entitlement programs that would make large groups of people dependent upon the government not just for assistance, but for subsistence.

Of course, one of the lowest income groups was African-Americans, who had been kept down on, and often kept off, the economic ladder. Democrats immediately saw them as potential consumers of welfare state benefits and artfully developed them as a constituency. Democrats came to be seen as the party of the poor, the struggling, the oppressed (forget that just minutes earlier they had been the oppressors). With Republicans generally opposed to expansive welfare programs, they became seen as threats to the minority community.

There was, however, more to it than just a disagreement on policy and economics. Just a decade earlier, Republicans had been determined to be "right wingers," the ones who opposed communism. Remember, too, that WWII had led us to define the opposite of communists to be fascists, or Nazis. At that moment in time, very fresh in the memory of every American, was our recent clash with Germany's most notorious racist of modern history and the poster child for "right wingers." So began the portrayal of Republicans, the right wingers, being opposed to welfare programs and helping minorities because they were inherently racist. After all, that's what it meant to be a "far right" person, and what could be more "far right" than saying you didn't want to feed poor African-American children living in Mississippi?

From that point on it got easy. Not only did Team Left attract African-Americans, but other minority groups began to join Team Left. These groups often felt, and still feel, sometimes rightly and sometimes wrongly, that they have been victimized or not given a fair shake, that they need a helping hand in the form of government assistance.

Today, it is nearly considered dogma that Team Left is the one that takes care of minorities and their interests and Team Right is constantly fighting its inherent racist tendencies, at best ignoring those minorities and, at worst, attempting to enact policy that will be deliberately detrimental to their interests.

Sadly for Team Right, while the remaining racists are a very small minority in this country, since having seen the minorities move *en masse* to Team Left, many of them decided that the only place they could be was Team Right. There aren't many of them around anymore but any time Team Left finds one hiding on the Team Right sideline (David Duke is an example), they point a bright shining light at them and say, "See. I told you they were there." When members of Team Left, like former Los Angeles Clipper owner Donald Sterling, show obvious signs of racism, the team suffers little or no damage and chalks it up to him/her having simply been a bad teammate.

Finally, when a minority group leader shows overt signs of reverse racism, they are seldom seriously criticized, certainly not by their teammates. After all, they have been loyal team members for more than 50 years, and isn't the reason that they joined the team in the first place because they were victims of racism from right wingers?

ꜿ   ꜿ   ꜿ

The other contribution that Johnson made to American polarization was the Vietnam War. It is easy to make the argument that the Vietnam War was the most significant event in American military history. You can make it not because of the outcome of the war (other wars, Revolutionary, Civil, WWII, would be more important in that regard) but because of the seemingly permanent effect it had on both dividing the country and governing how America would, and would not, wage war thereafter. The nation's wounds from Vietnam are still raw, open, and painful today.

Regardless of a person's opinion about the use of military power in general, or its use in Vietnam in particular, it is impossible to argue that the war itself was not a colossal example of mismanagement on the part of U.S. leadership. Started in the early 1960s under the Kennedy Administration and escalated under Lyndon Johnson, the war which ultimately claimed more than 58,000 U.S. casualties was fought as a containment conflict against an enemy that was striving for all-out victory. It was destined for failure before it ever started.

It was in 1961 that President Kennedy began sending in military advisors, and not until January 27, 1973, that the Paris Peace Accords were signed ending the fighting. The 12-year duration of the war made it the longest U.S. military engagement up until that time. America left after 12 years having essentially helped the South Vietnamese battle the North Vietnamese to a draw. Two years later, after the U.S. withdrawal, Saigon would fall to the North Vietnamese and America's waste of blood and treasure was complete.

Vietnam was the first war that saw television bring the battlefield into every American's living room on a nightly basis. The graphic images of American casualties, combined with the long duration of the war and the seeming lack of progress towards victory, led to anger on the part of many Americans. A significant portion of America, especially the youth who were being involuntarily drafted to go to Southeast Asia to fight, were becoming antiwar, antimilitary, and anti-U.S. in general.

Consider the change in American attitudes brought about by Vietnam. When our involvement started in earnest in 1961, we were only 16 years removed from having been victorious in one of history's most significant confrontations, WWII. Americans might have been war-weary after that victory but they were anything but antimilitary (there were isolationists leading up to, and even during WWII but that was a different kind of position than the one born during Vietnam). It took a protracted and bungled use of American wealth and excessive loss of American lives to split the nation on the matter of using American military power to create an impact overseas.

So how did the Vietnam War impact American right wing and left wing politics? It is very interesting to note that the war was started and escalated by two Democratic presidents (Kennedy and Johnson). This might seem ironic, or at least inconsistent, until you remember the slow evolution of America into teams. During the McCarthy Era, Democrats were not "pro-communist" per se. They were simply softer on the issue. Kennedy and Johnson were both Democrats who were concerned about the Soviet Union and its spreading of their form of government to other regions of the world. They saw Vietnam as a communist beachhead in the region that had to be stopped, if not rolled back.

In Vietnam we were fighting the North Vietnamese communists. Communists were the left side of the political continuum and anti-communists were the right. The movement that was forming against the war didn't need to find a political home; it needed to build one. The logical place for them to break ground and homestead was the Democratic Party, which had already shown its Team Left tendencies. So the antiwar, antimilitary, often anti-U.S. crowd began its takeover attempt of the Democratic Party in 1968 with riots outside of the DNC convention site in Chicago and completed that takeover with the nomination of George McGovern as the Party's presidential candidate in 1972. From that point forward the Democratic Party and Team Left would contain the antimilitary platoon.

Of course, many Americans who still believed in the rightness of American action wherever and whatever it might be were appalled to see the demonstrations against the war and the vocal protestations of people criticizing American soldiers. Those people supported our nation's efforts to ensure the sovereignty of the South Vietnamese and contain the "red menace" of communism. For these Americans, as they watched the antiwar crowd take over the Democratic Party, they felt that left them no place to go but the Republican Party to oppose them. From this split you can watch the news in 2015 and see party members and Team Right/Left commentators take almost reflexive positions when discussing any issue involving U.S. foreign intervention, and especially use of military power.

Vietnam also fortified the membership of the mainstream American media on Team Left. With the media on the ground in Vietnam for 12-plus years watching the self- inflicted failure of U.S. policy, and with it the death of American troops, reporters there and back home came to be very antiwar. No single figure represented that shift more than the American legend, and tragically flawed, Walter Cronkite. For years considered the "most trusted man in America," Cronkite anchored the *CBS Evening News* throughout the war and used his calming voice and dignified look to almost single-handedly turn Americans against the effort. His deliberate misreporting of the 1968 Tet Offensive by the North Vietnamese (a victory for U.S. forces that Cronkite characterized as a significant setback, even lying about the occupation of the U.S. Embassy) may have been the single most significant event hastening the ultimate withdrawal of U.S. forces.

With Watergate on the horizon and a Republican the villain, the Fourth Estate was on its way to permanent Team Left status.

¢   ¢   ¢

There is perhaps no single event in the last 100 years that divided America more than the 1973 Burger Court's decision on abortion.

In writing his majority opinion, Justice Harry Blackmun ruled that the due process clause of the 14th Amendment protected a woman's right to privacy and, as follows, her right to an abortion. This took a very controversial issue that had been a matter of individual state legislation for nearly 200 years and gave it blanket sanction under the Constitution.

It seems that both sides in the abortion debate like to cite U.S. history prior to Roe as an argument to support their case. Obviously, both sides can't be right, or can they?

The true history of abortion and the laws governing the activity in America is very complicated. It is important to consider that over a 200-year time span various factors have either changed or evolved. They include:

- The knowledge of when human life begins.

- The capability to save an unborn child.

- The methods available to safely perform an abortion.

- Moral views on the matter, both secular and religious.

The first actual state law prohibiting abortion was passed in 1821 in Connecticut. It involved proscribing the use of *poison* administered to expectant mothers to induce abortion. From that point forward states became increasingly inclined to pass laws to either prohibit or restrict abortion, then still a very dangerous medical procedure to the mother. (In fact, many of the regulations passed restricting abortion were meant to protect the mother, not the fetus/child.) These led to the passage at the federal level of the *Comstock Act* in 1873, which banned the dissemination of information about either abortion or birth control.

Antiabortion attitudes were prevailing in the United States up through 1967, when at the pro-life zenith, 49 states plus the District of Columbia had either severely limited or outright banned abortion. Then the momentum began to shift. In 1970, first Hawaii and then New York passed laws making abortion legal in the early stages of pregnancy. The Comstock Act started to be repealed in 1971 and prior to the Roe case (originating out of Texas), 14 states had legalized abortion in some form. Clearly, the tide was turning.

With *Roe*, the very imperfect and cumbersome process of state by state legalizations and restrictions was suddenly and surreptitiously replaced with a one-size-fits-all ruling. This seems like a good idea in some sense. For example, the U.S. does just fine with universal recognition of free speech, the right to a fair trial, and the elimination of slavery. Unfortunately, regardless of your opinion (really *because* of your opinion), abortion was different.

To those who consider themselves to be "pro-life" abortion is tantamount to murder. They hold to the position that life begins at conception and the taking of that life at any stage is no different than taking the life of a 22-year-old. This side considers abortion murder.

For those calling themselves "pro-choice" they see the right of a woman to control what happens inside of her own body as being intrinsic to her own humanity and something that should not be dictated to her by others. Some believe human life begins at birth and some concede that life has already begun inside of the woman. Regardless, they see the woman's right to decide for herself about her own health as superseding all other considerations. This side sees abortion as an elective medical procedure.

Solomon himself couldn't reconcile the difference between murder and cosmetic surgery.

When the Supreme Court took the decision out of the hands of the states, it removed the opportunity to craft 50 imperfect, but geographically confined, solutions and replaced that system with one winner and one loser. People could no longer "venue shop" to find the medical and moral climate to suit their liking. Now they were two distinct groups forced to fight on a national level.

Pro-choice members who had long felt oppressed by pro-life members took that natural "civil-rights-challenged" position and joined Team Left. Pro-life people came to Team Right so as to oppose the pro-choice group in full force. Since *Roe*, abortion has been a major issue (explicitly or implicitly) in every election held in the U.S. Candidates who run for office, even at office levels or positions that will not permit them to act on any abortion matters, will still be asked their position on the issue. People may well decide to oppose someone based upon their abortion position even if it doesn't relate to the job they'll be doing once in office. More than any other issue, abortion not only drives how a person might vote, it decides how they vote when the issue of abortion isn't even involved.

Ċ   Ċ   Ċ

In addition to the seismic movement-type events noted in the preceding sections, there were other events from the 20th century forward that have helped build and solidify Team Right and Team Left. While reasonable people can differ over the inclusion or exclusion of an event, or its relative importance, here are some that meet the criteria of being identifiable, polarizing, and having long half-lives within our social/political structure. Some of those events include:

- ▶ American Labor Movement of the 1930s
- ▶ Pursuit of the Equal Rights Amendment for women in the 1970s
- ▶ Watergate in the early 1970s
- ▶ Clinton-Lewinsky scandal of the 1990s
- ▶ Bush V. Gore: The 2000 presidential election
- ▶ Second Iraq War (with no WMDs)
- ▶ Battle over Obamacare
- ▶ Fight for same-sex marriage and other LGBT issues

That historical journey, commencing in 1789 France, has led us to the point where we now have two clearly formed teams in the United States battling with each other every single day. They battle on campuses, they battle in break rooms, they battle on streets, and they battle on legislative floors. Teams play to win, not to solve problems. Here is a fairly comprehensive list of how the teams line up:

TEAM LEFT	TEAM RIGHT
"Nth generation Democrats"	"Nth generation Republicans"*
Pro-choice	Pro-life
"Green groups" & climate change activists	Oil & gas supporters
Minorities	Middle-age white men
Gun control advocates	Second Amendment supporters
Animal rights advocates	Hunters
Activist atheists	Evangelicals/traditional Christians
Antimilitary	Pro military
Academia	Rural America
Criminal justice reformers	Strong law & order supporters
Economic "socialists"	Free market thinkers
Unions	Small business owners
Pacifists	Military "hawks"
Open borders	Strict immigration controls
Pro-Palestinian	Pro-Israel
Feminists	Tea Party "enthusiasts"
LBGT	
Mainstream media	
Entertainment industry	

*An "Nth Generation" Republican or Democrat refers to people who have always considered themselves to be Republicans or Democrats, most often inheriting their party affiliation from a long-standing tradition within their families, cultural/community influences, religion, etc. They are what they are simply because those around them are what they are. These people can be the most difficult to reach because they often have never given any serious thought as to why they believe what they believe. When we encounter them on college campuses it almost requires a deprogramming process.

The first thing you should notice is that people can belong to multiple groups listed under both teams. So how can they be on different teams at the same time? The short answer is that they aren't. When you sit and talk with people and run through a series of "litmus test" issues to determine their opinions (e.g., abortion, capital punishment, tax rates, etc.), what you will find is that people end up identifying with the team that embraces the single issue that is most important to them. For example, a person who feels the most important issue to them is a woman's right to choose will tend to become part of Team Left even if they agree with Team Right members on almost every other issue.

This team membership does something very interesting inside of a member's mind when confronted with a current event. This is something you can test on yourself any time you learn of a story in the news that makes you become aware of conflict inside your head as you watch the coverage. Let me share a personal example taken from the Ferguson, Missouri, shooting mentioned at the beginning of the chapter.

TV coverage during the attacks showed footage depicting mobs rioting in the street and police being the subject of insults and attacks. Without knowing any of the facts, I found myself almost instinctively siding with the police. As a defender of the Constitution and a full-fledged fan of the Bill of Rights, I frequently express concern over the periodic excesses of police and other members of the criminal justice system. So why was I jumping to the defense of law enforcement without knowing what was going on? In conversation with my associate author at the time, I realized it was because I was supporting my team. I'm a free market guy, which places me on Team Right. Law enforcement is on Team Right. I was just cheering for my teammates.

Have you ever found yourself arguing on one side of an issue or news story and realized as you were arguing that you weren't even sure if you really believed in, or agreed with, what you were saying? If that's happened to you it's likely because you were arguing for your team without even thinking about it. That shouldn't happen.

Every time you argue you should be thinking about it. This is what we encounter in trying to present arguments for freedom on college campuses. When this happens anywhere in society it is difficult, if not impossible, to have a rational debate over issues and events.

The groups broken out above represent the core "platoons" for each team. Each platoon supports the other if it comes into conflict with the other team. When a conflict develops between platoons or members of the same team, you can actually watch the team leaders create their own "hierarchy" of platoons, and it will determine how the entire team processes the conflict. The dynamics of "group think" are never more plainly seen than they are in such circumstances.

Because these teams have been developed over such a long period of time and so thoroughly cemented as platoons on one team or the other, there is virtually no issue that can come up for discussion that does not involve a platoon for one or both teams. As a result, there is almost nowhere where common ground can be found. Teams play to win whenever they play. It is our challenge at Turning Point and for every other group promoting individual liberty to get people to that common ground.

ϲ   ϲ   ϲ

So "right wing" and "left wing" as they are commonly used today have little to do with directionality and everything to do with two teams relentlessly competing, always seeking the win. If we don't break these teams apart, the future of the United States looks very bleak. We won't be able to solve problems because we can't discuss them rationally. Ultimately, from the chaos, some form of state-managed "order" will be imposed and Americans will find themselves anything but free to enjoy life, liberty, and their pursuit of happiness.

A key requirement for breaking Team Right and Team Left apart is to get people to understand what the real political continuum is. People can try to construct other models, either for pseudo-intellectual or propaganda/controlling purposes, but no matter what they construct there is an actual continuum along which we all move, both as individuals and as a nation, and we ignore it at our own peril. Consider the following representation of the true political continuum:

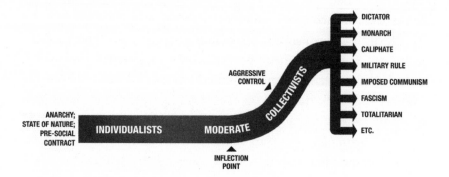

Just outside the far left edge of the continuum we have the "pre-social contract" period. The idea of a social contract and what people's lives were like prior to submitting themselves to governance by an authority has been the subject of debate among political philosophers for centuries. For our purpose that debate is of little interest because whatever the case regarding people's lives in a state of nature, we are certainly beyond that at this point. What matters is what happens as we move across the line and into civilized society.

At the far left edge of the continuum is the area that best reflects an environment that embraces the "Natural Law" written about by Bastiat and others. As people first consent to be governed, the most proximate form of government to "no government" is one where the only laws recognized as legitimate are those that do the minimum required to protect life, liberty, and property. This type of government would have as little control over the lives of people as possible. In contemporary language "libertarians" would be the closest defined group as they embrace Natural Law and grant very few, if any, extensions of power beyond that to government. But libertarians have given a political party that name and since we are trying to change language, a better term for people at this far left edge of the political continuum who place individual freedom and limited government at a premium is "individualist."

As you move along the political continuum to the right you are making trade-offs between individual freedom, choice, and responsibility for more government control over areas of life and commerce. Free-thinking and rational individuals can have these types of debates. Each such debate should be framed by using a similar type of question:

▸ How much of our individual privacy are we willing to give up in allowing the government to use surveillance for threat detection?

▸ How much of our individual income are we willing to part with in order to have a societal safety net for the poor?

▸ How much of our personal space are we willing to let police intrude upon in order to search for criminals and prevent potential harm to others?

As we move along this line from left to right we are deciding to trade individual control for group control. In a modern society, sound arguments can be made that many of these trade-offs are reasonable and beneficial, but all of them need to be viewed in this context and rationally analyzed. If citizens fail to do so it can lead to crossing the inflection point in the continuum (labeled above as moderates) where granting powers to the government to *supplement* individual rights changes into the government substituting its power for, and *supplanting*, individual rights.

Let's call people who believe that a society should be managed beyond that inflection point on the continuum "collectivists." They believe that individual choices are "nonoptimizing" and the decisions of a small group, or even an individual, should be imposed upon all individuals collectively within the society for the greater good and for their own good. The peril associated with this point of view is that almost inevitably their nicely planned and optimized society slips rapidly into a more despotic form of control. No matter the structural form of the suppressing government, regardless of whether it has a religious or secular foundation, no matter if it is ruled by a single person or a "star chamber," the outcome for the general population is always the same: slavery and persecution.

While this continuum represents a political continuum that a nation can use, it also can be used to represent an individual's life. The further someone is to the "individualist" side of the spectrum, the more likely they are to be self-reliant and take responsibility for their own lives and actions. As they allow themselves to become more dependent upon others, sliding towards the "collectivists" side for their decisions and their outcomes, the more likely they are to become dependent and feel like they have been victimized by others and are now entitled to some form of assistance. Julio is a shining example of the ideal individualist.

Right now it is hard to reach people and get them to understand new ideas, because not only are they on a team and taking their team's position, they likely don't even realize they are on that team. These people need to be reorientated in terms of how they think about the entire political landscape. The starting point with this is to ask them one very basic and critical question:

In general, do you believe that individuals should be primarily responsible for themselves with little or no help or restrictions from groups or government, or do you believe that groups or the government should be making decisions for individuals and limiting their actions whenever they think it's in the best interest of everyone?

Our experience on college campuses tells us that when we take the essence of that message and translate it into clever, memorable sound bites we get young people from both teams to be very receptive. Everybody wants to be free. We are essentially triangulating them away from their teams and their platoons and towards a different, shared ideal: freedom. It works. We just have to be relentless in executing.

Another good idea in creating awareness is to ask people what issues really matter to them, where they stand on those issues and why. Remember the hierarchy process discussed earlier that influences what "Team" people join? If you can make people aware of their views in total, you may help them come to see that in general they are, say, more individualists than collectivists. The person who is a member of Team Left strictly because they are "pro-choice" may discover that overall they actually embrace natural law beliefs and that they have been voting against individual freedom for years strictly because of that single issue. Create that kind of awareness in enough people and the entire world can change.

Right now, it is hard to change people's minds because of their team orientation. Have you ever gone to a party with a friend where they knew everyone and you didn't? Remember how it felt when they abandoned you at the door and you felt completely alone and out of place? That's how people feel now when they find themselves dropped in with the other team. Remember, they have been competing with those people. This can't change until the teams are destroyed completely and people begin to look at every issue from the simple perspective of:

How much of my individual freedom am I willing to give up in order to solve a problem?

So what we need to do at every opportunity, in every engagement we have with people discussing politics, economics, and issues, is simple:

- ▶ Ask them what they believe.
- ▶ Ask them why they believe it.
- ▶ Ask them why it matters to them.

By following that simple process, we can understand premises, confront biases, and have productive discussions with one another.

In the late 1980s and early 1990s, as the Berlin Wall fell and the Soviet Union crumbled, Karl Marx, the intellectual founder of communism, became a bit of a punching bag in many circles. Communism had failed! Marx, like Nietzsche's "God" before him, was dead.

But the Soviet Union wasn't a "true" communist state in the first place. Marx hadn't failed. He hadn't even been tried yet. Marx argued that communism was the inevitable, determinable, final state of a matured capitalist system. That's not what Russia was in 1917 and it is not what China was some 30-plus years later under Mao. The United States, however, is a matured capitalist economy. If Marx was right, and with the increasing amount of individual freedom we have surrendered to big government and to people who aggressively attempt to control every aspect of our lives, then the United States may be marching along the path towards communism. Have we crossed that inflection point in the political continuum?

Every story involving people traveling to the future ultimately asks the same question: Are they seeing things that *will* be or that *might* be? As you observe the United Sates becoming increasingly fractured in the fight between Team Left and Team Right, and drifting further along the curve away from the individualist side to the collectivist side (perhaps heading to Marx's future), that is the question we should be asking. It is also the issue we should be trying to address with every intellectual weapon we possess. I've shared Julio's future. I want to turn it from the future that might be to the future that will be.

I am committed to doing everything I can to help get us there. I know that we need to stop fighting and start talking. The work we've done on college campuses proves to me that we have more in common than our biases and beliefs allow us to understand. We need to look for the ties that bind, not keep tearing ourselves apart. Almost every person in the country lives somewhere on the continuum between individualist and moderate. For those people, we are just dealing with differences of opinion. We can bridge that gap with messaging and discussion if we can just get them to listen.

The hour is late. While we fight over differences in opinion, the people who want to have control over us, the collectivists, use our disunity as an opportunity to take control. They have been winning for a very long time. We don't just have a difference of opinion with them. We have a difference of values.

Enough! Join me. Please, join me.

Musings from my Homeric Travels during Interesting Political Times

Over the past few years, I have experienced so many events that have had an impact on me, it is sometimes difficult to put into perspective. After all, it was only a few years ago I was a high school student in a modest Chicago suburb. Now, I find myself in intimate social settings with presidential candidates, or speaking in front of groups of more than 1,000 people. There was no way I could have prepared or planned for any of this to have happened.

Along the way, I have had some interesting moments that have stood out for me, either as having been celebratory or introspective. I thought in closing out this book I would share some of these moments with you. They are just stories that have been important to me and are not tied to the book per se. Imagine this as being the end of a high energy rock concert where the front man comes out for an encore, picks up a simple acoustic guitar, and has a few last moments, one-to-thousands, with his audience.

ζ ζ ζ

I threw myself into the taxi cab and told the driver, "Hilton Hotel, overlooking Millennium Park, drive quick."

The streets were very eerily empty. It was only 7:01 p.m. but it seemed the world decided to take a deep breath before plunging into the icy waters of the unknown.

I was demolished. It was 10 days straight of little to no sleep. My closest friends and I had done everything we could do help elect Bruce Rauner as the next governor of Illinois. For more than a year and a half we dedicated our life and time to get a true conservative elected as governor of the most liberal state in the country.

Polls closed at 7 p.m. and I was now heading to the "victory party," or least I hoped it would be. We knocked on more than 50,000 doors as a team and made more than 100,000 phone calls. We barnstormed the state and mobilized students in every county to help Bruce defeat the Chicago political machine.

As the taxi cab rolled street after street I clearly remember how I first met Bruce Rauner. It was March of 2013, speaking at a Lincoln-Reagan Day dinner in Aurora, Illinois. Turning Point USA was nothing but a small group of dedicated, forward-thinking young entrepreneurs at that point and we were looking for a catalyst.

I was the keynote speaker that evening and I was blessed enough to have the opportunity to have Bruce Rauner in the audience. I expressed my vision for Turning Point USA, which included effective messaging and grassroots organizing.

I was given a standing ovation after the speech and Bruce told the audience that was the best political speech he ever heard given about the next generation. He went on to become a generous contributor to our organization and a close friend of Turning Point USA.

For months thereafter I forged a friendship with Bruce. I helped where I could, and I was incredibly grateful to have played a small part personally for him eventually securing the Republican nomination for governor. After that, it was all the hard work required to win. Now, at this moment, he was at the figurative doorstep of the governor's mansion, having fought hard against the Illinois/Chicago democratic political machine, the stuff of legends.

We pulled up to the hotel and I unloaded quickly out of the cab. My head was pounding with nerves and my stomach tightening by the minute. It was 18 months of tension, anger, frustration, and commitment all coming to catharsis.

I couldn't wrap my head around what another four years of Governor Quinn would look like. I ran in circles around the hotel trying to find screens that were reporting the results. I viewed the monitors and it had 5% reporting with Governor Quinn up 40 points. Chicago always reported first so I wasn't fazed by it. After about five minutes I said to myself, "Screw this, I am going to figure it out on my own."

I sprinted out to the lobby of the hotel, opened up my laptop and started to crunch projection numbers and precinct totals, and began to call county commissioner websites to get live reports. I learned how to do this during the 2013 primary, the 2012 presidential campaign, and the 2010 senatorial campaigns I had joined.

Quickly, the numbers started to come together. Chicago turnout was down, way, down. This was very good news for Bruce.

Soon, the collar counties came in. Bruce was leading by 14% in Lake County, 18% in DuPage. Every indication seemed Bruce was going to take this victory to the bank. It seemed too good to be true and I couldn't quite bring myself to realize that Bruce Rauner, a conservative, was going to be the next governor of Illinois.

Finally, the media called the race for Rauner: Victory!

Bruce won by 180,000 votes and far exceeded all the pundits' projections. It was a complete rejection of the Illinois political ruling class.

Even when the media called the race, Governor Quinn refused to concede. I, like him, couldn't believe what I was witnessing. During the victory celebration I was constantly checking my phone to see if there were votes about to be dumped that would somehow change the outcome. I simply couldn't believe Illinois elected a conservative as governor.

My phone was blowing up with texts, tweets, e-mails, and phone calls. It was a series of moments that I couldn't have designed. It was the beginning of the frustration the American people had with the political class as a harbinger for things to come. Bruce Rauner, a self-made billionaire who refused to take teacher union money and special interest favors, had propelled himself into office by running a campaign that was principled and focused on the issues.

If it can happen in Illinois, it can happen anywhere. There was something even deeper happening at the time that I didn't quite appreciate. I wouldn't fully realize it until Donald Trump stormed onto the national stage. There was antiestablishment fervor brewing in America that was ready to throw everyone out. I was sitting smack dab in the middle of it.

¢   ¢   ¢

I saw Trump coming, and I chose to ignore it.

I remember sitting in a living room in Palm Beach, Florida, in the spring of 2014. I was sitting with our host, who is a close friend and supporter of Turning Point USA, Pat Caddell, and then Senator Ted Cruz's chief of staff. We were discussing the 2014 political climate and the tone of the country. Naturally, the topic of the 2016 presidential election came up.

"I have never seen the American people so angry," Pat Caddell remarked. "This recent polling we have done is mind-boggling; the anger, the resentment for the Washington political class, the lack of trust. I can't believe what I am seeing."

At the time I didn't understand what Pat meant. He was so emphatic and so deliberate in the way he described the frustration the American people had for Washington, D.C., the ruling class, and GOP establishment.

A few weeks after, I saw exactly what Pat was talking about first-hand. In my home state of Illinois, I worked for and supported a much milder but similar type of candidate for governor in Bruce Rauner.

Bruce was not a politician, he never served in elected office and he owned it. Bruce ran TV ads that boasted he "couldn't be bought" and that he would "fight special interests." This message gave Bruce an unimaginable amount of support amongst blue collar Reagan Democrat voters and people who were frustrated at the corrupt Illinois political climate. Bruce was a self-made billionaire who wasn't afraid to defend his wealth or his experience in the private sector. Is any of this sounding familiar?

And even before 2014 we saw the rise of Governor Rick Snyder, Senator Rand Paul, Congressman Thomas Massie, and many others who used their nonpolitical background as an asset, not a liability.

But still, I had these signs around me and I did not connect the dots. I refused to come to grips that a singular candidate would translate this deep sense of anger amongst the GOP base and successfully turn it into votes. I failed to notice how being a nonpolitician was in fact the greatest advantage one could have when trying to seek elective office in 2016.

Then December of 2015 rolled around and Jeb Bush announced his prospective interest to run for president. Like dominoes, Scott Walker, Marco Rubio, Ted Cruz and others sprang their super PAC-building into action. Little did all of them know money would mean next to nothing in this political season.

Almost exactly a year later I found myself in that same living room again with Pat Caddell. This time, Pat was equipped with binders of information and polling that was dubbed the "Candidate Smith project." The premise behind the project was to analyze what sort of candidate would resonate with the American people in 2016 and what was the political climate for 2016.

"The anger, the rage, the fury, it has only gotten worse. People are ready for revolution. It doesn't matter who or what party they stand for, if the political class is not careful they are going to create a monster that will turn this entire system upside down," Caddell remarked.

Caddell was insistent that the landscape would dictate who was going to win, not the candidate. Caddell's observation, based on numerous rounds of polling, is that the political ruling establishment was so out of touch with the American people a "Candidate Smith" could come along and spark a wildfire that could change American politics forever.

Caddell called it the "Candidate Smith" project because he felt that a true outsider was the only type of candidate who could spark this sort of political revolution. Caddell even went so far as to say, "This election is not about ideology, it is about insurgency. This election is about who can build the bigger explosion to attack the political ruling class."

At the time it seemed a little farfetched. I had the opportunity to attend numerous fundraisers and hear from Governor Bush, Senator Rubio, Senator Cruz, Governor Walker, and many others. Their descriptions of how they were going to win the nomination seemed to make perfect sense. The confidence from their bundlers and staff made it seem like this was going to be a very standard political season. Things were going according to plan, Bush raised $100 million, Walker was atop in the polls, Cruz had a wonderfully choreographed announcement at Liberty University, and Rubio branded himself as the anti-Clinton. Everything seemed to be falling into place.

And then June 16, 2015, happened and everything I chose to ignore was set in motion.

From Rauner's successful outsider bid in Illinois, the disgust towards Washington I saw at Tea Party rallies, to Caddell's clairvoyance, I never actually put all the pieces together until recently. This improbable rise of Donald Trump was far less about Trump and far more about the political climate he parachuted into.

Trump found himself in a circumstance where a vast majority of the American people hate Washington, D.C., are fed up with political correctness, and disgusted by career politicians. And beyond that, the rage felt towards Obama and Hillary Clinton caused the GOP base to search for anything and anyone that would resemble their own frustration towards the system—and they found Donald Trump.

They say hindsight is 20/20. But in my case I had plenty of warning signs to indicate that a Donald Trump-type candidacy would have success. By the time other candidates and career campaign managers figured out what was going on (and some still haven't), it was far too late to do anything about it. He became destined to be the nominee (at least as of this writing in May, 2016) and the next challenge for him will be to replicate his success in a general election.

As Pat Caddell put it in that living room in 2014, "The American people are so angry they can't see straight. They just want someone who isn't part of the DC political elite and they don't care who they are, what they have done, or their stances. They just want to see the whole system turned on its head. They want an outsider. They want an insurgent."

A small handful of us who were able to be witnesses to the warning signs now understand the impact and the gravity of what we chose to ignore. Whether this trend will continue into the general election remains to be seen, but I do know the anger and disgust the American people have for D.C. sure hasn't gone away, and Trump isn't going to be the only one who benefits from it over time.

$$\mathcal{c} \quad \mathcal{c} \quad \mathcal{c}$$

I remember waking up at 4:30 a.m. telling myself, "This is the day Turning Point USA will either become a fixture with America's youth, or become just another conservative organization."

I sprang out of bed, sick to my stomach, threw on my running shoes and ran three miles in the way too early hours of the morning. I ran along the calm waters of the Potomac in National Harbor, Maryland. The Gaylord Hotel glimmered in the distance and I continued to pound the pavement trying to work off the nerves.

I kept saying to myself, "Cruz and Paul, Cruz and Paul, Cruz and Paul."

Around 5:20 a.m. I finally made it back to my hotel, showered, threw on my red Turning Point USA polo, and headed downstairs for breakfast. I was too nervous to eat. I could barely even drink water, let alone coffee.

Around 6:30 a.m. the TPUSA troops started to flood the lobby with their bright red polos. Each of them was excited, driven, energetic, and filled with a vibrant passion for America. I knew this was going to be the biggest day of my life, I just didn't realize at the time how big.

Around 7:30 a.m. we shuffled our 125 TPUSA ambassadors to our booth in the main exhibit hall. Over the entrance hung a massive banner with the words "CPAC 2015! The conservative movement starts here."

Just two years ago I was merely a speaker at CPAC. Now I was accompanied by 125 passionate and driven young patriots who each wanted to save their country. We had one of the biggest, if not the biggest, booths at the conference.

I vividly remember sliding down the escalator towards the main exhibit hall and asking myself, "What if it fails" What if no one shows up?"

We ran the ambassadors through their introductory marching orders and sent them out armed with tablets to go recruit other students attending CPAC.

Crystal Clanton, my incredibly loyal and talented Chief Operating Officer, approached me right after and said, "Charlie, the room opens for us at 4 p.m.; we can start letting people in at 5:30 p.m. What time will Ted Cruz and Rand Paul arrive?"

Just hearing those names uttered gave me the chills. These were the two biggest superstars of the conservative movement, and we had them booked for a featured event the first night of CPAC. It would be like booking the Rolling Stones and The Beatles in one night at Red Rock. It just doesn't happen.

We discussed logistics and I continued pacing aimlessly around the conference hall. Throughout the day I approached our ambassadors and asked them how many new students they had recruited to bring to our event that night. I kept asking them over and over like a child asking their parents from the backseat, "Are we almost there?" I was a total mess.

At 3:30 p.m. Tyler Bowyer came up to me and asked, "Charlie, you doing ok? It's going to be alright, we will kill it."

We had booked a room with a capacity of 1,300. We weren't sure if we would be able to fill it or even fill half of it. Just the idea of not filling a room and having Cruz and Paul speak drove me absolutely worried sick.

We began setting up the chairs and the Turning Point USA banners throughout the room. Our staff was committed to making this an excellent event. As I have said many times, we have the greatest staff in American politics. I am convinced of it.

Time started to move too fast; 4:45, 5:00, and 5:15 all rolled by. No one was coming yet. There was no line. Where was everyone?

Around 5:25 we had 15 people show up and start waiting in line. This wasn't even 1/100th of what we needed to have a strong showing. My stomach was combustible. Tyler is usually very calm, cool, and collected but even he, right at 5:30, said, "Ok, what's going on here?"

I didn't know what to do. I had to put down my phone and just walk away. This was the event of a lifetime and we were blowing it.

I walked out the doors of the Gaylord, down to the Potomac River and just stared into the distance at Alexandria, Virginia. I took 30 deep breaths in a row and gathered my thoughts. Finally, I turned back towards our event.

I came back eight minutes later and to my stunning amazement I saw a line of people nearly 200 feet long and growing. No way this could be for our event, could it?

It was. There were hundreds of young people waiting in line for a chance to see Rand Paul and Ted Cruz and eager to learn more about Turning Point USA.

The number just kept growing; up to 600, 700, 800, 950, and 1,000. No way. Could we actually fill the room? Still they kept coming, and coming. The room filled until the crowd spilled out the doors. In total, more than 1,500 people came.

It was a sensational relief for about 10 minutes, until Rand Paul's campaign manager approached me and said, "Hey Charlie, the Senator is running behind, we aren't sure when he will be able to come by."

Running behind? Are you kidding me? We have 1,500 screaming young people and we are going to lose them all. My thoughts were moving quicker than I could put words to them.

Twenty minutes passed; then thirty minutes. The clock kept ticking. I felt like I had a time bomb ticking inside of me.

It was the most nerve-wracking 40 minutes I can ever remember. Would he cancel? This could be worse than I ever imagined. Imagine if we got all these young people here and then Turning Point USA will be known as the group that let everyone down. I couldn't bear to think what this could possibly mean.

And then I got a tap on my shoulder. It was the Rand Paul body detail. "The Senator is in the building, we are good to go."

I sprinted backstage and met the Senator, where I briefed him on the event, the audience, and the magnitude. Senator Paul listened and then turned the corner to greet the audience.

When he saw the size and felt the energy he said, "Holy S***!" and sprinted on up the stage.

The young people in attendance were going nuts. Screaming in jubilation, hands in the air, rejoicing with pure adrenalin.

Senator Paul even said at one point in his speech:

"So what do you think of Big Government?"

And the students responded: "IT SUCKS!"

It was that moment I knew we made it. We cleared the bar. We were no longer a start-up movement. We had arrived on the national stage with flying colors. We had pulled off an event unlike anything previously seen in the youth political arena, and we did so in a way no one expected.

Senator Cruz followed with a 45-minute passionate speech where he told his life story and the importance of youth engagement in politics. He hit home run after home run.

Senator Cruz stayed after the event and took a picture with every person who wanted one. Senator Cruz had the patience to take those pictures with nearly 1,500 young people in front of our banner that said "BIG GOVERNMENT SUCKS!"

That evening was a "turning point" for our organization. We turned doubters into believers. We made everyone aware that Turning Point USA was here to stay, for a long, long time.

ʗ   ʗ   ʗ

I was driving through the slush on a gloomy winter day, firmly pressing north on I-90 to Madison, Wisconsin. It was January 30, 2014, and I had just finished a long multicity road trip. The last place I wanted to be was driving through the light snow northbound to the liberal paradise of UW-Madison.

I was delivering a few boxes of booklets and materials to our chapter leader at the university, Katherine Sodeika. Katherine needed extra material to help her with the recruitment event that was taking place as the spring semester was getting underway.

I arrived in Madison, parked, and began unloading my car. I walked 10 blocks in the 8-degree weather carrying several boxes of activism supplies to Kohl Center, which is where the recruitment event was being held.

Katherine met me outside the building and we went upstairs to begin setting up the table with our posters, banners, supplies, and activism material.

"You know, Charlie, it's a very hostile environment here. We will be lucky to get 15–20 people even interested in what we are doing."

I understood what Katherine was saying, and after a long drive from Chicago and a long travel-weary week, the last thing I needed was to have to listen to campus liberals rebuking free markets and the concept of limited government.

What happened next was truly extraordinary.

We began recruiting and attracting hundreds of new members and students. These were students of all different ethnic backgrounds and of varying socioeconomic levels. I saw a movement being created in front of my eyes.

Capitalism Cures, Healthcare Games, Game of Loans. These messages were resonating with UW students unlike anything I had ever imagined.

This was the very first time I fully realized the organizing potential of Turning Point USA. This was the moment that I began to see the entire picture of what Turning Point USA could start to create.

I was experiencing a similar level of enthusiasm, energy, and interest that I watched in person as Barack Obama evoked it on that same campus only two years earlier.

"I have been waiting for something like this!" exclaimed one student.

Yet another student came up and asked, "How do I get involved? I want to help."

Dozens of UW students were willingly giving us their cell phone numbers, e-mails, and contact info. They were inspired and moved by the message and they wanted to help.

After days of 14 hours of traveling and winter weather, I hardly expected to stumble upon the campus of UW-Madison and see our messages and materials be received with such widespread support.

We ended up recruiting nearly 200 new students and we were able to build a formidable activist army at UW-Madison that still exists to this day.

The movement didn't start on that winter night in January of 2014, but that is when it all started to make sense. That was the very moment when I made the firm commitment to do everything I possibly could to raise the money and garner the support to grow this field program and movement to its now unprecedented levels.

I got a glimpse into the future, and I've been chasing it ever since.

¢ ¢ ¢

My journey is going to continue. I will collect thousands of these stories over a lifetime. By the time I have finished, I am certain to feel like some odd combination of Homer, Chaucer, and the Brothers Grimm. I plan to continue to share the experiences with you and with others. It is my hope that you will become willing to share in the experiences with me.

ACKNOWLEDGEMENTS

This project was first discussed between us in November of 2015. Around New Year's Day, we spoke and decided that we would get to work on the project during the month of January. It was on January 20, 2016, that we had our very first meeting to start to scope out the project. A final manuscript got delivered to our publisher on May 30, 2016.

In that incredibly compressed period of time, a lot of different things had to come together and a number of folks had to pitch in.

I wish I could just take credit for this absolutely amazing book. The first thanks goes to my co-author and "comrade," Brent Hamachek, for his incredible intellect, grit, and vision putting this project together.

Many, many thanks to:

- Bill Montgomery, thank you for not letting me give up when things seemed so dark. Thank you for making me stick with it through the impossible and believing in me and the vision of Turning Point USA. Thank you for putting a crazy idea into my head and then not abandoning me when it got difficult.

- Crystal Clanton, for your endless belief in Turning Point USA. Also for the early mornings where you did the work when no one was watching, the late nights when you got proposals done that no one else could put together. You believed and bought into this idea, concept, and vision when everyone else thought it was crazy. You put in more work than anyone else to make this movement a reality. Turning Point USA could never have gotten off the ground without you.

▶ TPUSA's incredible staff, thank you for signing up to be part of this vision, idea, and movement. Thank you for getting up early, and going to bed late and hitting the daily grind. Thank you for showing the grassroots leadership that our movement sorely lacks, and thank you for doing more than is ever asked of you.

▶ Our donors, for putting their money where it mattered. Without your investments this organization could never have existed. Tom Patrick, Foster Friess, Mike Miller, Allie & Lee Hanley, Jack Roeser (we miss you Jack), Vince Foglia, Governor Bruce Rauner, Greg Gianforte, and countless others, thank you for investing in a vision that became a reality.

▶ To our advisors, for taking valuable time to listen, absorb, and help guide our organization to new heights. Larry Diamond; John Chachas; Doug DeGroote; Tom Cox; Bob Rubin; Larry Keith; Jim Young; Rip McIntosh; Gary Rabine; and Joe and Helene Walsh, thank you for always being there in so many different and extremely important ways.

▶ To our activists, this book is really written about you and for you. I am nothing more than the offensive coordinator of a football team. You are in the trenches doing the blocking and tackling when it isn't easy. You experience the pain and the sacrifice that comes with competing and winning. You are the ones fighting the campus totalitarian culture. This book is a tribute to you, we salute you!

▶ Moriah DeMartino, Tyler Bower, Joe Enders, Josh Thifault, Justin Carrizales, and Crystal Clanton again for being interviewed for this project and sharing their stories.

▶ To Paulette Kirschner and William Frech of Fisher, Cohen, Waldman, Shapiro LLP in Glenview, Illinois, for assisting with research and for proofreading for both content and structure along the way. Also to Cheri Rakowsky for assembling the chapters, formatting, and editing.

▶ Our literary agent, Jennifer Cohen, showed such enthusiasm for the project that she had a publisher lined up for us before we even had an agreement with her. She gave us tremendous guidance and brought positive energy to the project.

▶ Constitutional expert and author of *Constitutional Sound Bites*, and its Spanish language translation *Capsulas Informativas Constitucionales*, Dave Shestokas, provided facts, stories, and inspiration for the chapter dealing with First Principles.

ABOUT THE AUTHORS

Charlie Kirk is the Founder and Executive Director of Turning Point USA, a national student movement dedicated to identifying, organizing, and empowering young people to promote the principles of free markets and limited government. Since the inception of Turning Point USA in 2012, Kirk has grown Turning Point USA from nothing to having representation on over 1,100 high schools and college campuses nationwide and a full time field staff of over 75.

The 22-year-old Kirk has appeared on Fox News, CNBC, and FOX Business News over 200 times. In addition to his entrepreneurial political endeavors, Charlie plays every type of saxophone, was captain of his school's varsity basketball team, and is a proud Eagle Scout.

Brent Hamachek is the founder of Segueway, a Chicago-area consulting company that has been working with privately owned businesses since 2000. Brent has had over 120 engagements since then and has worked in 70 different industries. Brent is a professional speaker on a wide range of business, political, and economic topics. He is a high honors graduate from Lake Superior State University and an honors graduate from the Graduate School of Banking at the University of Wisconsin. He has also studied theology at Loyola University. Brent is a member of the Advisory Council to Turning Point USA, a member of Engaging Speakers, and a member of True Mentors, a Chicago-area group of business professionals providing guidance to young people.